HEBREWS OF THE PORTUGUESE NATION

THE MODERN JEWISH EXPERIENCE

Paula Hyman and Deborah Dash Moore, editors

HEBREWS
OF THE
PORTUGUESE
NATION

CONVERSOS AND COMMUNITY
IN EARLY MODERN
AMSTERDAM

Miriam Bodian

INDIANA UNIVERSITY PRESS

Bloomington • Indianapolis

The author and the publisher gratefully acknowledge
the financial support of the Lucius N. Littauer Foundation
and the University of Michigan.

Publication of this book is made possible in part with the assistance
of a Challenge Grant from the National Endowment for the Humanities,
a federal agency that supports research, education, and public
programming in the humanities.

© 1997 by Miriam Bodian

The paper used in this publication meets the minimum
requirements of American National Standard for Information
Sciences—Permanence of Paper for Printed Library Materials,
ANSI Z39.48-1984.

Manufactured in the United States of America

Library of Congress Cataloging-in-Publication Data
Bodian, Miriam, date
    Hebrews of the Portuguese nation : conversos and community in
early modern Amsterdam / Miriam Bodian.
        p.   cm. — (The modern Jewish experience)
    Includes bibliographical references and index.
    ISBN 0-253-33292-3 (cl : alk. paper)
    1. Sephardim—Netherlands—Amsterdam—History—17th
century.   2. Jews—Netherlands—Amsterdam—History—17th
century.   3. Marranos—History.   4. Judaism—Netherlands—
Amsterdam—History—17th century.   5. Amsterdam (Netherlands)
—Ethnic relations.   I. Title.   II. Series: Modern Jewish experience
(Bloomington, Ind.)
DS135.N5A5323   1997
949.2'3520049240469—dc21   96-48373

1 2 3 4 5 02 01 00 99 98 97

CONTENTS

ACKNOWLEDGMENTS

A number of people and institutions have been instrumental in bringing this book to fruition. To paraphrase a rabbinic saying, without bread there is no research—and so I am grateful to the Lucius N. Littauer Foundation and the Rackham School for Graduate Studies at the University of Michigan for financial support which made possible two research trips, and to the Littauer Foundation and the University of Michigan for subvention funds. On those trips and on many other occasions, the dedicated staffs of the National and University Library, the Institute for Microfilmed Hebrew Manuscripts, and the Central Archives for the History of the Jewish People, all in Jerusalem, have offered unfailing assistance. I owe special thanks to Renato Spiegel of the Central Archives. I have also benefited informally from the scholarly expertise of Jonathan Israel, Gerard Nahon, Harm den Boer, and H. P. Salomon. During my visits to Amsterdam, I was kindly assisted by Dr. Odette Vlessing at the Municipal Archives, Dr. F. J. Hooge-woud at the Bibliotheca Rosenthaliana, and Mr. I. S. Palache, chairman of the board of the *Dotar* society.

A number of people have read drafts of the manuscript. The book has incorporated, with changes, several passages from an article published in *Past and Present* 143 (1994). For their encouragement and suggestions I want to thank David Bien, Laura Downs, Valerie Kivelson, and Susan Juster. To Sabine MacCormack, my heartfelt thanks for good counsel. I owe a very special debt of gratitude to Todd Endelman, who has read the manuscript in various stages and has been a constant source of helpful advice and criticism. Finally, I would like to thank the anonymous reviewers of the manuscript and my editor at the Indiana University Press, Janet Rabinowitch, whose sound suggestions I have tried to incorporate.

PREFACE

This book is about the making of a community. It will investigate both the concrete and intangible aspects of community formation: both the organizational enterprise of institution building and the ideological and imaginative enterprise of self-conceptualization. The particular community under scrutiny is the Portuguese Jewish community in Amsterdam (known in its formative years as the "Portuguese Nation" for reasons that will be explained below).

The community had its origins in the stream of conversos (descendants of baptized Jews) emigrating from the Iberian Peninsula in the late sixteenth and seventeenth centuries. To be sure, this stream did not flow exclusively to Amsterdam. In the early modern period, conversos settled and established Jewish or crypto-Jewish communities in Venice, Hamburg, Bordeaux, London, and other European cities. Any one of these settlements might provide fertile ground for a study of identity. However, the Amsterdam community was chosen as the focus of this study for two reasons. First, no other converso community rivals Amsterdam for the wealth of its archival material. The records of the Spanish and Portuguese Jewish community of Amsterdam, now housed in the Municipal Archives of Amsterdam, are unequaled in their richness and depth by those of any other European Jewish community. Important material can be found elsewhere in the Municipal Archives as well, particularly in its rich collection of notarial deeds. And then there is the extensive literary legacy of the Amsterdam "Portuguese" (as they referred to themselves): polemical tracts, apologetic works, occasional poetry, sermons, and chronicles.

It is not by accident that the Amsterdam archives are so rich. The second reason for making the Amsterdam "Portuguese" community the focus of this study is that by the mid-seventeenth century it had risen to a position of international importance in the Jewish and commercial spheres. Its printing presses, merchants, and freedom of action made it a nerve center for a commercial, ethnic, and religious network of considerable complexity.

Thus, this book ranges far beyond the confines of the Dutch milieu, and it does so in a two-pronged fashion. The ex-conversos of Europe belonged to two far-flung diasporas. On the one hand, they belonged to "the Nation"—the population of conversos and ex-conversos with roots in post-Expulsion Spain and Portugal. Within the orbit of the "Men of the Nation"[1] in northern Europe, the Amsterdam community rose quite early to a position of virtual hegemony. On the other hand, the ex-conversos of Amsterdam belonged to the collectivity of the Jewish people, united, despite dispersion, by what was viewed as the covenantal bond of rabbinic law. Within this diaspora, too, Amsterdam became a major Jewish community in its own right, holding its own with older Jewish centers like Venice, Prague, and Salonica. The tensions inherent in this double affiliation, and the efforts to resolve them, are central to the issues explored in this book.

My work owes much to existing scholarship, recent and otherwise. But it is also an effort to break out of the mold of converso research among Jewish historians, who insofar as they have touched on issues of identity have focused on religious issues. At least in its early years, converso research was also deeply ensnarled in polemical and apologetic battles. This is evident in Cecil Roth's pioneering work on the conversos, *A History of the Marranos* (1932). (The term *marrano* will be discussed below.) Underlying Roth's work is the impulse to tell a narrative of crypto-Jewish sacrifice, suffering, heroism, escape from the Peninsula, and return to Judaism. The story of crypto-Judaism, for Roth, is thus primarily a vehicle for celebrating Jewish national greatness and steadfastness. Needless to say, viewing the conversos within the confines of such an idealized conception of Jewish history deprives the story of much of its richness. Comparing the crypto-Jews' vestigial practice to Jewish life outside the Peninsula, Roth found that "the doctrine of the ordinary Marrano [cryptojudaizer]" was "pathetic in the extreme" and that "Marranos could not be expected to appreciate Judaism in its comprehensive whole."[2] Indeed. But the effect of Roth's conceptualization was to ignore *converso* experience "in its comprehensive whole."

A similarly narrow view of converso identity persisted in the 1950s and 1960s. It is reflected in what became an emotion-laden controversy among Jewish scholars of that generation: the question of whether the conversos in the Peninsula were steadfast in their loyalty to their ancestral faith and thus an integral part of the Jewish people,[3] or whether they were really assimilated Spanish Catholics.[4] Behind this polemic were vexing issues of contemporary Jewish national and collective identity—particularly the relationship between the diaspora and the new State of Israel. For Israeli historians who wished to perpetuate a sense of continuity with the diaspora experience—an experience which had so recently turned horrific—the themes of Jewish solidarity, martyrdom, resistance to persecution, and the struggle to maintain a distinctive Jewish way of life were of paramount importance. The history of the Jews and conversos of Spain struck many as an archetypal story of Jewish suffering and heroism in the diaspora.[5]

Those on the other side of the debate attempted to strip converso suffering of the meaning conferred on it by the heroic school, arguing that inquisitorial charges of cryptojudaizing were fabricated. These scholars have undoubtedly contributed to better understanding the unreliability of inquisitorial evidence. However, their work has tended to rely on a dogmatic interpretation of the evidence, and their most sweeping conclusions have been widely discredited.

Interestingly, early Spanish research on the conversos was also deeply enmeshed in a national polemic. When in the 1950s the scholar Américo Castro took the unorthodox step of placing Jews, Muslims, and conversos at the very heart of Spanish culture and history, he set off an ongoing, heated debate with his colleague and opponent Claudio Sánchez-Albornoz over the importance or unimportance of "semitic" influences for the evolution of Spanish national life.[6] For these polemicists (to simplify greatly), the focal question was whether Spanish society had been "orientalized" by Muslims and Jews, or whether it possessed an enduring Roman-Christian character—a question with major implications for Spanish national consciousness. Both historians, however, remained captive to their own grand theses (and prejudices), and enraged Jewish scholars by attributing to Jewish/converso influence both the methods of the Inquisition and Spanish racialism.

Fortunately, research on conversos outside the Peninsula has been less tendentious. Still, it has usually been conducted with the unwitting premise that what matters about conversos and ex-conversos is their relationship to Judaism. Carl Gebhardt, for example, coined the oft-quoted formula defining the converso as "a Catholic without belief and a Jew without knowledge, but by will, a Jew."[7] I. S. Révah, too, in his influential article "Les Marranes" (1959) regarded converso identity as a function of religious loyalties (or lack thereof).[8] A somewhat teleological conception of converso history also led Révah to conclude that the "marrano religion" was essentially a "potential Judaism," realizable only after re-settlement outside the Peninsula—a conceptualization that discouraged any consideration of the important functions of distinctively "converso" ways of thinking in the Iberian milieu itself.[9] (Let me hasten to add, however, that this criticism is not meant to detract from the work of a scholar who was a model of intellectual integrity and judiciousness.)

In recent years a more complex picture of converso experience has emerged. The host of scholars now pursuing research on one or another aspect of converso society have tended to avoid ideologically driven generalizations, even when their loyalties are apparent. Together they have breathed realism and life into the converso past. In my own work on Amsterdam, I have been especially indebted in this respect to the contributions of I. S. Révah, Y. H. Yerushalmi, Yosef Kaplan, and Jonathan Israel.

No attempt has yet been made, however, to make converso identity and ethnicity the focus of a historical study. Recent scholarly interest in the historical foundations and genealogy of ethnicity would seem to point the way to such an inquiry.[10] The present book is an attempt to answer some of the questions suggested by such research, often in fields far removed from converso history. It will view converso identity as a changing cultural construction, evolving over many generations and answering a variety of needs. As such, it will examine how conversos defined themselves vis-a-vis other groups over time, and how a distinct conception of "the Nation" crystallized among the ex-conversos of northwestern Europe as a response to their specific historical experience and given predicament.

Our own all-too-acute awareness of the persistence of ethnic allegiances and conflicts, despite all efforts to suppress them, gives the subject an immediacy and familiarity that is both compelling and deceptive. I have tried to make use of insights gained from reflection on other ethnic phenomena (and their frequent entanglement with religious loyalties) without, I hope, misrepresenting the particular experience of the "Men of the Nation." It is precisely the particularities of this case that it is hoped will contribute to understanding—in a historical context—issues that have been richly researched in contemporary society: responses to stigma, responses to the suppression of ethnic or religious expression, conceptions of ethnic difference, strategies among immigrants and refugees to adapt to a new environment, the social control of dissent, and the maintenance of coherent diaspora societies. It will also, I hope, contribute to understanding issues of religious adaptation in an era in which this has become an increasingly arcane subject.

There are no doubt many ways in which the story of the reconstruction of "Portuguese" identity in Amsterdam could be told. I have tried to do so in a way which favors coherence over strict conformity to chronological progression. The first two chapters of the book provide the historical framework for the discussion of identity, describing first the Iberian experience which led to the wave of "Portuguese" emigration in the late sixteenth and seventeenth centuries, and then the early history of the community in Amsterdam.

Each of the subsequent chapters deals with a distinct set of problems which faced the "Portuguese" in Amsterdam in the process of clarifying their identity. The encounter with Dutch society is discussed in chapter three—an encounter whose outcome was initially uncertain. The way in which the Portuguese Jews negotiated their way as minor players in the power struggle between the ruling regent class and the Calvinist clergy, as well as the way in which they responded to a new and unfamiliar cultural and religious environment, had an important bearing on the crystallization of their collective sense of self.

But the common legacy the "Portuguese" brought with them from the Peninsula also shaped their thinking; and chapter four proceeds with a discussion of how communal leaders mined and recast the Iberian legacy, its *hidalguísmo* as well as its experience of persecution, to serve new needs. The book then explores in chapter five one of the key collective goals prompted by this legacy—the "rejudaization" of the community, which is to say, the transition from the ill-defined, shadowy existence of the "Portuguese" in the Peninsula to life within the framework of a carefully demarcated community committed to maintaining normative rabbinic Judaism.

Such a goal was fraught with conflicts, both theological (coming to terms with a tradition that was in many ways alien) and social (establishing ties with a wider Jewish world which had distasteful aspects); and the efforts to resolve these conflicts had much to do with the shape the community ultimately assumed. Finally, in chapter six, the book examines the delicate issue the community faced of dealing with "Portuguese" loyalties which cut across religious lines. Could the community be fully committed to Judaism and yet maintain itself as part of a diaspora that included friars, nuns, and skeptics?

How communal leaders and the rank and file of the community dealt with these issues forms the core of the book—both how they envisioned their enterprise and how they actually behaved. By way of closure, the book concludes with some reflections on the fate of the community in the eighteenth and nineteenth centuries, as it was forced to confront dramatically changed demographic, social, and political realities.

HEBREWS OF THE PORTUGUESE NATION

1

Introduction

The Portuguese conversos who made their way to Amsterdam in the late sixteenth and early seventeenth centuries would not have been conspicuous upon arrival, despite their ignorance of Dutch and their Iberian dress. Foreign immigration to the United Provinces was at a peak in these years. In at least one quarter of the city, around the Bloemstraat, it was easier to make oneself understood in French or Flemish than in Dutch.[1] Later in the seventeenth century the German poet Philipp von Zesen described the Amsterdam Exchange as a place where "almost the whole world trades"—one could find there "Poles, Hungarians, Walloons, Frenchmen, Spaniards, Muscovites, Persians, Turks, and even, occasionally, Hindus."[2] Some of the foreigners were temporary residents, but by the late sixteenth century thousands of foreigners had already settled permanently in Amsterdam. Some had fled war, some religious persecution; others were drawn by economic opportunities in the bustling metropolis on the Amstel.

It was into this milieu that a few Portuguese converso merchants and their families introduced themselves in the last years of the sixteenth century. By 1603 one could speak of a tiny ex-converso community which had established Jewish worship with the aid of a rabbi from Emden. Not long thereafter, in 1609, the community entered a period of extremely rapid growth. In that year the Twelve Years Truce ended a Spanish embargo on Dutch commerce and shipping which had also blocked Dutch trade with Portugal, then under Spanish rule. The truce opened up rich possibilities in Amsterdam for "Portuguese" immigrants, who brought with them experience in Portuguese colonial trade.

What had begun as a small nucleus of merchant families had developed by 1639 into a relatively conspicuous community of well over a thousand persons. Portuguese Jews could be seen entering and leaving the public synagogue they had built, burying their dead at the cemetery they had established just outside the city, and negotiating on the Stock Exchange floor. A governing board of seven officials, appointed mainly from within the merchant elite, supervised communal life in virtually all its aspects, from taxation to excommunication. This rather autocratic regime could be oppressive. But there were certain advantages to having a powerful and centralized communal government, given the broad array of welfare, educational, and financial matters it was expected to administer. And it fit quite naturally into the oligarchically structured political world of seventeenth-century Holland.

During its heyday in the 1670s, the community had a population of about 2,500; its wealth was given concrete expression in the form of an elegant and monumental new synagogue (still a landmark in Amsterdam); and with its Hebrew printing presses, diaspora-wide welfare activity, and distinguished rabbis, its reputation in the Jewish world was firmly established. It would have taken a canny observer indeed to perceive that the community was in fact facing a precipitous decline.

Because of the rapid changes the community underwent, it is not easy to give an accurate portrayal of its social character in the decades following its establishment. The sources inevitably distort as well as reveal. They tend to throw into relief two social types in particular: the international merchants who dominated the community, and the intellectuals who produced treatises, sermons, poetry, and other literary works. Other social elements are seriously underrepresented in the sources, especially women, the "middling" classes, and the poor.

It is true, of course, that much was shared among the different strata. If that were not so, the merchant leadership would not have been able to cultivate a sense of ethnic and religious solidarity, as it did. Certain communal occasions reinforced the sense of community. On sabbaths and holidays, at least, and at major funerals (and more intimately at the *mikveh*, or ritual bath), midwives and barber-surgeons would participate alongside wealthy merchants and their wives in the ritual life of the community. Certain events were also likely to stir a feeling of unity. Dramatic news from elsewhere in the "Portuguese" diaspora—a mass auto-da-fé in Spain, for example, or the Portuguese reconquest of Dutch Brazil—would reverberate within the community and accentuate its separateness from the surrounding society. And yet the gulf between the great merchants and everyone else (including the most eminent of rabbis) was immense.

Contemporary etchings and paintings offer a vivid representation of the way of life of the greatest merchant families. The Dutch artist Romeyn de Hooghe produced striking images of the palatial homes of the baron Manuel de Belmonte (known in the synagogue as Isaac Nunes), Jeronimo Nunes da Costa (Moseh Curiel), and the De Pinto family. The gravestones of the wealthy also say more—and have drawn more attention—than other gravestones in the "Portuguese" cemetery of Amsterdam. They are likely to display a family coat of arms along with baroque biblical scenes and symbols of death—complex statements about status, belief, and aesthetics. In the realm of work, too, we know more about these figures than others.

The home of Isaac Nunes, Baron of Belmonte. Etching by Romeyn de Hooghe, c. 1675. From the collection of the Jewish Historical Museum, Amsterdam *(on loan from J. van Velzen).*

Scholars have described their commercial and diplomatic enterprises in detail, and have measured their degree of Jewish commitment by their presence or absence on lists of communal officials.

But such figures were few. Much of the burden of communal obligations fell on the many lesser merchants whose names appear in notarial deeds, on the pages of Exchange Bank records, in lists of stockholders of the East India Company, as well as in communal records, where they appear as *parnasim* (communal leaders) or as officials of such welfare societies as Bikur Holim (which tended to the sick and dying) and Chonen Dalim (which gave aid to widows and the sick). These so-called "merchants" in fact engaged in a wide spectrum of commercial activity—international trade, speculation on the stock market, shipowning, lending, manufacture, brokerage, or various combinations of these. They might participate in modest commercial ventures or operate huge and multifaceted concerns. But generally, in the first half of the seventeenth century, they tended to specialize in Portuguese colonial wares such as sugar, tobacco, spices, and diamonds, trading almost exclusively with Lisbon, Porto, Madeira, and the Azores. Being engaged in this branch of commerce, it was highly advantageous for them to be located in Amsterdam, which was the main northern entrepôt for colonial commodities. But as a result they were also highly vulnerable to the vicissitudes of Dutch-Iberian relations. This situation changed, however, in the second half of the century (after the signing of the Treaty of Münster in 1648), when Spanish and Spanish-American ports were opened to Dutch "Portuguese" merchants. The focus of their activity shifted in this period to two new routes: trade between the Caribbean and Spanish America, and the wool trade between Spain and Amsterdam.[3]

"Portuguese" merchant families, great and small, constituted a somewhat closed group even within the confines of Portuguese-Jewish society. This is most obvious in their marriage patterns. Marriages between merchant families (or between cousins in the same family) were quite common. The very wealthy tended to marry among themselves (Pintos, Suassos, Da Costas, Pereiras), and smaller-scale merchants followed the same pattern. The absence of unions between the rabbinic and merchant elites is especially noteworthy. Unlike Jews elsewhere, a "Portuguese" merchant would not seek to marry his daughter to a promising rabbinic scholar.[4] Rabbinic learning might be admired (and supported), but it did not bestow social status.

In its early years, the Amsterdam community was in many respects simply a merchant colony like others in northern Europe. But it did not remain so for long. Once communal institutions had been firmly established, the city became a magnet for other Jews. Yiddish-speaking Ashkenazi Jews trickled in—then flooded in—from Germany and Poland, most of them poor and unlearned. They were not welcomed by the Portuguese Jews and lived, for all practical purposes, a separate collective existence. The "Portuguese" community grew almost entirely from converso immigration. Over time, however, the demographic character of this immigration changed. In the period of the Twelve Years Truce (1609–1621), the new immigrants included not only merchants, but persons who served as rabbis, cantors, sextons, school teachers (*rubissim*), physicians, apothecaries, midwives, printers, and diamond cutters.[5] From time to time, a Sephardi Jew from the Mediterranean region would also settle in the community, usually in a rabbinic or quasi-rabbinic role. The change such immigrants brought to the complexion of the community was sociologically important, but not inherently problematic.

Conflict developed only when the changing pattern of immigration produced a growing "underclass" whose members lived off communal support. This was almost inevitable. Once it became known that the community's welfare institutions provided for the poor of "the Nation," poor conversos (of whom there were many) began to flock to Amsterdam.

Relatively little is known of this population. It appears to have been socially heterogeneous, including impoverished widows and orphans from "respectable" families, victims of inquisitorial confiscations, disabled persons, and the chronic poor who were accustomed to seeking assistance. Some succeeded in being integrated into the community. But because of what communal leaders perceived as an excessive burden on communal resources, many were sent away as a matter of policy—in the early years, to the east (Italy or Turkey), and later to the Americas.

What united the community demographically was its "ethnic" unity. The overwhelming majority of the emigres had origins in Portugal, though many had settled subsequently in Spain or Antwerp. Notarial and marriage documents indicate that many were from Lisbon and Porto. But they also came from smaller towns like Bragança, Trancoso, Viseu, or Mogadouro.

From whatever stratum, members of the community were likely to have relatives living in the Peninsula and in other parts of the "Portuguese" diaspora—in Hamburg, Rouen, Salonica, Pisa, Livorno, Tunis, Jerusalem, Brazil, Curação, or Surinam, to name some prominent places of settlement on the map of the "Portuguese" diaspora. Many members of the community had lived for a time in one or more of these places, and others would leave Amsterdam (by choice or otherwise) to settle elsewhere. The geographical dispersion of a single family studied by I. S. Révah—the Bocarro Francês—offers a vivid, if impressionistic, illustration.[6] At the time when a member of this family, Gaspar Bocarro, testified before the Lisbon Inquisition in 1641, he had close relatives living in Lisbon, Madrid, Hamburg, Livorno, Turkey, Pernambuco (Dutch Brazil), and the Portuguese Indies. This dispersion reflects to some extent deep religio-cultural divisions in the family. Bocarro had an aunt who was married to an Old Christian; in 1641 the couple was living in the Portuguese Indies, and raised a daughter who like her mother married an Old Christian. But he also had a first cousin named Mordecai who had been circumcised in infancy in Hamburg, the child of "rejudaized" parents. Gaspar Bocarro himself crossed multiple geographical and religious boundaries in his lifetime. A native of Portugal, he fled from Madrid to St. Jean de Luz after a brawl, and lived as a Jew in Hamburg, Amsterdam, Livorno, and Florence before returning to Portugal in 1641 and reverting to Catholicism. Such persons could be members of "the Nation" in Amsterdam, but they could just as well be members of "the Nation" somewhere else: their sense of affiliation extended far beyond the confines of their visual horizons. It also extended, as we shall see, deep into the past.

Iberian Origins and Vicissitudes of "the Nation"

The past was embedded in the very terminology used to identify the Portuguese Jews, particularly in the term "the Nation." But a distinction should be made between the use of the term "nation" as the Dutch used it and as the "Portuguese" used it. In Amsterdam as elsewhere in Europe, foreign residents tended to be identified according to their religio-ethnic origins. This was sometimes expressed in the term "nation" (e.g., "the English Nation in Antwerp") or the term "church" (e.g., "the French Church in Amsterdam"). The Dutch authorities generally referred to the colony of converso immigrants in the early seventeenth century as "the Portuguese Nation" (*Portugeesche Natie*). The term "nation" used in this way was directly derived from the use of the word in Roman antiquity to mean a local community of foreigners (never one's own community), and this usage was also common in the medieval period.[7]

The emigres, among themselves, used a category of self-definition that appears at first glance to resemble that used by the Dutch authorities. They, too, used the term "nation" to refer to themselves, but did so in a way that was by no means generic: they called themselves "those of *the Nation*." It was the term "nation" that carried the affect. Especially in its Portuguese form—*os da nação*—the term evoked an aura, drama, and historical experience which outsiders could not grasp.

The term harked back to sixteenth-century Spain and Portugal,[8] but among the converso emigres in seventeenth-century Amsterdam it quickly gained new connotations and came to serve new purposes. To understand how the term was transformed, it will be helpful to examine its earlier meanings within the changing Iberian cultural system. Let us go back briefly, then, to the beginnings of converso collective life.

A distinct converso population first emerged in the Peninsula in the wake of the popular anti-Jewish riots that spread through Spain in the summer of 1391. Riots like these, although not unprecedented in medieval Europe, were unique in their long-range consequences. The many Jews who accepted baptism during the riots in order to escape violence became the nucleus of a permanent subgroup of "conversos" in Spanish society.[9] Earlier anti-Jewish disturbances had also left in their wake large numbers of forced converts to Christianity. But this time the converts were not absorbed into Christian society. On the contrary, they developed into a distinct, conspicuous element in Spanish life, recognized as such by all strata of Spanish society. Moreover, the group had a continuing existence, since descendants of the converts continued to be regarded as conversos, or converts, for many generations. And the ranks of this group grew. Fresh converts joined the group periodically as a result of economic and psychological pressures, as well as outbreaks of antisemitic violence. The combined pressures peaked in the period from 1391 to 1415, but violence and the pressure for conversion persisted up to the time of the Expulsion.[10]

The numerous terms by which Castilians referred to the converts and their descendants in the fifteenth century are revealing. In official documents, Catholics of Jewish lineage were referred to as *conversos, confesos,* or *cristianos nuevos* (New Christians). These are concise and reasonably appropriate terms for Jews who had undergone baptism. Had their usage been limited to this sense, the terms would soon have disappeared, since there were no Jews on Spanish soil to be converted after 1492. But in fact the terms showed a surprising resilience. In the century between the riots of 1391 and the Expulsion of 1492, these terms were just as often applied to persons who had never undergone conversion—that is, to *offspring* of baptized Jews who had been raised as Catholics from birth. And after the Expulsion, when there was no one left to convert, the terms *converso, confeso,* and *cristiano nuevo* were never used in their literal sense. The status of converso became, curiously, an *inherited* status—a fateful development. Clearly the terms had assumed certain connotations that justified their continued use.

The primary connotation was "insincere Christian." This assumption about Christians of Jewish origin was expressed quite openly in street parlance, where conversos became known pejoratively as *tornadizos* (renegades) or *marranos* (a term probably alluding to pork).[11] The fact that Castilian legislation of the fourteenth century prohibited the use of these terms indicates that conversos considered them insulting in the extreme.[12] Some of them had obviously complained.

Spanish hostility toward the converts to some degree reflected the persistence of old anti-Jewish sentiments, which did not disappear when a Jew was baptized. The awareness that New Christians had only recently worshiped in synagogues and that they continued to fraternize with their Jewish friends and relatives aroused uneasiness about their place in Spanish society. In this society where group boundaries were clearly drawn—where modern ambiguities of identity were unknown—the conversos violated boundaries in an unprecedented way. In many cases, conversos continued to live in the Jewish quarter; their existence remained connected in the most concrete way with the Jewish realm. And the same New Christian who was seen at mass might be found shortly thereafter at the Jewish burial ceremony of a friend or relative who had not converted. The *mezuzot* (ritual objects placed in the doorways of Jewish homes) would be removed from the doorposts of the new converts' homes, but the place where they had been affixed would be visible, a symbol of everything that baptism alone could not efface. The conversions, a desirable thing in the abstract, became a source of disquiet in Spanish society, a disturbing change in the socioreligious status quo.

Hostility to conversos and their offspring was sharpened by the anger and confusion caused by reports of cryptojudaizing among them. Inquisition files from the late fifteenth century record allegations of conversos practicing a wide range of Jewish ritual acts. Judaizers commonly tried to observe the sabbaths, holidays, and fasts; refrained from eating pork; recited Jewish prayers; and initiated their children, when they felt it was safe, into Jewish beliefs and practices. Needless to say, the Inquisition files in which such behavior is reported must be read with a critical eye.[13] While these files undoubtedly report many actual cases of intentional crypto-judaizing, inquisitorial notions of "judaizing" can be misleading. Officially, the Inquisition sought to prosecute only active heretics. But in fact all conversos came under scrutiny and suspicion. The inevitable result was that various types of nonconformist religious behavior, when observed in conversos, were regarded as "judaizing." Skeptical or relativist ideas about religion in general, blasphemous expressions about the Church, the denial of an afterlife (the widespread expression was that "in this world you will not see me suffer and in the next one you will not see me punished")—all of these were associated with "judaizing" although, strictly speaking, they are clearly not.[14] Inadvertent, vestigial "Jewish" behavior might also be regarded as "judaizing," as, for example, when conversos spontaneously swore "by the Law of Moses" or "by God"—that is, *para el Dío,* using the traditional Jewish singular form of *Díos.*[15]

In the period between 1391 and the Expulsion, it was possible for conversos to fraternize with unbaptized, openly practicing Jews. Where a Jewish community existed alongside a converso community, sustained intimate contact could be maintained between the two groups.[16] Moreover, among the conversos themselves, those who were recently converted remembered Hebrew prayers and the details of Jewish practice. In other words, crypto-Jewish life was informed by normative rabbinic Judaism—its Hebrew liturgy, theology, ritual, and legal precepts. Even in the town of Ciudad Real, where Jewish communal life was completely eliminated in 1391, crypto-Jewish life in the late fifteenth century reflected considerable knowledge of details of rabbinic practice. There is evidence of cryptojudaizers in this period who not only observed the fast on Yom Kippur (a biblical injunction), but went barefoot on that day (a relative detail of rabbinic law). Not only might they attend a Passover *seder,* they might also recall eating the *karpas,* the vegetable dipped in salt prescribed by rabbinic custom.[17]

In this period, up to the establishment of the Inquisition in Castile in 1481, Old Christian attitudes toward conversos were relatively relaxed and lacked the obsessive quality they later acquired. Though hostility existed, it did not prevent ambitious converts and descendants of converts from penetrating social and economic elites in major cities of the Spanish realms. New Christians negotiated marriage alliances with Old Christian families, including those of the high nobility. Many were able to fan out occupationally from their base in traditional Jewish administrative and financial functions (though many, it should be added, remained humble artisans or small-scale merchants). As members of the converso economic elite expanded their functions, they also gained entry into hitherto unattainable offices in municipal government. Those offices could be transformed into an inherited family asset. The rapid accumulation of social prestige, wealth, and political power among the converso elite continued unchecked until the mid-fifteenth century. Inevitably, it stirred new fears and resentments.

Such new fears contributed to the first outbreak of violence against conversos in 1449. A popular uprising in Toledo, led by a noble who had become disaffected with the crown, culminated in rioting against the local conversos and legislation aimed at excluding conversos from public life.[18] This act, the Toledo "purity of blood" statute (revoked after the revolt was quelled) was one of the earliest statements of the idea that conversos posed a threat to Spanish society beyond that of religious nonconformity: the conversos had accumulated power "in order to destroy the holy Catholic faith as well as the Old Christians who believe in it."[19] The statement reflected a significant shift in attitude: an emerging ethnic hostility to conversos—and fear of their imagined malevolence.

From this time until about 1474, anticonverso violence was a common event. Bands formed, and conversos took up arms to defend themselves.[20] Religious suspicions fueled the unrest, but no less powerful a role was played by strong popular resentment at the success of conversos in obtaining lucrative municipal offices.[21] Growing hostility created a new basis for converso solidarity, thus intensifying converso chariness toward Old Christians. A great deal more needs to be understood about converso–Old Christian relations in this period. It seems evident, however, that it was a time when converso accommodation to Catholic life was proceeding, while at the same time converso-Old Christian tensions along socioeconomic and political lines were being heightened.

With the establishment of the Inquisition and firm centralized royal control in the late fifteenth century, the civil strife between conversos and Old Christians subsided. Indeed, the state's assumption of responsibility for monitoring converso behavior may have been intended in part to check popular violence. But if violence ceased, the process of isolation and stigmatization continued. In fact, inquisitorial activity gave it considerable impetus. Thus, despite the fact that by the late fifteenth century a great many conversos in Castile had accommodated to Spanish Catholic life (they were not necessarily pious Catholics, but neither were they purposeful judaizers), the highly public activity of the Inquisition fed the popular conviction that all conversos were religiously suspect. As mentioned, the Inquisition sought to prosecute only active heretics, but all conversos came under scrutiny, with the result that cases of "judaizing" were uncovered and hostile attitudes reinforced. And, as the Inquisition forced cryptojudaizing underground, fears about conversos intensified: the hidden, unseen threat was felt to be greater than the easily identifiable one.

Two royal measures toward the end of the fifteenth century caused a surge in the number of conversos: the Edict of Expulsion issued by the

Catholic Monarchs in 1492, which triggered a wave of conversions among Jews reluctant to face the hardships of exile, and the forced baptism en masse of Portugal's Jews in 1497.[22] These measures not only swelled the ranks of the conversos, but also eliminated the open practice of Judaism from the Peninsula. This meant that from this point onward converso life in the Peninsula evolved in almost complete isolation from traditional rabbinic life. This is not to say that there was no contact whatsoever between conversos in the Peninsula and Jewish communities elsewhere. Evidence indicates that a number of Jews did make their way to the Peninsula, generally under disguise, to conduct business or proselytize among conversos.[23] But sustained contact with Jewish life elsewhere ceased.

In the absence of institutionalized Jewish life, ideas and attitudes about Judaism among the conversos assumed a folkloristic, unlettered character. A vivid example is the crypto-Jewish grasp of the minor holiday of Purim, which conversos elevated to the status of a major holiday. The holiday is a symbolic celebration of the Jews' victory over their enemies, with its source in the Book of Esther.[24] This story had widespread appeal to Jews everywhere, but it had a particular hold on conversos. It is a story of the systematic religious oppression of Jews, and its heroine, Esther, is forced for a long period to conceal her Jewish identity, but at last reveals her origins and saves her people from a violent slaughter.

The appeal to conversos of this story, available to anyone who could read the Vulgate, is obvious. The weight conversos gave it was expressed not only in the centrality Purim assumed in the crypto-Jewish year, but also in the crypto-Jewish observance of the Fast of Esther. Rabbinically this was a one-day fast in memory of the three-day fast Esther observed in the biblical story. But crypto-Jews, following the biblical account, observed a three-day fast. This was a deviation from rabbinic practice but few crypto-Jews in the post-Expulsion period could have known this.

A striking particular example of the importance attached to Purim appears in the testimony of an accused Portuguese "judaizer," Leonor de Pina, interrogated in March 1619. Her testimony included only one brief remark about the major holiday of Passover, but went on at great length about the minor Fast of Esther. Leonor and her daughters, like other conversos, observed three days of "fasting," as she put it, "without eating if it was not dark, or else eating things other than meat." She was well aware of the origins of the fast. She said that it

> was observed by Queen Esther when, at the order of Haman, the king Ahasuerus decreed to massacre the Jews. Mordecai begged his niece Esther to ask Ahasuerus to revoke the decree. She fasted three days, then went to the king. The latter, though it was ordained that no one ask him anything, kissed his scepter when he saw her and, upon her request, revoked the order against the Jews and executed Haman.[25]

Introduction

The Inquisition files of Spain and Portugal are rich with material throwing light on the symbolic and ritual lives of "judaizers." To be sure, testimony extracted under coercion cannot be taken at face value, and highly generalized, standard confessions must be regarded with special caution. But there can be no doubt that among "judaizers," whose numbers varied greatly over time and in different parts of the Peninsula, types of religious sensibility emerged which differed greatly from late medieval Spanish-Jewish piety.

Cryptojudaizing proved, however, to have rather shallow roots in Castile. A generation or two after the Expulsion, it died out quite quickly. By the mid-sixteenth century, the vast majority of Castilian conversos entertained only the vaguest ideas about Judaism and had effectively assimilated into Spanish Catholic society. Cryptojudaizing continued to live as a reality—with fateful consequences—mainly in the Spanish-Catholic imagination.

As converso society changed in the period following the Expulsion, so too did Old Christian attitudes about conversos. This is reflected in shifts in terminology in the sixteenth century. The terms that had been common at the time of the Expulsion referred to the converts and their descendants as individuals with a certain religious history. By the mid-sixteenth century, there was an increasing use of collective terms like *gente del linaje, esta gente, esta generación, esta raza* ("those of this lineage," "this people," "this lineage," "this race"), as well as *los de la nación* ("those of the nation"). These terms reflected an emerging view which emphasized the conversos' purported ethnic or racial traits.[26]

The increasingly ethnic view of the conversos added a new dimension to the antiheresy rhetoric of "purification." Many in Spanish society, including concerned ecclesiastics, came to believe that even the propensity to judaize was an inherent racial characteristic. Religious fears, instead of disappearing, became increasingly generalized and obsessive. This shift meant that religious suspicions merged with the general configuration of anticonverso thinking, which pointed to the conversos' tainted blood as the source of their many evils.

This shift in perception was stimulated by the gradual spread in Spanish society of statutes discriminating against conversos on racial grounds (the *estatutos de limpieza de sangre*, or "purity of blood" statutes), which became common in sixteenth-century Castile. In effect, they established a separate and inferior social status for all persons with Jewish blood of whatever degree. Conversos with profound Catholic beliefs were now faced with exclusion from various institutions, among them military orders, religious orders, municipal councils, and confraternities. The statutes were not adopted by all such bodies, nor were they always strictly enforced.[27] But the spread of these statutes affirmed the implicit social inferiority of conversos.

The stigma of being a converso had become a racial stigma, tied primarily to values of honor and social prestige.[28]

The institutionalized attitudes to conversos which evolved in Castile were in some ways unique to that kingdom. But they reverberated throughout the Iberian Peninsula and had important consequences for the conversos of Portugal, a group central to this study. It was in response to pressure from the Spanish crown that the Portuguese monarch carried out the forced baptism of Portugal's Jews in 1497. And it was in imitation of Castilian patterns that Portugal dealt with its "converso problem." Portugal, too, established an Inquisition and instituted "purity of blood" statutes. Conversos there came to be identified by terms which were the Portuguese equivalents of the Castilian terms: *cristãos novos* ("New Christians"), *gente da nação,* and *homens da nação* ("Men of the Nation")—with or without the identifying adjective *hebrea.*

But the terms coined for conversos, insofar as they suggested a group with genuine collective traits, had a real human referent in Portugal in a way they did not in Castile. In Portugal the perceived "Jewishness" of converso society was not so unequivocally a product of the imagination. Here the "Men of the Nation" tended to cling tenaciously to Jewish identity, and actual judaizing among them was not unusual.

The reasons for this difference are easily understood. The conversos who remained in post-Expulsion Spain had already been subjected as a group to a century-long assault on their psyches. The assault continued after the Expulsion. Most of those who clung to Jewish memories and practices were eventually beaten into submission by the Inquisition (or terror of it). In Portugal, in contrast, Jewish life among Portugal's native Jews and its emigres from Spain had been allowed to proceed without interference until the sudden forced baptisms of 1497. Among the converts in 1497 were many exiles from Spain, that is, Jews who had had the strength to resist pressures to convert and, ultimately, to flee Spain.[29] They were not easily cowed by a "baptism" that was a matter of royal expediency. Moreover, the crown took a relatively realistic attitude and did not begin to crack down on "judaizers" until the establishment of an inquisition in 1536. By this time, Portugal had on its hands an experienced population of "converts" who regarded themselves as Jews and were prepared to resist attempts to intimidate them.

As a result, crypto-Jewish life in Portugal retained its vitality for generations, whereas in Castile it became increasingly enfeebled. But toward the end of the sixteenth century the neat bifurcation of development on opposite sides of the border was upset by political events. In 1580 Portugal was annexed to the Spanish crown, and the Spanish border was opened to the Portuguese New Christians. This was virtually an invitation to the latter to migrate to the large commercial centers of Castile, especially to Seville and

Madrid—either to escape the Inquisition (in Spain one could not be tried for crimes committed in Portugal) or to seek out economic opportunities. The migration reached major proportions after 1621, due to stepped-up inquisitorial activity in Portugal which coincided with particularly favorable conditions for conversos in Spain.[30]

The immigration of thousands of Portuguese New Christians to the great commercial and political centers of Spanish life was laden with consequences. A relatively quiet Spain became a refuge for significant numbers of crypto-Jews, among them prominent royal financiers (*asentistas*). Spanish society was not slow to respond. The Spanish Inquisition began to expose what it claimed to be episodes of "judaizing" among the Portuguese newcomers, not always on strong evidence.[31] Many of these New Christians were in fact from "judaizing" families, but had learned well the art of dissimulation. They also tended to be wealthy. The Inquisition acted on what was perhaps a combination of intuition and greed. In any case, the "revelations" aroused growing hostility among the public. As a result, the "Men of the Nation" who had immigrated from Portugal were perceived as a distinct and increasingly suspect element in Castilian society.

The appearance of this new group on the Castilian scene gave rise to a new term. The need to distinguish these conversos from native Spanish conversos was obvious. This need was soon satisfied with the terms *portugueses de la nación hebrea,* or, in ellipsis, *portugueses de la nación.*[32] Significantly, by the seventeenth century, the term "Portuguese" was applied even to Castilian-born conversos whose parents or grandparents had Portuguese origins.[33]

Since the crypto-Jewish tendencies of the families who crossed the border from Portugal to Spain were notorious, the term "Portuguese" became virtually synonymous with "judaizer." Collectively, the Portuguese conversos were known as *la nación portuguesa* or *la gente portuguesa.* These terms were adopted in European countries outside the Peninsula as well. The Portuguese Jesuit theologian António Vieira lamented the misunderstanding this produced, noting that "in popular parlance, among most of the European nations, 'Portuguese' is confused with 'Jew.'"[34]

Responses to Stigma in the Peninsula

It was thus by a long process, over many generations and through various historical vicissitudes, that there emerged a view of the Portuguese converso as both an intimate, familiar presence and an alien element in Iberian society. The elliptical term "the Nation" suggests both familiarity and foreignness, intimacy and phobia. One could despise conversos, but one could also enjoy them: as a butt of jokes, for example, or as a convenient group against which to flaunt one's own superiority. They were also useful in their roles as bankers, merchants, and physicians, especially since Spanish and Portuguese Old Christians shrank from these now racially stigmatized functions. Some were also powerful in municipal government and at court. This may partially explain why they were discriminated against but not, like the *moriscos* (converted Muslims and their descendents), expelled.[35]

To such a complex situation there was naturally a wide range of responses on the part of conversos themselves. The group—if it can be called that—had few of the characteristics that generally define social groups. It had no contrasting social environment—no distinct language, culture, or religion against which to define itself. It had no territory. It possessed no institutional structures. It included sincere Catholics, crypto-Jews, and skeptics, thus lacking one of the most important characteristics that define social entities in premodern societies: a common religious identity.

But all conversos shared the stigma of Jewish blood, except perhaps for the unknowing descendants of those who had obtained spurious certificates of *limpieza* (purity of blood). Given the psychological and social rejection experienced by conversos, there was a certain inevitability that despite the lack of clear boundaries defining "the Nation"—and despite the fact that this group was created primarily as a result of hostile outside impulses—a genuine sense of affiliation to "the Nation" developed among many conversos.

To be sure, not among all. Indeed, many New Christians in the urban elite, particularly in Castile, seem to have thoroughly internalized the Spanish-Catholic ethos and accepted the routine disgrace of possessing Jewish origins. The stigma was tolerable to such conversos as long as they reaped significant economic or other benefits by participating in Spanish society. That there were many conversos who succeeded in doing so is indicated by the rapid upward mobility of Castilian conversos in the fifteenth century and their concomitant accommodation to Catholic life.[36]

But there is also evidence that at least some conversos developed subtly defiant postures toward the society that stigmatized them. They sought to cast "the Nation" in a positive light without challenging the basic religious and social values of Old Christian society. An early example can be found in a fifteenth-century work of Juan de Lucena, who attributes the following fictional words to the converso churchman Alonso de Cartagena:

> Don't imagine that you injure me when you call my fathers Hebrews. Of course they were, and thus I want them to be. For if nobility lies in antiquity, who goes back further [than the Jew]? And if [nobility lies in] virtue, who is closer to it [than the Jew]? And if—by the standards of Spain—wealth is nobility, who is more wealthy in his day?[37]

As the passage hints ("by the standards of Spain"), the author was affirming, not challenging, Iberian values concerning ethnicity and lineage; but he was rearranging the hierarchic order in a way that permitted him to cultivate a sense of adequacy, even superiority, vis-à-vis Old Christians.[38] It is possible that this line of argument was persuasive to conversos because of the lingering medieval aristocratic pride of the Spanish Jews. The dominant Jewish families of medieval Spain, who had played important roles at court, were able to imitate the aristocratic lifestyle of their environment; eventually, an aristocratic self-image was projected onto Spanish Jews in general.[39] After the conversos were forcibly integrated into Spanish Christian society, they would have had every reason to hold on to such notions, adapting them, as Juan de Lucena did, to their new conditions of life.

The most categorically defiant response to the converso plight was to engage in "judaizing" of one form or another. Such activity (or thinking) was, to be sure, a matter of belief—or at any rate, compliance with the will of other family members for whom it was a matter of belief. But it also served to provide the "judaizer" with an affirmative inner sense of self and group. To cling in some way to the Law of Moses entailed not only a denial of the claims of the Catholic Church, but also a rejection of religio-national claims which linked Iberian imperial expansion to notions of religious superiority and chosenness.

The renunciation by some Iberian conversos of the religio-national identity paraded in the streets and represented in the churches took different forms. Conversos sometimes idealized their condition by identifying with the Jews in Egypt, oppressed and surrounded by idolatry (i.e., Catholic ritual).[40] A poignant example of such identification is a prayer produced in testimony before a Portuguese inquisitorial tribunal. The brief supplication was a prayer, in effect, for a new Exodus: "Lord, just as You liberated those of Egypt, opening the sea for them in twelve places, thus liberate me from these prisons [sic] I am in."[41] (The allusion to the Red Sea parting "in twelve places" derives, interestingly, from an early rabbinic *midrash*, or homiletical commentary on the Torah.)[42]

As we have noted, "judaizing" conversos also identified with the story of Esther, with its strong elements of identity concealment, systematic religious persecution, and ultimate victory. Both the Exodus and Esther stories involve religious and national self-affirmation vis-à-vis an oppressor. Identifying with their protagonists allowed conversos to situate themselves in the mainstream of Jewish history and tradition. It also served to elevate Jewish history to a metahistorical plane, thus rendering early modern Spanish *grandeza* ephemeral and meaningless. Finally, it suggested the possibility of deliverance and "return" to the open observance of Judaism.

Many possessed a hope not only of deliverance, but also of redemption. Expressions of Jewish messianic hope among the Iberian exiles and conversos[43] (a characteristic of Jewish society at the time)[44] are a clear indication of alienation from and defiance of the theological and political messages of the Spanish-Catholic world. Conversos expressed the wish to go (or be transported) to the Holy Land. In Calatayud, a converso believed his son was destined to be a page in the service of the Messiah and declared he would not cut his son's hair until the Messiah came.[45]

There is an abundance of evidence of this sort that "judaizers" among the conversos in the Peninsula developed countermythologies powerful enough to sustain their sense of dignity in a milieu saturated with the symbols and rhetoric of Spanish superiority. To be sure, such conversos could not have developed any single countermyth. They were too dispersed and too constrained from freely communicating to create a common discourse. Yet the mobility, ingenuity, and "networking" of Iberian conversos should not be underestimated. The historian I. S. Révah isolated three more-or-less universal elements in crypto-Jewish traditions: a) the rejection of Catholicism as a form of idolatry; b) the awareness of belonging to a Jewish people which worships the only true God and which will be redeemed by the Messiah, its remnants being conducted to the Holy Land; and c) the belief that salvation could be achieved only through the Law of Moses.[46]

But crypto-Jewish ideas tended to be transmitted not in the colorless style of the scholar seeking to generalize, but in vivid, popular images which possessed the power to inspire and be retained. By way of illustration, let me discuss a single idea with strong emotional elements that crops up in two radically different contexts. It appears in a passage in a fifteenth-century chronicle by the Castilian priest Andres Bernáldez (not himself a converso) and in a seventeenth-century family history by a Portuguese ex-converso living in Amsterdam. Bernáldez reports the following belief among conversos:

> All of them [the conversos] were Jews and clung to their hope, like the Israelites in Egypt, who suffered many blows at the hands of the Egyptians and yet believed that God would lead them out from the midst of them, as He did with a mighty hand and an outstreched arm. So, too, the conversos looked upon the Christians as Egyptians or worse and believed that God had them in His keeping and miraculously preserved them. They held steadfastly to their faith that God would guide and remember them and bring them out from the midst of the Christians and lead them to the Holy and Promised Land.[47]

Bernáldez's text (with its typically undifferentiated view of conversos) is strikingly echoed in a passage from the family history composed by Isaac de Pinto, an ex-converso living as a Jew in seventeenth-century Amsterdam. The author relates that his great-grandfather Gil Lopes Pinto (active in the mid-sixteenth century), when he revealed the family's origins to one of his children, stated that he was "a Jew, and was known as a person belonging to this nation," and furthermore "that God is performing a greater miracle for us than the Exodus from Egypt, for we continue to maintain ourselves among people who know [unlike the Egyptians] that we killed the one they believe in."[48] This story was preserved in the family (and a large and far-flung family it was) for at least four generations.

The common elements of these two reported beliefs would have resonated powerfully among crypto-Jews in the Peninsula. There was an implicit denial that God was on the side of the Iberian monarchs (the mighty Pharaoh in the Exodus story), even though the Spanish and Portuguese made such claims and drew reinforcement for them from their political and military successes. Identification with the Israelites in slavery reassured crypto-Jews that God was on their side despite their apparent helplessness, that their suffering was part of a divine plan, that deliverance would come at the appointed hour and the enemy would be humiliated, destroyed, and exposed as fraudulent.

Interestingly, vivid countermythic material with an anti-imperialist thrust can be found in works written by emigres who had escaped the Peninsula. It is difficult to establish whether or not the authors were making use of ideas that had been cultivated clandestinely in the Peninsula. In general, we are likely to find such ideas in apologetic works aimed at the ex-converso population, such as Isaac Cardoso's *Excelencias de los Hebreos* or João Pinto Delgado's autobiography.[49] The need such authors felt to contrast Jewish virtues with Iberian pretensions suggests that there existed some conflict among ex-conversos. Iberian national claims still held sway among this rejudaized minority and aroused ambivalence even after emigration.

Among conversos there might exist, then, both a wish to identify with the prevalent values of Iberian society and a need to defy them. This led, in some cases, to a kind of inversion—an acceptance of the Iberian esteem for lineage, for example, along with the insistence on the special merit of Jewish ancestry. Others suffered inwardly from insulted pride and feelings of alienation, while appearing outwardly well integrated into Old Christian society. Responses to stigma and religious persecution varied greatly, but certain problems seem to have haunted the population of Portuguese conversos, whether they had to do with social prestige or eternal salvation. These problems continued to play a role in identity formation long after members of "the Nation" settled outside the Peninsula.

On Free Soil: The Ideology of Restoration

Attitudes and ideas formed in the Peninsula proved persistent, but they inevitably underwent change among the emigres after they settled in Amsterdam. The ex-conversos were now free to define themselves as they chose. Indeed, for some, the wish to do so had been an important motive for leaving the Peninsula. Settlement in Amsterdam was an act of liberation and an opportunity to repossess the past. From this point of view, the efforts of the Amsterdam "Portuguese" to reconstitute their Jewishness bear comparison to the efforts in modern times of once-colonialized or otherwise culturally dominated peoples to restore an "authentic" lost heritage.

The emigres did not, however, feel a need to renounce their Iberian "nature." The thought would never have occurred to them. Living in Calvinist Amsterdam, they were more conspicuously Iberian than ever before. This was a source of pride and an important component of their developing sense of collective self. As practicing Jews in a Christian environment, there was also a clear religious boundary separating them from the majority society. Both in the habits they had assimilated from Spanish and Portuguese society and in their practice of Jewish law, they suddenly became what they had never been before, a well-defined group.

But while the boundaries of the group were clarified in some ways with emigration to the Netherlands, they became more confused in others. True, the term "the Nation" continued to be used to define the population of conversos and ex-conversos. But it now came to incorporate a far-flung and expanding diaspora. In this new context, the danger of open religious conflict within "the Nation" was far greater than it had been. In the Peninsula, no converso had been an openly practicing Jew, and there had been a continuum of religious affiliation, from ardently Jewish to ardently Catholic, with a large ambiguous cluster in between. Once on "free soil," religious differences among conversos became more dichotomized, and vacillating became more difficult. Moreover, with the reestablishment of "normative" rabbinic communal life, there was a need to establish theological and religious-legal authority and to institute enforceable boundaries of behavior.

This was especially problematic given the psychological and cognitive problems ex-conversos faced in adapting to "normative" rabbinic life. When conversos left the Peninsula after generations of isolation from traditional Jewish life, they brought with them notions of Judaism that were anomalous and rudimentary. They were not necessarily ashamed of this or repentant of their "Catholic" past (though some were). Since the Iberian "judaizers" of later converso generations, having been baptized in infancy, had not themselves betrayed Judaism through conversion, and since in any case they had taken daily risks and made sacrifices to maintain a Jewish identity, they did not usually feel that their level of Jewish knowledge and observance—however folkloristic—was less than admirable. What their Jewishness lacked in organic connection to historic Judaism, it made up for in its steadfastness in the face of systematic persecution.

Introduction

The decision to draw boundaries in the Amsterdam community on the basis of adherence to rabbinic Judaism thus threatened unity even within the ex-converso group. It also threatened the viability of diaspora-wide solidarity. Once rabbinic norms were established in Amsterdam (or Hamburg or London), the sense of affiliation with conversos without Jewish commitments in the Peninsula, including those who were nuns and friars, became problematic.

Yet failure to draw such boundaries also posed a danger. It would undermine the cherished goal, rooted in crypto-Jewish lore, of a collective "return" to mainstream Jewish life and historical experience. It would threaten the community's integration into the wider Jewish world—and this integration could not be taken for granted. Iberian Jewry's centuries-long experience of religious repression was the experience of a relatively small and isolated sector of the overall Jewish population. Meanwhile, outside the Peninsula, Jewish life had continued to develop as it had for centuries within the framework of rabbinic law and autonomous communal institutions. The emigres' encounter after they left the Peninsula with Jews whose links with rabbinic tradition were unbroken inevitably aroused conflicts, cultural as well as religious.

Not only its religious ambiguities, but also the increasing dispersion of "those of the Nation" threatened the survival of this entity, with its intangible and tangled boundaries. With the loss even of continental boundaries—with "Men of the Nation" dispersed from Pernambuco to Cochin, from Safed to Zamosc, from Seville to London—could a persuasive idea of community be constructed and maintained at all? And was there a sufficiently strong emotional need to sustain such an idea?

In the new circumstances, the peninsular crypto-Jewish ethos, built around resistance to inquisitorial persecution, lost much of its affect and power. The ex-conversos faced challenges of another type. True, they had kin and friends in the Peninsula who were still in "Egyptian bondage." But defiance of a remote oppressor was not a suitable emotional impulse for community building in an atmosphere of well-being and relative freedom.

A set of ideas emerged as central, by no means entirely new but thrust into a position of new importance. They are prominently represented in the founding legends of the community, recorded in the late seventeenth and eighteenth centuries. These legends were part fact and part fancy, woven together over time as such collective myths are. They compressed and distorted actual events, but reveal much about the community's understanding of its own history. Before examining the historical record, it is worth examining the stories of the community's founding, and the ideas they embodied.

The organizing notion in these stories was that of restoration. The founding of a Jewish community represented the fulfillment of dreams and expectations that had been harbored secretly in the Peninsula: the escape from enforced conformity to a false belief system, and a return to the true ancestral faith. There was nothing new in the structure of this idea. The phenomenon of straying, suffering, and returning had roots in Scripture, in the Exodus story and in the later prophets. The message spoke directly to judaizers in the Peninsula, reassuring them that their predicament was temporary. Had not Moses prophesied both this predicament and redemption from it? "And the Lord shall scatter you among the nations. . . . And there you shall serve gods, the work of men's hands, wood and stone. . . . But if from there thou shalt seek the Lord thy God, thou shalt find him" (Deut. 4:27–29). This passage, rich in its evocation of exile and crucifixes, suggested that their own "restoration" was not only possible but written into the divine script.

The restoration myth of the Amsterdam emigres—like the more secular ones of modern anticolonial and nationalist movements—had its legendary heroes and symbols. Emotionally it had both a rebellious, rejecting aspect (vis-à-vis Catholicism) and an affirmative aspect (vis-à-vis Judaism). This is evident in one of the early images used by emigres in Amsterdam—the phoenix, used as the symbol of one of the early congregations (Neve Salom, 1612) and revived as a symbol of the united community (though perhaps not until much later).[50] The image of the rebirth of the bird out of its own ashes—the ashes suggesting the autos-da-fé (the image is much used in converso martyrdom literature)[51]—gave poignant expression to the idea of restoration.

The most important early elaboration of the myth of restoration can be found in a rambling, diffuse work by Daniel Levi de Barrios, a former New Christian who joined the Amsterdam community in about 1662. The entire work, a collection of essays with the imposing title *Triumpho del govierno popular* (Triumph of Popular Government), is a description of, and tribute to, the Amsterdam community. It is dedicated to the communal leaders ("the very illustrious *señores, parnasim* and *gabay* of the *Kahal Kados* of Amsterdam")[52]—whose patronage, incidentally, De Barrios needed badly.[53] With its transparent flattery of the communal leadership, the work clearly does not reflect the candid observations of a solitary intellectual. De Barrios was constructing an idealized conception of the community which he believed would be attractive to the elite.

Of great importance to the perpetuation of lore concerning the founding of the community is the story related in the essay "Casa de Jacob," although important material is found elsewhere in the book as well. De Barrios is the earliest source for this story (though not the sole one) and must have learned it from people with early roots in the community.

According to De Barrios, Jewish observance and worship were first established in Amsterdam by an Ashkenazi rabbi from Emden, Uri Halevi,

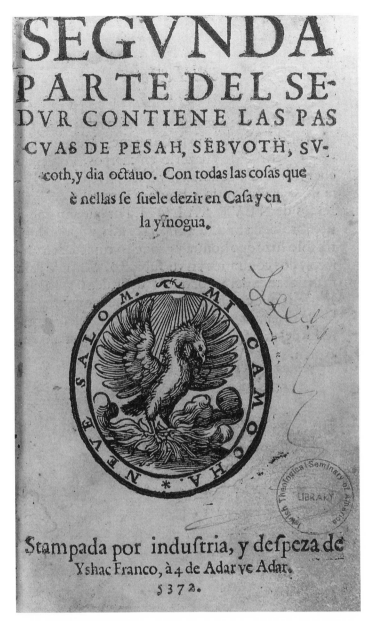

SEGVNDA

PARTE DEL SE-
DVR CONTIENE LAS PAS

CVAS DE PESAH, SĒBVOTH, SV-

coth, y dia octáuo. Con todas las cofas que

è nellas fe fuele dezir en Cafa y en

la yſnogua.

Stampada por induftria, y defpeza de
Yshac Franco, à 4 de Adar ve Adar.
5372.

Title page of part two of a prayer book in Spanish published at the initiative of the merchant and communal leader Isaac Franco for the Neve Salom congregation (Amsterdam, 1612), showing the emblem of the congregation, the phoenix, and a transliteration of the Hebrew "Who is like thee?" (Ex. 15:11). *Courtesy of the Library of the Jewish Theological Seminary of America.*

in 1580.[54] As this story would have it, the Jewish practices of the group around Halevi were kept private and were not discovered by the authorities until 1595. In that year, on the solemn day of Yom Kippur, the group was found during the dramatic culminating prayer of the day (*Ne'ilah*) by the "rigorous police of Amsterdam," who, seeing the worshipers prostrate in prayer, believed they had come upon a group of idolatrous "papists." Since public worship of Catholicism was prohibited in Amsterdam, there was a certain plausibility to this story but also, of course, an irresistible irony. The police demanded that the worshipers hand over their hosts and crucifixes; but when they searched for such articles they found only some books in Hebrew, indicating that they had come upon a group of Jews. Upon realizing this, the sheriff asked them to pray to the God of Israel on behalf of the government of Amsterdam. The Jews gladly consented through their representative Jacob Tirado (an important figure in the community's lore, said to be the founder of the first congregation in Amsterdam). When the incident was reported to the magistrate, the latter declared on the spot that Judaism could be practiced openly.[55]

In its broad strokes and in its detail, this is a fascinating story—all the more so since we have documentation about what actually happened. The lore reported by De Barrios depicts the converso colony in Amsterdam as a fully observant Jewish community from its inception, which he dates at 1580. Moreover, it presents Jewish practice as immediately acceptable to the Dutch authorities when they became aware of it. This offers an idealized, simplified picture of what was in fact a complex process whose long-term outcome was ambiguous for many years.

What actually happened on that Yom Kippur is somewhat different. Uri Halevi was very much a historical figure (and was in fact an Ashkenazi rabbi from Emden), and he did take part in such an episode. The episode occurred, however, on Yom Kippur of September 14, 1603—a full eight years after the date De Barrios gives. (Moreover, the first evidence of a converso presence in Amsterdam is from 1595.)[56] Rabbi Uri Halevi and his son were arrested, imprisoned, and brought before the authorities. Halevi was charged not with conducting Catholic rites—but with receiving stolen goods and circumcising adults! Clearly, it was in part the group's *Jewish* activity that was disturbing to the authorities.[57] However, Halevi and his son were released and allowed to continue their activity.[58]

What the distortions in the narrative seem aimed to achieve is to produce a perfect restoration story in a compressed, simplified way. The story leaves no room for the question, What were the practices and loyalties of the conversos who came to Amsterdam before Uri Halevi's arrival? And concerning the attitude of the authorities it produces an impression quite different from the reality. (The evidence indicates that the authorities refused to sanction Jewish practice in Amsterdam until 1614, when they did so only implicitly.)

Introduction

In addition to the Yom Kippur story, De Barrios recounts a more romantic piece of lore. He tells of Mayor Rodrigues and Gaspar Lopes Homem, conversos in Lisbon, who sought to escape "the horrors of the cruel Inquisition" by fleeing Portugal for Holland. In 1590 (the Hebrew date De Barrios gives) or 1593 (the Roman date he gives) their daughter Maria Nunes and son Manuel Lopes Pereyra embarked for Holland with an uncle, Miguel Lopes. The English, who were at war with Spain, seized their ship. Maria was wooed for her beauty by an English duke. In London, the Queen drove her through the city in a carriage to show off her beauty. But "not yielding to amorous entreaties or honorific and alluring gifts," she renounced wealth and royal privilege and chose to revert to Judaism in Amsterdam, where she married the ex-converso Manuel Lopes Homem.

Documentary evidence from several sources points to a kernel of historical truth in this story. Maria Nunes, the daughter of Mayor Rodrigues and Gaspar Lopes Homem, did indeed marry Manuel Lopes Homem in Amsterdam; according to the Amsterdam municipal marriage registers (*Puyboecken*), this occurred on November 28, 1598.[59] A good deal is known about her family, including the fact that her parents were indeed incarcerated in an inquisitorial prison.[60] A remarkable letter from Noël de Caron, agent of the States of Holland in England, to the States-General of Holland in 1597, reveals more. He relates that Dutch ships on their way from Spain were seized and boarded by the English. He continues:

> One of the said ships, from Vlissingen, under Master Willem Pieters, was stripped and its entire cargo taken to the Queen's warehouse. Four Portuguese merchants were discovered upon it and a Portuguese maiden dressed in a man's habit. . . . They were seemingly making for Amsterdam, where the Portuguese maiden (who is of noble descent) intended to marry, her parents being confined by the Inquisition.[61]

In view of the corresponding details, it is difficult to see this as anything other than a record of the Maria Nunes episode, which must have occurred not in 1590 or 1593 but in 1597. The fact that Maria's marriage took place in 1598 tends to confirm this.

Not surprisingly, we find nothing in De Caron's account of royal carriages or ducal proposals. Like other founding legends, the story was enhanced in the telling. The Jewish motivations of the Nunes family were underscored: so powerful were they that Maria spurned an English duke (of whom she was naturally worthy).

Why, though, does the tale related by De Barrios push the events back in time, to the imagined early days of the Jewish community in 1590 or 1593? (Even later, at the actual time of Maria Nunes's arrival in 1597, there was no organized Jewish community in Amsterdam.) This served a possible function which we have seen with the Uri Halevi story. The messy possibility that there was a period of limbo during which no real effort had been made by the conversos to reestablish Judaism in Amsterdam was neatly eliminated.

Equally notable is the fact that De Barrios eliminated later events in the history of Maria Nunes from his story. A notarial deed of November 1612 reveals that Maria's husband, Manuel Lopes Homem, had by then left Amsterdam and gone elsewhere—first to Lisbon and then to Seville![62] Perhaps Maria (who would have been 37 years old in 1612) accompanied him, although we have no evidence for this. In any case, the idealized picture of the family's loyalty to Judaism, as transmitted by communal lore, is thrown into serious doubt by the (at least temporary)[63] return of the heroine's mate to the "lands of idolatry," as Spain and Portugal were known to the emigres. The picture is further tarnished by the astonishing fact that Maria Nunes's brother Antonio Lopes Pereyra, who married in Amsterdam like Maria and became a pillar of the Jewish community, also returned to Spain, and became a figure of some stature at the court of Philip IV.[64] (Incidentally, this latter development was not ignored by De Barrios, who with some exaggeration elevated Lopes Pereyra to the office of "*contador mayor* of the king of Spain.")[65] This should not obscure the fact that some members of the Homem-Nunes-Pereyra group became—and remained—pillars of the Jewish community.[66]

The two embellished stories told by De Barrios, and repeated with variations by later authors, are elaborations of a single fundamental myth. Along with the usual functions that founding myths serve—the creation of a shared, idealized past in order to perpetuate the community as a meaningful entity and project its destiny into the future—these stories also served to smooth over some of the less heroic aspects of the early years of the community. They suggested a harmonious, unconflicted, natural transition from the Iberian Catholic experience to normative Jewish life in Amsterdam. They created the illusion of a continuous, uniform Portuguese-Jewish ethnic existence, from the time of the forced baptisms in the Peninsula onward, with two dramatic stages—the period of oppression and the period of restoration.

Such founding myths reflect important beliefs about a society's past. But they typically fail to reflect the complexities of the context in which new social groups crystallize, or the more pedestrian aspects of their adaptive strategies. Fortunately, in the case of Amsterdam's "Portuguese" community there are quite a few early archival sources which allow us to scrutinize the legends and place them in context. We will attempt in the next chapter to reconstruct that context and, insofar as we can, the early events of communal organization.

2

⬥

The Forging of a Community

EARLY YEARS IN AMSTERDAM

The Background to Settlement

In the early seventeenth century, Portuguese conversos in the Peninsula found themselves weighing a host of new conditions. They had to try to calculate what their fate would be if they stayed in the Peninsula—commercially, socially, and in the orbit of the Holy Office—and balance that against their chances of successfully building a new life elsewhere (in a Jewish community or otherwise). If an opportunity to leave presented itself, they would have to decide whether to seize it (perhaps at the risk of their assets) or delay (perhaps at much greater risk).

The Inquisition was an ever present factor in these calculations. It was not merely a dramatic flourish when De Barrios depicted Maria Nunes's family fleeing "the horrors of the cruel Inquisition." As already noted, Inquisition records show that members of the family had indeed suffered considerably. Maria Nunes's parents, Gaspar Lopes Homem and Mayor Rodrigues, had both spent time in inquisitorial prisons. Mayor Rodrigues, first arrested in January of 1594, insistently denied having judaized during the three years she was in prison; as a result of her refusal to confess (assuming there was anything to confess) she was condemned to death in 1597. She escaped death only by implicating her husband, who was thereupon arrested and spent three and a half years in prison. The couple's goods were confiscated and after their release they were required to wear the humiliating *sambenito*, a garment publicizing their guilt. In the wake of these sufferings, they carefully planned to flee Portugal on March 19, 1601, but were discovered and tried once again by the Inquisition. That they took the first opportunity to flee the Peninsula after these harrowing events is hardly surprising.[1]

It is significant that the entire family of Maria Nunes was able to leave the Peninsula in the years following 1601. In general, it was becoming less risky in the seventeenth century for conversos to leave. This was partly due to the accumulated experience of conversos in organizing escape. But it was also due to changes in royal policy. It had long been illegal for conversos to leave the Peninsula, even in order to travel to Iberian overseas territories. Indeed, being caught doing so was not only a violation of a royal decree, but prima facie evidence of judaizing. But in the early years of the Amsterdam community's existence, a shift in royal policy caused the gates to open, allowing most conversos to emigrate freely for almost a decade.

Greatly simplified, what happened is this. After Philip II's death in 1597, his successor Philip III, more a compromiser in personality than his father, found himself in dire need of revenue. In 1601 the king's favorite, the Duke of Lerma, worked out an agreement whereby in return for a payment of 170,000 cruzados collected by the New Christians among themselves, the ban on emigration would be lifted. For so high a sum, the government even agreed to make the order irrevocable.

The agreement immediately set off a wave of emigration. The exodus caused some alarm in official circles. A debate opened as to whether an "irrevocable decree" could perhaps be revoked. As deliberations about this took a serious turn in 1609, anxiety grew among conversos. Their insecurity may have been intensified by the January 1608 decision of the council of state to expel the *moriscos* (descendants of baptized Muslims), and by the actual implementation of this decision in 1609.[2] In any case, the wave of emigration swelled.[3]

Certainly fears of various kinds were a factor in the emigration of many of those who settled in Amsterdam. But not all of those who came to Amsterdam were fleeing the Inquisition, and not all who fled the Inquisition were judaizers, since one did not have to be a crypto-Jew to run afoul of the Inquisition. A mere rumor or an anonymous accusation by an enemy could place a person in danger of arrest. And if one member of a family was arrested, all of his or her relatives were also in danger. Given the extensive ties among members of extended New Christian families, few could feel truly secure. The Maria Nunes legend suggests that those who fled the Peninsula did so in order to revert to Judaism, but in fact many fled with no such intention.

Closely following upon these events was the signing in 1609 of the Twelve Years Truce between Spain and the Netherlands, an agreement forced on Spain by its chronic financial crises. For converso merchants, the immediate significance was clear: commerce between the two countries would now be unhampered, and business between Amsterdam, the major entrepôt for colonial goods, and the Peninsula, the major target of "Portuguese" emigre commerce, could proceed as usual. This made Amsterdam increasingly attractive to converso merchants contemplating emigration. In fact, it was partly due to the heavy migration of "Portuguese" merchants to Amsterdam, where Spanish officials anxiously perceived them as enriching the enemy, that the order permitting free exit was revoked in 1610 and the ban on emigration reinstated. This did not, however, bring emigration to a halt: there were ways of evading the authorities that were by now well established.

If the merchant founders of the Amsterdam "Portuguese" community were as ardent in their desire to practice Judaism as legend would have us believe, one must wonder why they settled in a country (the United Provinces) where Judaism was not officially tolerated. Why did they not choose to leave the Peninsula for such well-known "Portuguese" destinations as Venice, Livorno, or Constantinople?

The complexity and diversity of converso experience, and the lack of reliable evidence about it, has produced different views about the motivations of the "Portuguese" elite who fled the Peninsula in the seventeenth century and settled as Jews in Amsterdam. These views belong to a wider scholarly polemic about conversos and the Inquisition in which, unfortunately, conclusions have often been drawn on the basis of insufficient or poorly interpreted evidence. The debate focuses on the question of whether inquisitorial persecution of conversos in the Peninsula was motivated by religious or socioeconomic concerns, and, concomitantly, whether those condemned by the Inquisition were actually "judaizers" or not. While thinking has in some ways been enriched by the debate, the adoption of rigid partisan positions has led to representations of converso experience divorced from the realm of real life.[4]

The issue of the extent of converso "judaizing" has inevitably colored views about converso emigration. According to one view, emigration from the Peninsula was an act of Jewish affirmation, religious and ethnic. The urge to leave Iberian lands drew its force from unbroken crypto-Jewish family traditions going back to the fifteenth century.[5] According to another, flight from the crisis-ridden commercial centers of the Peninsula to the thriving new commercial centers of the Atlantic states was a shrewd economic move, further stimulated by a wave of inquisitorial arrests of wealthy conversos.[6] In fact, the experience and actions of conversos were far too complex to lend themselves to sweeping conclusions of this kind. A closer look at the evidence and the circumstances surrounding immigration and rejudaization of Portuguese conversos will help give a more realistic picture of motivations.

The emigres who settled in Amsterdam were only part of a larger northbound wave of immigration to places where the practice of Judaism was formally forbidden. Many had settled earlier in Antwerp, and others established "Portuguese" colonies in southwest France, Germany, and (in small numbers) London, in none of which places could they live openly as Jews.[7] In fact, northward migrating conversos did not settle in Amsterdam for quite a long while. According to Jonathan Israel, the reason was mercantile: commercial activity in sixteenth-century Amsterdam was concentrated in the shipping of bulky products of relatively low value, such as grain, timber, and salt—an enterprise in which Portuguese conversos (or for that matter Jews in general) had never played a role. Rather, the "Portuguese" had developed commerce in certain "rich" Spanish and Portuguese colonial commodities, especially sugar, spices, bullion, diamonds, and tobacco. Under the Habsburgs, northern trade in these commodities was heavily concentrated in Antwerp, and it was there that a Portuguese colony developed which attracted both Old and New Christians.[8] By 1571 there were about eighty-five Portuguese New Christian families in Antwerp.[9] Of these, it appears that many were crypto-judaizers: there is persuasive if sporadic evidence that a clandestine synagogue existed in Antwerp during the period from 1564 to 1594 (though perhaps not continuously).[10]

This situation changed in the 1580s, as a result of the siege of Antwerp by the Dutch rebels, who were seeking to drive the Spaniards out of the Netherlands. The siege precipitated a mass exodus of merchants and craftsmen of all origins, many of whom headed for Amsterdam. It might be supposed that New Christians would be among them, since as a result of the siege, Antwerp lost access to the "rich" trades. But at this juncture, New Christian emigres were still not attracted to Amsterdam. The probable explanation for this lies in adverse conditions for colonial trade created by the military struggle in the Netherlands. From 1585 to 1590 Philip II of Spain imposed an embargo on Dutch ships. For the conversos, so heavily concentrated in the Spanish colonial trade, this made Amsterdam an unattractive place.[11] Instead, from about 1585 to 1595, Hamburg became the center of colonial trade in northern Europe, as well as a place of "Portuguese" settlement.[12]

This may explain why it was only after the lifting of the embargo that we have the first evidence, from a notarial deed of 1595, of a "Portuguese" merchant active in Amsterdam.[13] This was Manuel Rodrigues Vega, an importer of sugar and spices. He was born in Antwerp, the son of Luis Fernandes, apparently a crypto-Jew.[14] Significantly, after leaving Antwerp, Rodrigues Vega lived in France for some years. It can hardly be a coincidence that only after the Spanish embargo was lifted—that is, when Amsterdam began to take a leading role as an entrepôt for sugar and spices—did he settle in Amsterdam.[15] It was in the mid–1590s that both regional and local circumstances made Amsterdam a strategically advantageous place for such merchants to settle.

Many of the emigres had judaizing inclinations. Yet the earliest "Portuguese" to arrive in Amsterdam could not have been attracted solely, or even primarily, by the dream of building a Jewish community there. At the time, there was no reason to be confident that open adherence to Judaism would be tolerated in Amsterdam. To be sure, the emigres knew that under the republican rule established after the revolt against Spain in the 1570s, there was no threat of inquisitorial persecution. But for conversos driven primarily by a desire to revert openly to traditional Jewish practice, there were better places to go than late sixteenth-century Amsterdam: Safed in the Land of Israel, Constantinople, Salonica, or Venice. True, these places were becoming increasingly less attractive from a commercial point of view (and, with regard to post-Tridentine Italy, from a religious point of view). But they had long drawn Jewish immigrants and refugees not only from the Peninsula but from elsewhere in Europe as well. Thriving communities of Spanish-Jewish exiles were established there from the time of the Spanish Expulsion. Converso emigres to these centers almost invariably settled in Jewish communities where patterns of authority and community were fully established. Even if they founded their own separate congregations for worship—as they did in a number of places[16]—they lived within a larger communal framework dominated by Jews with an unbroken tradition of Jewish communal life. In such settings, the task of "restoration" for ex-conversos was undoubtedly simpler.

In contrast, for those who wished to make an immediate transition to the practice of rabbinic Judaism, Amsterdam was not, until about 1603 at the earliest, an appropriate destination. The most basic institutions and functionaries necessary to sustain rabbinic life did not exist: there was no ritual slaughterer, no ritual bath, and no rabbinic figure to guide the "return" to Jewish life. Then, too, it was not clear whether Jewish institutional life would be permitted. After the signing of the Union of Utrecht in 1579 the United Provinces (and particularly Amsterdam) became a haven for the religiously persecuted—Huguenots from France, Protestants from Antwerp, and English dissidents. But what was true for nonconformist Christians did not necessarily pertain to Jews. The thrust of the crucial article 13 of the Union of Utrecht, ensuring that "each individual enjoys freedom of religion and no one is persecuted or questioned about his religion,"[17] was open to interpretation: the provision had been intended to prevent disorder between Catholics and Protestants, not to grant refuge to Jews.

There was little opportunity to test this article regarding Jews. The Low Countries had few Jews in the medieval period, and the few settled there had left by the mid-sixteenth century. Although by the 1570s some Jews were tolerated in the villages of Groningen,[18] their formal status was unclear. The guarantees of the Union of Utrecht could thus not be assumed to include Jews. This seems to have been clear to the earliest "Portuguese" emigres—or at least the judaizers among them—who were careful to conceal their Jewish ways (whatever these may have been).

Certainly the emigres desired freedom from persecution. How they would choose to behave with that freedom, however—what kind of communal life they would choose to establish—was not obvious, even regarding those with deep Jewish loyalties. In the Peninsula, the latter had evolved a religious ethos of their own. Although aware that it was impoverished from a ritual point of view, they could not have known how far from traditional rabbinic Judaism it had wandered. Accustomed to their own ways, to which they were deeply attached emotionally (particularly since they had suffered for them), they were not always receptive to the changes in thinking, behavior, and self-perception required from them to conform to norms of rabbinic Judaism. It could not always have been easy to relinquish cherished converso patterns of judaizing for alien rabbinic practices.

To be sure, rabbinic Judaism itself was not without variations in matters of both ritual and outlook. The Jewish diaspora was too far-flung and spanned too many cultures to be otherwise, especially given the decentralized nature of rabbinic authority. But a considerable degree of uniformity had been maintained, despite centrifugal forces.

The chief means by which uniformity was achieved and sustained in the medieval period was through the dissemination of the Babylonian Talmud and the universal acceptance of this text's authority. In the early modern period uniformity was again ensured by the nearly universal acceptance of a code of Jewish law, the *Shulhan arukh*, composed in sixteenth-century Safed. From Warsaw to Fez, from the Galilee to Alsace, the *Shulhan arukh* established the *regula* by which Jews were expected to live. It was virtually impossible for a community to reject the norms it set (although there were always deviant individuals).

Such highly institutionalized Judaism was a novelty to the early "Portuguese" settlers in Amsterdam, for whom the "Law of Moses" was often more a symbol than a reality, and who had been almost entirely cut off for generations from the rabbinic scholarly and legal establishment. It was virtually self-evident that they would establish their own self-governed merchant colony. How they would interact with the rabbinic world, though, and whether or to what degree they would accept its norms as a basis for communal life, could not have been immediately apparent.

Emigre Attitudes to Rejudaization

Unfortunately, the early "Portuguese" merchant settlers (and later ones, for that matter) did not leave much evidence of their religious attitudes and impulses. What appears evident is that there was great variation among them. There were those for whom religious issues were matters of intense interest, who suffered guilt for the transgressions they believed they had committed and entertained hopes for messianic redemption. There were those who lived quite this-worldly lives, but for whom ingrained family patterns and an ancestral religious loyalty gave them the motivation to accept rabbinic Judaism. And there were those who viewed belonging to the Portuguese-Jewish community a mere practical necessity, who remained at the fringes of its life and, in some cases, eventually left it, sometimes returning to Catholicism in the Peninsula. I will try to illustrate the diversity in attitudes by looking at a few cases for which there is documentation.

The wealthy merchant Diogo Nunes Belmonte, who arrived in Amsterdam prior to 1607 and adopted the Hebrew name Jacob Israel Belmonte, has left an intriguing document: a prayer he composed in October 1599, while on the Portuguese island of Madeira—possibly just prior to his flight.[19] At the time he was about thirty-four years old, already an affluent merchant who owned several houses in Lisbon.[20] The prayer, though vague about the circumstances of its writing, gives us an inkling of Belmonte's state of mind and his convictions at the time:

> I have prayed for special mercy from the almighty God of Israel, with much confidence and devotion, [praying] that, persuaded of the great devotion with which I worship Him, He will answer me, and that knowing I shall always give Him thanks without measure, as well as [perform] certain deeds which I have vowed to perform (which if He so wills shall certainly be performed), that He grant me the mercy that I never offend Him. With great love for Him I express gratitude for these acts of mercy, as well as for many others I have received at His omnipotent hands when my hour was near; and they give me hope that I may improve my life, and that I shall not be ungrateful, and that I shall seek to achieve this, with His compassion and glorious grace [grassa gloria] with which I was created.

The prayer is simple, sincere, and, alas, exceedingly general. It displays a conspicuous absence of specifically Jewish content. Aside from Belmonte's invocation of "the God of Israel," there is nothing to indicate the prayer is Jewish at all. Indeed, his invocation of God's "glorious grace" sounds unwittingly Christian. It is what the prayer lacks in terms of *Christian* content—that is, any reference to Jesus, Mary, or the Trinity—that renders it a "converso" prayer par excellence.

There is little to be learned from the fact that at a difficult time in his life Belmonte formulated an emotional prayer, reminding God of his merits and asking for help. What is significant is that Belmonte afterward regarded the prayer as a concrete record of a moment full of mystery and meaning, a moment in which he found himself passing out of one life into another, as it were. After his arrival in Amsterdam, he copied it, adding that

> these very words, written above, I wrote on the island of Madeira on a sheet of paper, on that very day, October 12, 1599. But because [the sheet] tore, I have made a copy here in Amsterdam on October 23, 1607. God help me to merit prosperity, now and in the future.

It is tempting to conclude that the anxiety Belmonte expressed in the prayer had to do with fear of capture and trial by the Inquisition. Unfortunately, no copy has survived of a poetic work (or works) which Belmonte wrote in Amsterdam and which might throw more light on this subject. The themes of this work were, according to De Barrios, Job and the Inquisition.[21] The choice of subject matter speaks volumes in its own way. It seems likely that Belmonte was haunted, like so many other emigres, by memories of suffering inflicted by the Inquisition and was moved to express himself through a classic text on suffering from the Hebrew Bible.

The diary Belmonte kept in Amsterdam gives an impression of him as a steady, pious person who sought a spiritually rich life and was satisfied with what he found in rabbinic Judaism. In Amsterdam he followed the course of many emigres: he adopted a Hebrew name (Jacob Israel Belmonte), married a Portuguese-Jewish woman, and started a family. In 1614, he was the wealthiest person in the community[22]—though this was not the case for long. His wealth and his commitment to rabbinic Judaism—a commitment which is quite evident in his brief diary—made him an ideal candidate for communal office, and he held various offices from 1614 until his death fifteen years later.[23] Most significantly, he was one of the first members of the *Imposta* board, an institution crucial to the overall governance of the community and the establishment of communal norms.

Given the paucity of evidence on the early "Portuguese" merchants, a rather primitive engraving of Belmonte's wife Simha by their son Moses is revealing. Clearly she, too, was of a pious disposition. She is dressed spartanly, her hair thoroughly covered, clutching what is probably a prayer book in her right hand[24]—the very antithesis of the fashionable "Portuguese" women depicted in contemporary engravings. Whether or not she shared her husband's piety and the eschatological hopes expressed in his diary, she evidently accepted a rabbinically regulated way of life.

Not all the early settlers were so apparently unacquainted with rabbinic Judaism as Belmonte when they arrived. For example, the merchant Garcia Pimentel arrived in Amsterdam in 1596 from Venice, where he had lived for some time. According to Jonathan Israel, "the Pimentel were an extremely prominent Sephardic family at Venice and Constantinople where one of Garcia's brothers was a rabbi and it is safe to assume that he [Garcia] played a conspicuous part in the early judaization of the Marrano immigrants at Amsterdam."[25] Whether this was so or not, Garcia Pimentel does reflect early ties to Venice that were crucial in shaping communal life in Amsterdam.

Other early settlers maintained a conspicuous distance from Jewish communal life. There is, for example, the case of Manuel Carvalho. In 1643, Carvalho stated that he had settled in Amsterdam "more than forty years ago" (i.e., before 1603), but that he "had not professed Judaism in any way until 1616."[26] And there is Henrique Garcês, a grandfather of Baruch Spinoza. Garcês had been in Amsterdam as early as 1598, though he may not have settled there permanently before 1605.[27] Yet by 1614 he was still living outside the ritual life of the community: he was taxed for the purchase of land for a cemetery by the administrators of both existing Jewish congregations jointly, "since he belonged to neither."[28] And he was circumcised only after his death in 1619, in order to permit burial in the Jewish cemetery.[29]

Likewise there is the case of Antonio Lopes Pereyra, who was in Amsterdam before 1610 but joined a congregation under the name Joseph Israel Pereyra only in 1616. In testimony before Lisbon inquisitors in 1642, he stated in his defense that while in Amsterdam he had gone to the synagogue several times to participate in the service but had not put on phylacteries or a prayer shawl because only the circumcised were allowed to do so, and he was not circumcised.[30] Suspect as such testimony might be, there is the possibility it is true, since Pereyra's claim of having resisted circumcision could easily have been checked.

Expectations and intentions about how to live collectively thus varied considerably among the early settlers. There were, however, powerful forces pushing the emigres to embrace the rabbinic world. Certainly they knew that their community would never gain legitimacy in the wider Jewish world unless they accepted rabbinic norms. They would be relegated to a netherworld once more, with an undefined identity and a doubtful future as a community. They would have a doubtful status in the Christian world as well. The regents and clergy of Holland, like Christian authorities elsewhere, recognized rabbinic Judaism as the legitimate (however erroneous) contemporary expression of the religion of the ancient Israelites. It is inconceivable that a religiously split community of "judaizers" and Catholics, with no clear authority structure, would have been acceptable.

Furthermore, the Mediterranean region offered visible and long-established models of converso rejudaization. News of the integration of "Portuguese" emigres into Jewish communities in Italy, North Africa, and the Ottoman Empire must have reached Amsterdam even before a Venetian rabbi settled there in 1608 (and must have been known to the emigres long before they left the Peninsula).

If the emigres in Amsterdam were to follow suit, the obvious model for their organization would be the well-known Spanish and Portuguese Jewish community of the Venetian ghetto. This community's organization became familiar to the Amsterdam "Portuguese" via persons like Garcia Pimentel, mentioned above, who came to Amsterdam from Venice, and Jacob Tirado, who had a brother living in Venice. The particular suitability of the Venetian community as a model for the Amsterdam "Portuguese" has been summed up by Jonathan Israel. He describes it as "the crucible of a new hispanic Judaism forged from a mixture of intellectually dynamic but unstable and unformed Marranism and traditional, orthodox, Balkan Spanish Judaism."[31] That is, the ex-converso population of Venice tended to assimilate into the larger Sephardi group and lost some of its anomalous and "unstable" characteristics.[32] By virtue of this, the "Portuguese" of Venice provided an important link for the Amsterdam community to the traditional world of the Mediterranean Sephardim.

Finally, individual religious and emotional forces favored the reestablishment of Jewish life in Amsterdam on rabbinic foundations. There were those who felt a strong inner sense of obligation such as that expressed so vividly (if vaguely) in Jacob Israel Belmonte's prayer. Such a feeling in some cases stemmed from an intense experience of personal and religious crisis; in others it arose from a long family tradition of judaizing and/or inquisitorial persecution, and identification with the goal of "return." The variety of emotional catalysts involved can best be illustrated with a few well-documented cases from the merchant emigre population. The paths of "return" were individual, but common elements are evident. Let us look at the paths taken by members of three merchant families: the conscience-wracked David Abenatar (Fernão Alvares) Melo; the more robust brothers Jacob and David Curiel, who became simultaneously pillars of the Amsterdam community and loyal servants of the crown of Portugal; and Isaac de Pinto, whose account of the judaizing patterns in his family explains much about the underlying loyalties of this practical, worldly man.

The merchant Fernão Alvares Melo, like so many others who became emigres, belonged to a family with a history of entanglement with the Inquisition. Most of those involved were probably "judaizers" to one degree or another, since there seems little reason to doubt Melo's statement that his parents had taught him and his siblings "the Jewish faith" when they reached the age of eight or nine. In any case, his father was arrested by the Évora Inquisition in 1542 during the early stages of inquisitorial activity in Portugal. His mother died a professing Jew in Safed. His half-uncle Henrique de Melo was arrested in 1581. (He confessed that he had told his wife and daughter that Jesus was a prophet rather than the son of God—an interesting example of converso "judaizing.") His aunt Mor Dias died in an auto-da-fé in Évora in 1584, and other family members were also molested by the Inquisition.

Fernão Alvares Melo thus shared the fate of others in his family when he was arrested in Lisbon in April, 1609. He insisted in his defense on being a dutiful Catholic. In fact it seems, from a piece of verse composed in Amsterdam, that before his arrest Melo was indifferent to both Judaism and Catholicism.[33] The poem, possibly composed by his brother António Rodrigues Melo who had settled in Amsterdam by 1597, urged Fernão to leave the Peninsula before the Inquisition seized him, and appealed to him as his brother knew him to be—an overconfident, reckless, worldly person. Among his arguments to Fernão to flee, the author wrote:[34]

> The bread is not as hard here,
> And less risky! [*sem osso*]
> And meat of high quality.
> One can also earn one's keep,
> And with less hardship [*sobroço*]. . . .
> Beware of the den, of the lair,
> Something's brewing!
> Don't wait to be seized.
> Let pure self-interest move you,
> Since God does not!

While languishing in prison, Melo seems to have undergone a personal and spiritual conversion. After being released, he fled to Holland, where he adopted the name David Abenatar Melo and engaged in the shipping trade. He also produced a deeply personal and revealing literary work. It is a Spanish rhymed paraphrase of Psalms, *Los CL Psalmos de David en lengua española, en varias rimas*, published in 1626.[35] In the dedication, Melo describes his conversion:[36]

> You came to search for me,
> For I was fleeing from You,
> Knowing I owed You
> A debt I cannot pay.
> Many times You have called me
> With overwhelming indulgence,
> At times by drawing blood
> From my soul, which now I feel.
> All because I did not follow
> That which my ancestors gave me,
> The everlasting heritage
> Which leads to the knowledge of You. . . .
> Then You, seeing I was to be lost
> To You, came to my rescue,
> And in the Holy Inquisition
> Placed me in obeisance. . . .
> From there, O Lord, I called You,
> The eyes of my soul having opened,
> For then I knew the soul.
> I had thought that all was body.

The intensity of guilt that accompanied Melo's conversion may have triggered his later uncompromising, absolute rejection of worldly leisure pursuits—in great contrast to the inclinations of most of the emigres. He urged his readers to "abandon the foolishness of . . . comedies and romances of foreign peoples, and develop an appetite for what is our own."[37] And he criticized those who although they professed Judaism continued to "delight in reading profane books of contrived and lying fancies, abandoning the continual sacrifice of prayer at set times in favor of games which deprave one's soul and erode one's fortune." His rationale for composing his verse version of psalms in Spanish was, he said, "to awaken you [the reader] to the divine literary legacy of my people, so that you will apply yourselves to it, abandoning and suppressing the desires which prevail upon us due to our evil inclination, such as having a greater taste for frivolous than for sacred writings, for games than for prayer."[38] Melo's remorse and demanding religiosity may have to do with personality traits of which we know nothing; but it is interesting that he perceived a direct connection between his punishment for acts of "judaizing" he had not engaged in and the awakening of his Jewish religious sensibility.[39]

The piety of "Portuguese" merchants was often more ambiguous than Melo's. Let us turn, by way of illustration, to one of the most richly documented merchant families in Amsterdam, the family of Jacob and David Curiel.[40]

These brothers' ancestors have been traced back to a Jewish woman of Lisbon who bore an illegitimate son fathered by an Old Christian nobleman. This son, a great-grandfather of the Curiel brothers, became a merchant in Coimbra. One of his two male children departed for Turkey in 1560 where he lived as a Jew. The other, Duarte Nunes, stayed in the Peninsula. His wife was arrested by the Coimbra Inquisition on vague charges of judaizing and was compelled to pay a fine in order to avoid permanently wearing a *sambenito*, the garment signifying guilt. Duarte Nunes himself was denounced to the Inquisition in 1573 but died before matters could be taken further.

Among Duarte Nunes's many children were several who eventually emigrated and lived in Jewish communities. His eldest son, a Lisbon merchant, migrated to Tripoli in Syria, where he lived as a Jew and took the name Curiel. Another son joined Jewish communities in Venice and elsewhere, and also took the name Curiel. He was condemned to death in absentia by the Lima Inquisition in 1601 and died in Safed in Palestine. A third son was arrested by the Inquisition in 1578 and tried, though not on charges of judaizing, but of violating Inquisition secrecy.

A fourth son of Duarte Nunes was the physician and merchant Jeronimo Nunes Ramires, father of the Curiel brothers of Amsterdam and Hamburg. His wife, Maria da Fonseca, belonged to a family that had militant crypto-

Jews among its members, among them the eminent "Portuguese" physician Eliahu Montalto who married Maria's sister and who reverted to Judaism in Venice in about 1611.[41] A half-sister of Maria was burned at the stake in 1582 for judaizing. Shortly after her husband's death in 1609 a brother of hers was seized by the Lisbon Inquisition. This led Maria and her sons to flee to Madrid and then, a few years later, to St. Jean de Luz in southwest France. Maria died there, but her remains were brought to Amsterdam by her son Lopo da Fonseca Ramires and she was buried as Sara Curiel.[42] This son, known in the synagogue as David Curiel, became one of the most important "Portuguese" merchants in Amsterdam. The other son, Duarte Nunes da Costa, spent time in Tuscany before moving north; he then spent five or six years in Amsterdam before settling as a merchant in Hamburg in 1626, where he lived as Jacob Curiel.[43]

Back in the Peninsula, the Curiel brothers' cousin Duarte Nunes Vitoria and two of their sisters were seized by the Inquisition. They were interrogated, tortured, imprisoned, and exhibited at autos-da-fé before escaping Portugal and formally reverting to Judaism in Holland. In their confessions before the Inquisition, they reported clandestine Jewish religious gatherings in the home of Jeronimo Nunes Ramires, and attested that their family's spiritual guide in Lisbon had been Dr. Felipe Rodrigues Montalto (Eliahu Montalto).[44]

The Curiel brothers, then, were born into a family with strong crypto-Jewish leanings and a long history of inquisitorial persecution. By fleeing the Peninsula with their mother, they were following not only a crypto-Jewish scenario but a well-established family pattern. Their mentor Eliahu Montalto, a man of learning and deep Jewish loyalties, would have offered them persuasive arguments for leading a life governed by rabbinic norms. In any case, after joining Jewish communities in Amsterdam and Hamburg, Jacob and David Curiel established themselves as important merchants, and so, possessing the appropriate credentials, proceeded to play a part in communal government. Jacob appears to have been a key figure in one of the critical developments in communal life in Amsterdam: the establishment in 1622 of the *Imposta* board, on which he, his brother David, and their cousin Duarte Nunes Vitoria (Abraham Curiel) all served at various times. In the next generation, when the *Imposta* board was replaced by the *Mahamad* of the united community, Jacob's son Moses assumed a similar role, serving six terms on the *Mahamad*.[45]

Yet both Jacob and Moses Curiel also served the Portuguese crown, however surprising that might seem. Jacob served as its agent in Hamburg from 1641 to 1664. In return for his services, João IV of Portugal made him a knight of his royal household (*cavaleiro fidalgo*), a rank later granted to his eldest son Moses (Jeronimo Nunes da Costa), agent of the crown of Portugal in the Netherlands from 1645 to 1697 and a figure of considerable political influence. Both father and son appear to have harbored genuine patriotic feelings about Portugal. Like other Portuguese Jews, Moses championed the Portuguese cause when that kingdom gained its independence from Spain in 1640,[46] and once stated that he would always be "a good Portuguese and faithful servant of His Majesty."[47] Despite their family's sufferings at the hands of the Lisbon and Coimbra tribunals, and despite their indisputable Jewish loyalties, Jacob Curiel and his son never relinquished the conviction that they were Portuguese—without quotation marks.

As suggestive as the Melo and Curiel histories are, by far the most revealing document is the family history written by Isaac de Pinto. The Pintos arrived in the Netherlands more than a generation after the others we have discussed. There have been contradictory views about the motivations for emigration of this family to the Netherlands. H. P. Salomon argues that the family fled from Antwerp to Rotterdam out of economic considerations alone.[48] The economic historian James Boyajian likewise argues that the Pintos made the move "from financial motives rather than from deepseated religious convictions."[49] But Jonathan Israel rejects this conclusion, arguing that "only a strong leaning toward Judaism could have swayed [the Pintos] to adopt so drastic and otherwise improbable a course as flight to Holland." Israel maintains that from the point of view of the Pintos' material interests, it was prudent to flee from a city threatened by the French advance in 1646, but it would have been no less prudent to maintain their ties to the Spanish crown by resettling as Catholics in Brussels, Liège, or Cologne.[50]

Let us put aside such arguments and look at what we know about the Pintos. Like many Portuguese New Christian families, they took advantage of the union of Spain and Portugal after 1580. All six brothers and brothers-in-law born in the generation of the union left Lisbon to settle in either Antwerp or Madrid[51] and were among the many "Portuguese" merchant families that made their fortunes this way. But the family's great fortunes were made after 1621, when the reformist, mercantilist regime of the Count-Duke of Olivares came to power. Having by then amassed sufficient capital, the Pintos and other "Portuguese" merchants were in a position to replace the Genoese crown bankers, whose financing system had become increasingly expensive.

One of the first "Portuguese" crown bankers or *asentistas* (a term referring to the contracts, or *asientos*, they negotiated) recruited a member of the Pinto clan, a native of Lisbon, whose half-sister he had married.[52] This in turn led to connections with members of the Pinto family in Antwerp, the brothers Gil Lopes Pinto and Rodrigo Alvares Pinto. It was these two brothers who made the decision to flee the Spanish Netherlands for Holland in 1646, and it is their decision we shall examine.

There were surely economic considerations favoring their flight. By the 1640s, the contracts with the Spanish crown were becoming a less sure source of profit. Amsterdam now rivaled Antwerp as a financial center, and the course of the war was beginning to favor the Dutch. By the mid–1640s there was a real danger that Antwerp would come under siege during the hostilities with the Dutch; and conditions there grew more insecure in 1645, when French forces threatened. By this time some of Antwerp's leading correspondents had already left the city. João da Rocha Pinto (a distant relative of our Pintos) had been the first to leave, in late 1643. From this time on, the Pinto brothers began planning their flight, transferring large sums of money to Rouen, Venice, and Amsterdam.[53]

The economic aspect of the decision to flee cannot, however, be seen in isolation from other considerations. The Pintos must have shared with other "Portuguese" in Spain and Antwerp the recognition of having lost the important protection and patronage of Olivares with his fall in 1643. Feelings of insecurity increased when this event was followed by a fresh outbreak of anticonverso inquisitorial activity. In July 1646, three important *asentistas* were seized in Madrid. Another was seized just after he had negotiated a contract with the crown to forward 400,000 ducats to Flanders, indicating that no financier, however important to the crown, was safe.[54]

The Pinto brothers in Antwerp were less directly vulnerable to molestation. But that does not mean they were untouched. The prosecutions in Madrid and Seville jeopardized the entire *asiento* network. Fearing prosecutions and confiscations, several of the original *asentistas* dropped out, and inquisitorial arrests discouraged investors. These developments must have had a profound effect on their morale and financial expectations.

The fate of the *asentista* network throws light on the timing of the Pinto brothers' flight, but offers no insight into the Pintos' ethnoreligious thinking. Fortunately, we possess the autobiography and family history of Isaac de Pinto (Manuel Alvares Pinto),[55] a son of Gil Lopes Pinto and a nephew of Rodrigo Alvares Pinto, the brothers who fled Antwerp for Rotterdam. This work, composed in Amsterdam in 1671, shows that the idea of fleeing the orbit of the Inquisition emerged in the Pinto family long before the 1640s.

There are certainly problems with the reliability of a source like this. The author selected his material from his conscious memories of events long after they transpired, recounted stories he had heard second- or even third-hand, and harbored aristocratic pretensions which may have led him to enhance the status of his family. (It is significant that members of the family added a "de" to their name when they settled in the Netherlands.) But there is also reason to respect the historical integrity of Pinto's work. Its primary aim was to transmit genealogical information to members of his family. It was not intended for publication and thus was not written under pressure to conform to communal conventions.[56] Moreover, the author revealed a readiness to question some of the family lore he recorded. Certainly there is no indication that he was fantasizing or fabricating.

Pinto related that some time before 1604 his grandmother, many of whose siblings and relatives had already been arrested by the Inquisition, was seized, whereupon her husband and son (the author's father) left for France. They returned to Lisbon in 1604, when the so-called General Pardon bought by the Portuguese conversos allowed them to do so safely. In Lisbon the head of the family, a physician, resumed his practice, which flourished. But according to a family story, his young son Henrique fell ill and urged his family on his deathbed to leave Portugal. The boy's father— the author's grandfather—"remembering what his son Henrique had announced, as well as his wife's imprisonment and the risk of her being arrested again," left Portugal and settled in Antwerp in 1607.[57]

If this was a family of crypto-Jews, it is not obvious from their behavior. Yet Pinto recorded family lore about Jewish attachments stretching back several generations to the author's great-great grandfather, a native of Castile who died in 1540 in Lisbon and was believed to have been baptized as an adult.

His son, Gil Lopes Pinto, a physician to the king of Portugal, had strong Jewish loyalties although he apparently did not practice Jewish rituals. The author describes him as being "timorous and cautious as regards Judaism, which he always professed in secret."[58] *Professed* in secret, not *observed* in secret. As a rule he told his children of their Jewish origins when they reached adulthood. Once, however, circumstances forced him to tell one of his children while he was still a youngster that he was "a Jew, and was known as a person belonging to this nation" and furthermore (a remark we have quoted in chapter one in a different context) "that God is performing a greater miracle for us than the exodus from Egypt, for we continue to maintain ourselves among people who know [unlike the Egyptians] that we killed the one they believe in."[59]

Was the transmission of such typical converso ideas in the Pinto family inconsistent with the family's lingering in Antwerp until 1646? The answer is affirmative only if one assumes that the "Egyptian condition" was intolerable. By the seventeenth century, "judaizing" in the Peninsula had become part of a way of life with its own power. Ideas like those of Gil Lopes Pinto worked to make conversos feel more comfortable *in their problematic condition:* Iberian society was rendered alien and the converso condition idealized—for judaizers and nonjudaizers alike. This is vividly expressed in a fantastic story related by Pinto about an in-law of his father, António Enriques, whom Pinto described as "a very devout Christian."

> A couple of years before the Inquisition arrested him, an apparition appeared to him in his house while he was alone in his consulting room (he was a celebrated doctor of law), and spoke with him, warning him to change

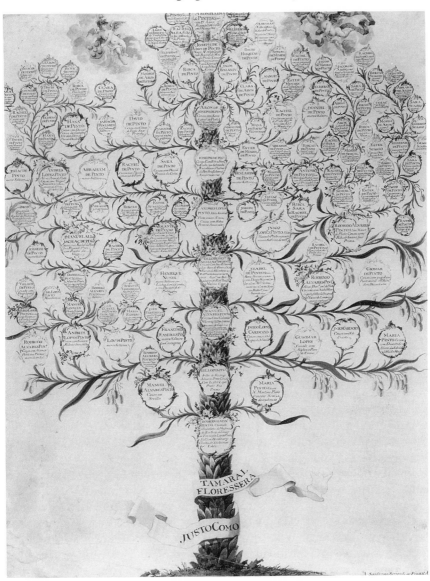

Family tree of the De Pinto family, drawn by A. Santcroos in 1758. From a
private collection, through Premsela & Hamburger, Amsterdam. *Photograph
from the Jewish Historical Museum, Amsterdam.*

his religion because only thus could he obtain salvation. The apparition predicted that if he did not do so, he would be burned at the stake. On this matter the apparition held several conversations and disputations with him. As long as the appearances of the apparition continued he was convinced it was the devil come to tempt him and he refused to be persuaded of anything.[60]

Pinto did not hide his skepticism about this story. "It is said," he wrote cautiously, "that [António Enriques's] wife heard these conversations many times but had never seen anything, had only heard the words which she later repeated to her daughter." Two or three years after the apparition's appearance António Enriques was arrested on what the author believed were false charges. Pinto wrote that António Enriques was sentenced to be burned at the stake because he was not willing "to make up lies, which is what their confessions consisted of." As to the reported response of the condemned man, Pinto was again cautious:

> [António Enriques] said, on his way to the auto-da-fé to be burned, that he was suffering the fate predicted to him by the vision (if, indeed, it happened this way, for I am only reporting what his daughter used to recount at the home of Aunt Sara Soares, where she lived so many years and finally died). She considered this story to be quite extraordinary and my aunt confirmed it as one well known among the relatives.

The story has an intriguing ending, whether true or not. At the auto-da-fé, António Enriques saw his wife, who was being "reconciled" and wearing a *sambenito*, and said to her, "You well know, because I have told you so many times, that it was predicted to me that I would come to this, and that I never believed it." He added poignantly, "What it all meant, God knows, may He always be praised."[61]

Such dramatic stories of the uncanny and miraculous played an important role in a clandestine judaizing sub-culture which lacked traditional means of cultural transmission. The only Jewish ritual Isaac de Pinto mentioned having practiced was the recitation of the *Shema*, taught to him by his grandfather (in what form it is impossible to know). In rabbinic practice, the *Shema* is said during the morning and evening prayers and before sleep. But the circumstances in which Pinto reportedly was taught to say the *Shema* indicate that this Jewish religious obligation was transformed into an act of resistance against Catholicism: he was to recite it (under his breath) when he entered a church.[62]

Pinto's work reveals that although the family's "judaizing" occurred in total isolation from synagogues, rabbis, and other institutions of rabbinic life, his father maintained ties to the Jewish world outside the Spanish realm and felt a part of it. Pinto told of an elderly relative in Jerusalem to whom his father in Antwerp sent a yearly pension. This relative, after being imprisoned by the Inquisition, had gone to France, where he changed his name to Moses Cabessão; he lived for many years in Jerusalem where he died at the age of ninety.[63] The author's father also sent a monthly allowance and provided dowries for the daughters of two relatives living as Jews in an unstated place.[64] Such gestures suggest not only family solidarity but also an appreciation of the hardships suffered by emigres who returned to Judaism and a willingness to accept the risks (admittedly not great in Antwerp) of sending them financial support.

Evidence from an institutional record book confirms that the Pinto family had strong attachments to the "rejudaized" converso diaspora outside Iberian lands. In 1616 the grandfather of the author, living in Antwerp, became a secret member of the prestigious *Dotar* confraternity in Amsterdam,[65] which accepted secret "Portuguese" members living outside Amsterdam even if they were not practicing Jews as long as they held basic Jewish beliefs.[66] Taking the risk to join this society clearly reflected an attachment to "the Nation" and to its free center in Amsterdam.

For Isaac de Pinto and others in his family, belonging to "the Nation" and having an obligation to practice Judaism were not easily separable. Certainly Pinto was neither the stuff of which martyrs are made nor a deeply searching or pious man. But highly revealing is a passage in which he expressed his dismay at Pinto intermarriages with Old Christians. Concerning a Pinto woman who married an Old Christian man, most of whose grandchildren became either canons, friars, or nuns, he remarked, "May God forgive them, for all the descendants of Guiomar Lopes have profaned His Holy Name as a result of her marrying Doctor Afonso Peres." He seems to have agreed with his father that responsibility for the presence of friars and nuns in the family lay with those who arranged opportunistic matches "in order to ally themselves with Old Christian gentry."[67] For Pinto, then, religious beliefs were not a matter of individual conscience and choice; nor were they particularly a matter for reflection. They were an inheritance, an ancestral obligation, closely linked to lineage and ethnicity.

Institutional Beginnings

Given the meager evidence about the attitudes of the first converso settlers, what can we know about the earliest efforts to create community among them? Much of the very early history of the "Portuguese" in Amsterdam is a matter of speculation. There is no body of sustained documentation until 1614. Yet if we want to understand the emergence of patterns of community and authority, we must cautiously consider the fragmentary evidence that exists.

The arrival of Uri Halevi in 1602—whatever the actual circumstances of his settlement—was the first clear indication that at least some emigres wished to adopt rabbinic Judaism. Halevi had performed a rabbinic function in the small Ashkenazi community in Emden. He may have met "Portuguese" merchants in Emden when, from 1598 to 1608, the Spanish embargo led Amsterdam "Portuguese" merchants to settle there temporarily so that they could import Iberian goods.[68] Among the "Portuguese" whose early ties to Emden are documented is Manuel Rodrigues Vega. In September 1603, he appears in a notarial deed granting proxy to a son of Uri Halevi in Emden to demand payment of a debt owed him by an Ashkenazi merchant to whom he had sold spices and pearls.[69]

Uri Halevi may have been a crucial figure in the establishment of rabbinic practice in Amsterdam, but little is known of the life of this obscure figure. One might wonder what could have induced him to leave the Ashkenazi community of Emden for the (at the time) inconsequential neophyte Sephardi community in Amsterdam. A look at conditions in Emden at the time suggests an explanation. After 1595 the position of the Jews in Emden had deteriorated seriously. A number had left the city and those who remained were periodically threatened with expulsion. In 1602, the year Halevi left for Amsterdam, threats of expulsion were renewed.[70] Under such circumstances, the Ashkenazi rabbi might well have chosen to accept the patronage of a group of wealthy conversos who intended to settle in Amsterdam.

Uri Halevi was, so to speak, the first Jewish institution in Amsterdam. He must have received a salary from a group of early "Portuguese" settlers in return for his religious services. Given his own commitments, he would have tried to obtain a *minyan* (a quorum of ten adult males) for prayer, at least on sabbaths and holidays. It was certainly for that purpose that he brought with him from Emden an essential ritual object for communal prayer—a Torah scroll, which he donated to the congregation in late 1606.[71] There is every reason to accept the testimony about Halevi given by communal leaders a generation later. In 1631 he was described as "a person . . . of whom it could be said that he introduced [Judaism] in this place."[72] But to what degree his congregants accepted his authority and, for that matter, how many among the emigres became his congregants—these are matters for speculation.

It does seem that Uri Halevi played some role in the first congregation to be established, known as Bet Jacob. But we know nothing about the organization of this congregation. Its founder was said to be the merchant James Lopes da Costa, that is, the aforementioned Jacob Tirado—hence "Bet Jacob." It may be recalled that Tirado appeared in De Barrios's description of the Yom Kippur incident. We know that Tirado was in Amsterdam by 1598 and that he left in 1612. There is evidence from 1610 that services were held in his home: in judicial proceedings of that year, a witness testified that the defendant (Simão de Mercado) had said that he attended religious services in the house of James Lopes da Costa, also known as Jacob Tirado.[73] In fact, Tirado was involved in the services well before this. After Uri Halevi donated a Torah scroll to the congregation in 1606, Jacob Tirado and his wife Rachel donated a silver Torah breastplate decorated with the crown of the Amsterdam coat of arms.[74] Tirado's role of communal leadership is also indicated in a Castilian prose version of a French poem[75] printed in Amsterdam in 1612 or early 1613:[76] it is dedicated to "the very illustrious *señor* Jacob Tirado, *parnas* [elder] of the Portuguese Nation residing in this noble and opulent city of Amsterdam."

Initially Uri Halevi probably served only the group that contributed to paying his salary. He certainly did not represent the "Portuguese Nation" in Amsterdam. If he had authority, it was highly circumscribed and accepted voluntarily. All of this was symptomatic of the community's transitional character in its early years. It did not belong to the wider world of organized Jewish communities, nor did Uri Halevi, a figure of little stature in that world, bestow significant legitimacy on it. Halevi also lacked the characteristics that might have given him a certain natural authority among the "Portuguese": his native tongue was undoubtedly Yiddish, and he possessed no Sephardi roots.

The impulse to establish a normative rabbinic community developed a kind of sociological and psychological momentum of its own—if only because those with the resolve to do so seized the leadership. As consensus emerged in the community, some of the reluctant or indifferent may have felt uncomfortable and moved elsewhere. Once consensus was achieved in the community, newcomers had little choice but to accept established norms. Social patterns including synagogue attendance, communal service, and charitable giving became entrenched rather quickly. And once the community was accepted as part of the wider Jewish world, with its time-honored structure of authority, powerful sanctions could be exercised to control dissenters, as we shall see in chapter five.

Consensus seems to have been achieved by 1608, when a rabbinic figure of a different stripe from Uri Halevi settled in Amsterdam: Joseph Pardo, a Sephardi rabbi and merchant from Venice.[77] In Venice, Pardo had been an avid doer and organizer, as well as a merchant. These aspects of his personality made him well suited to the task of establishing community life in Amsterdam. He had grown up in Salonica, one of the thriving Sephardi communities in the Mediterranean basin, and settled in Venice before 1591. In Venice, his talents were respected by one of the weightiest figures in the rabbinic orbit, Rabbi Leon de Modena.[78] It might seem odd that such a figure would leave the established Sephardi center of Venice to join an embryonic community of neophytes, were it not for the fact that bankruptcy forced him to leave Venice in 1608.[79] Leon de Modena expressed it more elegantly, lamenting that "the wheel of fortune turned against him and he suffered losses in his trade and was forced to leave this place and settle in Amsterdam."[80] In Amsterdam Pardo, having apparently been sufficiently cautioned by experience, did not engage in commerce. At some point he was appointed the rabbi or *hakham* of the Bet Jacob congregation and dedicated himself to serving that congregation and later the Bet Israel congregation. With his arrival, Uri Halevi's role may have been reduced to that of ritual slaughterer.[81]

A liturgical work printed after Pardo's death gives some indication of his role in the rejudaization (or re-rabbinization) of the community. The author relates that Pardo's congregants were in the habit of gathering in the synagogue on the three sabbaths preceding the fast of the Ninth of Ab to mourn the destruction of the Temple. Pardo prohibited this custom and instructed the members of his congregation rather to observe the Ninth of Ab with greater strictness. This included saying the traditional *kinot*, or elegies, which Pardo introduced in the form used by the Provençales congregation of Salonica.[82] This brief anecdote indicates that Pardo probably played a strong role in establishing the ritual norms of the community, using the full weight of his considerable rabbinic authority to do so.

The year of Pardo's arrival, 1608, seems to have been a turning point. In the same year two other important figures arrived with the intention of transferring their families there. These were the brothers Joseph and Samuel Palache, Sephardi Jews of Fez and members of a distinguished rabbinic family. Samuel Palache served as agent of the king of Morocco in Amsterdam from 1609 until his death in 1616. It has been argued, convincingly in my view, that as a learned Jew, Samuel Palache would not have been satisfied with the Bet Jacob group under Uri Halevi, presumably conducted according to Ashkenazi rite. Since Palache brought with him ritual articles for the synagogue, he was able, along with the important communal leader Isaac Franco (Francisco Mendes Medeiros), to establish a second congregation, Neve Salom, which reportedly met in Palache's home.[83]

The community was also developing demographically. It began to grow rapidly in 1609 as a result of the lifting of the Spanish embargos and the signing of the Twelve Years Truce between the Netherlands and Spain, which made possible unfettered trade with the Peninsula. As mentioned, the flow of immigrants was apparently also stimulated by fears among conversos in the Peninsula in 1609 that the decree granting freedom to emigrate would be rescinded. As many as fifty "Portuguese" a year made their way to the new community on the Amstel—only a fraction of the total number of emigres leaving the Peninsula. The first reliable data about the number of "Portuguese" in Amsterdam are from 1614, at which time there were about 164 families.[84] If correct, this would mean that a tiny colony had been transformed in two decades to a Jewish community of some size.

From the earliest years of settlement, the emigres settled almost exclusively in the Vlooienburg neighborhood and in the adjacent Breedestraat (today, Jodenbreestraat). The acute shortage of living space in Amsterdam had led to the city's expansion into this area beginning in 1593. Not only "Portuguese" emigres but many of the numerous other immigrants settled in this new quarter, where housing was available.[85]

Population growth may have provided the impetus for the next stage in the institutionalization of the community: the construction of a synagogue in 1612. Up to this time services were held in private homes. The contract for constructing the synagogue, negotiated with a Dutch builder by the Neve Salom congregation, appears in a notarial deed of January 31, 1612, with detailed instructions, providing even for a privy in back.[86] The synagogue was to be built on a piece of land situated on the Houtburgwal behind the Breestreet, that is, in the heart of the "Portuguese" quarter. It was to be 60 by 30 feet (pez)[87]—not a very imposing structure. Like other buildings along Amsterdam's canals, it was to be built on piles (the contract stipulated use of 200 piles of about 50 feet long). Inconspicuous as it may have been, it represented an important step in the process of communal institutionalization.

Acquiring a local site for burial of the dead was also an important institutional step. It was achieved only in 1614. From 1602 up to this time, the community had used a cemetery on land it had purchased in Groet, about 40 kilometers north of Amsterdam. Twice, in 1606 and 1608, Portuguese Jews petitioned the Amsterdam authorities to permit them to purchase land for a cemetery within Amsterdam's municipal boundaries, but were refused. The approval in 1614 of the purchase of land just outside Amsterdam, in Ouderkerk, signified, among other things, the stronger bargaining position the community had gained in this period of rapid growth. All community members (including those not belonging to a congregation) were assessed and taxed for the land. The records dealing with the purchase reveal a high degree of cooperation between the two congregations as well as the congregations' apparently unquestioned authority to impose such a tax.[88]

It was at this point that the community, having established its basic conformity with longstanding patterns of Jewish communal life, gave expression to its "Portuguese" distinctiveness. Until 1615 there was nothing in the institutional life of the community that could not be found in other Sephardi (and with some modifications, Ashkenazi) communities. The orthodoxy of its educational, welfare, and religious institutions was reflected in the familiar Hebrew names given them—*Talmud Torah, Neve Salom* (i.e., *Shalom*), *Bikur Holim*. But in 1615, communal leaders made a striking departure, establishing a prestigious institution which reflected in the most startling way the complex ideas of community and identity among the "Men of the Nation": a society for dowering poor brides, the *Santa Companhia de dotar orphas e donzelas pobres*, known as the *Dotar*. This was the first communal institution in Amsterdam to bear a non-Hebrew name. The idea for its foundation came from the otherwise undistinguished Portuguese-Jewish merchant Jacob Coronel, who had lived in Amsterdam but moved to Hamburg in 1612.[89] Its founders were all active as merchants or brokers, among them three of the wealthiest "Portuguese" in Amsterdam at the time: Joshua Habilho, Samuel Abarbanel, and Joshua Sarfati. In a short time, its membership came to include most of the established families in the community.

The truly novel aspect of this society, of which more will be said in chapter six, was the communications network it created with the crypto-Jewish communities of France and Antwerp. The scope of its operations was not limited by political, religious, or geographical boundaries. Girls living anywhere in the "Portuguese" diaspora outside Spain might apply for a dowry, whether they were practicing Jews or not, and membership was open in a similar way. Thus, although the *Dotar* was a body within a rabbinically orthodox community, it gave institutional expression to its members' affiliation to that most unorthodox entity, "the Nation."

This affiliation was affirmed by the criterion of ethnicity or lineage the society established in determining eligibility. A Jew who was not of "the Nation" could not participate. This is made clear in a remarkable preamble to the society's statutes. The society was to be

> a society of Portuguese, established with divine favor, to marry orphans and poor maidens of this Portuguese Nation, and the Castilian, among residents [in the region stretching] from St. Jean de Luz to Danzig, including France and the Netherlands, England and Germany; [a society] to which may be admitted all those who agree to aid in this pious work belonging to our Hebrew Nation, Portuguese or Castilian, or their descendants by the masculine or feminine line, residents in every part of the world.

Such grandiose aims seem inappropriate for a dowry society which granted only one to four dowries a year. But the *Dotar* appears to have served symbolic functions far more important than its welfare and mutual aid functions. Indeed, if there is any single institution in the Amsterdam community which offers insight into the specific character of the Amsterdam "Portuguese" merchants' attachment to "the Nation," it is this one.

In the years following the establishment of the *Dotar*, the community's standing was enhanced by the appointment of two more rabbinic figures of some stature. The first was Isaac Uziel, scion of a distinguished rabbinic family in Fez. It appears that when famine hit Fez in 1604–1605, Uziel left and settled in Oran, Algeria, where he served as rabbi.[90] It is not known when he arrived in Amsterdam, but in 1616 he was appointed *hakham* of the Neve Salom congregation.[91] He proved to be somewhat intolerant of the relatively lax standards of observance among Amsterdam's Portuguese Jews, but his very presence in the community was significant, symbolizing as it did a meshing of the old Sephardi world and the new "Portuguese" world.

The second figure was the youthful but talented Saul Levi Mortera, also from Venice. Though not Sephardi—he was probably of Italian-Jewish origin[92]—he was culturally much closer to his Sephardi congregants than the Ashkenazi Uri Halevi and possessed stature in the rabbinic world. He arrived in Amsterdam in 1616 accompanying the body of the ex-converso physician Eliahu Montalto from Paris for Jewish burial. As Montalto's rabbi and companion in Paris, he had already developed strong ties in "Portuguese" circles and possessed a command of both Portuguese and Castilian.

The community now had two congregations with governing boards, and three rabbinic figures of some weight—Joseph Pardo, Isaac Uziel, and Saul Levi Mortera. But it was not yet fully secure in the Jewish world. When two serious conflicts erupted in the years 1616 to 1618, the communal leadership turned to Venice for guidance.

In the first of the two cases, both the lay and rabbinic leaders were divided. A physician and prominent member of the Bet Jacob congregation (most likely David Farar) was charged by some members of the community with holding heterodox views. Although he had never challenged the rabbinic tradition in legal matters, he was openly critical of homiletic, aggadic interpretations of Scripture and of kabbalistic practices. The party opposed to Farar, including Joseph Pardo, chose to secede in 1619 and establish a new congregation, soon known as Bet Israel. The split led to a new dispute over the division of the congregation's property between the two parties. At some point the two sides, unable to resolve the dispute, turned to the lay and rabbinic authorities of the Venetian Jewish community. With considerable diplomacy, the Venetian *bet din* (rabbinic court) held that while Pardo was not at fault for his accusations, neither was Farar to be blamed for his opinions. The court took steps to bring other aspects of the dispute to an end as well. The blaze, however, was not immediately extinguished and sputtered on for some time, since the losing side on the issue of division of property, after accepting the Venetian court's ruling, appealed to authorities in Salonica. This, too, was a reflection of the internal weakness of the young community.[93]

The second case involved a far more heterodox figure, Uriel da Costa, who had fled Portugal and settled in Amsterdam with his family sometime between 1612 and 1615, but moved shortly thereafter to Hamburg. There, in 1616, Da Costa wrote a tract in which he enunciated radically heterodox ideas about the rabbinic tradition. Clearly aware of the relatively minor stature of the Amsterdam community, not to mention Hamburg, he sent this tract to the Sephardi communal leaders in Venice—who eventually responded by imposing a ban on him. While the climax and denouement of the Da Costa affair were played out in Amsterdam (and will be discussed in chapter five), what is important to note here is the crucial role played by the Venetian community, with its greater clout and prestige in the Jewish world.

Within quite a short time, however, the Amsterdam community made itself a power to reckon with in the Jewish world—even before the Da Costa affair came to a head there in 1623. A critical step in this process was the consolidation of authority achieved in 1622. In that year the communal leaders established a governing body which became the institutional basis of the unified community established in 1639. This body, the *Imposta* board, was governed by a joint body of six *deputados*—two *parnasim* from each of the three congregations. It was established to administer communal welfare but possessed much wider powers than this would imply, both legislative and administrative.[94]

The advantages of unifying the three congregations must have been evident to many of the communal leaders at this point. But there were a number of obstacles to achieving this end. There were the entrenched interests of each congregation, with its *parnasim* and rabbis. There was the question of merging the assets of the congregations, which would benefit one congregation at the expense of another. And there was the issue of providing a synagogue that would accommodate the entire community.

Presumably these were some of the issues that delayed for years a step that was clearly in the community's interest. In the late 1630s, however, circumstances conspired to convince even the reluctant. Toward the end of the Twelve Years Truce in 1621, when renewed war with Spain and the interruption of commerce between the Netherlands and Spain seemed inevitable, the community suffered a population loss as merchants left for Hamburg, Glückstadt, and elsewhere. It did not begin to grow again significantly until the 1640s.[95]

At the same time, Amsterdam's population of Ashkenazi Jews was growing. Until 1628, their numbers had been very small. But the devastations of the Thirty Years War in the German states brought Ashkenazi refugees to Amsterdam in increasing numbers. By the late 1630s it is estimated that there were about 500 Ashkenazim in Amsterdam[96]—this at a time when there were perhaps 1,000 "Portuguese." Witnessing the demographic growth of the Ashkenazim, at a time of their own demographic stagnation, must have encouraged the "Portuguese" to unify.

That the step was nevertheless a difficult one is reflected in a story, perhaps apocryphal, told by David Franco Mendes in his eighteenth-century chronicle. He related that Rabbi David Pardo (Joseph Pardo's son) had to resort to a ruse to obtain the agreement of the *parnasim* of the three congregations on unification. Predictably, when the matter seemed to be settled, a dispute broke out about who among the *parnasim* would sign the merger agreement first. In his wisdom, Pardo had three copies of the document drawn up and presented one of them to each of the congregations, whose *parnasim* all eagerly accepted the opportunity to sign "first."[97] The essence of the story is more important than its historical veracity: unification was an obvious step but, given human nature, a difficult one.

The merger agreement was signed by the congregational leaders, but also by "the entire Nation, heads of households"—218 additional signatures. It was no doubt important to obtain unanimous approval. But given the terms of the agreement, these signatures represented a relinquishment of power, an agreement to accept the virtually dictatorial powers of the *Mahamad,* or governing board of seven. The members of the community had no choice in the composition of the *Mahamad*: the first *Mahamad* was elected by the fifteen *parnasim* of the three dissolving congregations. Moreover, the document provided that in the future each outgoing *Mahamad* would elect the incoming *Mahamad,* making it an entirely self-perpetuating institution.[98] Such procedures were not unknown in Jewish communal life.[99] They were, however, also entirely consistent with the values and norms of a patriarchal elite of wealthy international merchants. Members of that same elite—or at least those who were committed to rabbinic Judaism—became the natural leaders of the rejudaized community. While rabbinic and popular lay approval of its measures was certainly needed and desired by the *Mahamad,* power and authority were entirely concentrated in its hands.

The statutes, like so much else in the early community's organization, were based on those of Venice, which unfortunately are not extant. Significantly, the unified community was given the same name as the "Ponentine" (ex-converso) community of Venice: *K. K. (Kahal Kadosh) Talmud Torah.* But this was in a way a final act of homage to Venice. The community now had the demographic strength, wealth, and rabbinic stature to steer its own course.

After unification was agreed upon, a set of statutes was drawn up which along with those of the merger agreement were to regulate the governance of the community. The first statute of these *Haskamot* (a Hebrew term for communal statutes) makes clear at the outset what the guiding principle was to be: "The *Mahamad* shall have authority and pre-eminence in all matters. No person may defy the resolutions made by this *Mahamad* . . . and those who do so shall incur the penalty of the ban."[100] As we shall see, the unghettoized nature of the Jewish community in Amsterdam occasionally undercut the absolute authority that the *Mahamad,* dominated by the merchant elite, arrogated to itself. But in general the principle laid down in the *Haskamot* was the principle by which the community was governed.

Just how, in subsequent generations, the *Mahamad* chose to establish boundaries—to include and exclude, to prohibit, permit, or turn an indifferent eye—tells a story of how identity was institutionally elaborated among the "Portuguese" of Amsterdam. Clearly, when the first *Mahamad* of the united community took office in 1639, two basic affiliations were affirmed: to the Jewish people and to "the Nation." These affiliations were not entirely compatible. Compatible or not, though, they were maintained, justified, and transmitted to subsequent generations. In the seventeenth century, a sociologically innocent time, there was never an attempt at systematic articulation of what it meant to be a "Hebrew of the Portuguese Nation." Insofar as the nature of this identity was articulated, it was done through the web of everyday contacts the "Portuguese" established with other groups: Dutch merchants and Reformed clergy, "old" Sephardim from the Mediterranean and neophytes to Judaism from the Peninsula, Ashkenazi and Italian Jews, other "Men of the Nation" wherever they lived and other Jewish communities throughout Europe and the Mediterranean. In the following chapters, "Portuguese" identity as expressed in these interpenetrating but distinct spheres of contact will be analyzed.

3

❖

The Dutch Context

WORKING OUT A MODUS VIVENDI

Relatively little attention has been devoted to the encounter between the "Portuguese" and the Dutch.[1] True, a number of scholars have examined the legal and political status of the "Portuguese" in Amsterdam, usually with an interest in the nature and extent of Dutch toleration.[2] Important as the legal status the Dutch authorities granted the "Portuguese" undoubtedly was, it did not define their relationship to Dutch society; to address this issue in isolation leaves important issues unanswered. To what extent, for example, did the Portuguese Jews measure themselves against the Dutch? How did they respond to Dutch mores, to the Calvinist world, to Dutch "golden age" culture? How did their leadership choose to regulate "Portuguese" relations with the Dutch? Was the relationship a utilitarian one, or did a sense of genuine affiliation to Netherlands society develop?

Certainly, in the first years, the merchant settlers were primarily interested in issues of commercial and legal advantage. In this respect they were like members of other merchant diasporas, little attached to a particular place of residence but rather seeking maximum opportunity and well-being (including religious freedom). It was with this in mind that the "Portuguese" merchant families had their first important experiences with Dutch society, in the encounter with its complex political structure.

The political institutions of the new republic bore little resemblance to those in the Peninsula. One significant difference the "Portuguese" discovered early on was that the political waters they had to navigate were largely municipal. Compared with the court-centered political life found elsewhere in early modern Europe, the central role of municipal and provincial government in the Dutch political structure was somewhat anomalous. Persistent Netherlands particularism might seem odd given the protracted, unifying campaign the Dutch waged against the Spanish. It is less so when one considers that what provided the rallying cry for the Dutch rebels were

Spanish violations of their provincial and particularist liberties (as they saw it).[3] It was not to a monarch, then, or to a centralized bureaucracy, or even to local representatives of a central government that the "Portuguese" looked to secure their status. It was to the magistrates of Amsterdam, representatives of the merchant ruling class (the so-called "regents").[4] This was not only unusual in early modern Europe; it marked a break with a centuries-old European pattern according to which Jews were dependent upon a single ruler and closely associated with his (or occasionally her) interests.

The Amsterdam regents generally welcomed immigrants (at any rate, those with skills). And immigrants had already streamed in: English textile workers, German sailors, tapestry weavers from Brabant, tinkers from Liège, Calvinist preachers from Flanders. In 1662 the Leiden cloth manufacturer Pieter de la Court underscored the need for the young and vulnerable Dutch republic to draw foreigners:[5]

> Here [in Holland] it is very necessary to attract foreigners. . . . Although this is disadvantageous to some old residents who would like to keep the profits all to themselves and who claim that a citizen [*borger*] should have advantages over a stranger, the truth is that a state which is not self-sufficient must constantly draw new inhabitants or be ruined.

As De la Court notes, not everyone welcomed the strangers. He ascribed the hostility shown by "some old residents" to fear of competition. This was no doubt true to some extent, judging by native efforts to restrict foreigners' entry into certain occupations. But many Netherlanders, even if they were not obsessive xenophobes, did distrust outsiders and engaged in the usual negative stereotyping of them.[6]

What constituted a "stranger" to the Netherlander was in itself revealing and significant and a symptom of persisting provincialism. In the first half of the seventeenth century even southern Netherlanders, whether Walloon or Flemish, were considered "foreign" in the north. Indeed northern Netherlanders who were from a different *province* were regarded as "foreigners."[7] But with so many many gradations of "foreignness" in the Dutch mind, the boundaries between "us" and "them" were never clear cut and categorical, especially in the cosmopolitan world of Amsterdam.

Among the groups of foreigners, the "Portuguese" were not conspicuous. They were a tiny minority in the city, even when their population peaked in the second half of the seventeenth century. In 1615, there were about 164 "Portuguese" families—perhaps 550 persons—at a time when the population of Amsterdam was approaching 100,000. By the 1670s, when the community reached its numerical peak of about 2,500, the population of Amsterdam was about 200,000.[8] Certainly the number of "Portuguese" was never large in comparison with other groups of foreign origin, such as Germans, Flemings, Brabanters, and Walloons.[9]

But the Portuguese Jews were anomalous. The complex religious com-position of the Netherlands was an outgrowth of the upheaval of the Protestant Reformation. However tense relations remained between Cal-vinists and Catholics, between Calvinists and Anabaptists or Lutherans, and (within the Calvinist camp) between orthodox Calvinists and the more liberal Remonstrants, all of these groups had their roots in late medieval Latin Christianity. Indeed, it was precisely because of their underlying closeness that they were intensely engaged with each other, as rivals and claimants to the truth. The Jews lay outside these conflicts. They had played no part in the formative struggles, religious and political, that brought the United Provinces into being.

The distance of the Jews from the core conflicts in Dutch society is nicely illustrated by the remark of the sixteenth-century Flemish Catholic poet Anna Bijns, who said of the despised Protestants that they had "strayed even further than the Turks and the Jews."[10] Among the Protestants, the same comfortable aloofness to the non-Christian was expressed in the motto of the early rebels known as the Sea Beggars, *liever Turcx dan Paus* (better Turk than pope).[11] This attitude was in good part rhetorical—but it was not without real consequences. It explains, for example, why the Jews of Amsterdam were allowed to conduct entirely public worship almost two centuries before Amsterdam's Catholics were allowed to do so.[12] It may also explain why the Jews, though attacked on occasion by zealous clergy, were not singled out as the enemy, the dangerous outsider. When pesti-lence or flooding occurred, the Calvinist *predikants* did not blame the Jews but rather the backsliding of the Christians. In times of rioting, too, Jews were not a target of attack.[13] It was Catholic churches, not synagogues, that suffered damage at the hands of angry mobs, and it was a demonized "popery" against which Protestant preachers fulminated.

Moreover, the racial stigma the "Men of the Nation" had encountered in the Peninsula—a stigma which was psychologically more punishing than rejection on religious grounds—was absent in the Netherlands. Differen-tiation on the basis of "blood" was alien to the Dutch. It is impossible to know how the residual effects of Peninsular "blood" stigma lingered among the emigres—there are signs of it, as we shall see—but routine, everyday exposure to it had disappeared and with it the need for constant mobilization of defensive strategies.

While most Dutch judged Jews in a negative light for having rejected Jesus and the Gospels, many identified them more-or-less positively with the Israelites of the Hebrew Bible. For Bible-reading Protestants, the more scholarly of whom were often Hebraists, Jews thus acquired a certain mystique as well, paradoxically, as a certain humanity. The visual represen-tations of Jews—contemporary or biblical—in seventeenth-century Hol-land show that whatever the Dutch thought of rabbinic Judaism, they did not demonize the Jews as peoples elsewhere in Europe did. In the many paintings and engravings in which Jews figure—Rembrandt's are the best-known—they appear altogether human, their ceremonies exotic but dignified.[14] The portraits are especially revealing—the warm, reflective glance of the physician Ephraim Bonus, etched by Jan Lievens; the stern, scholarly, ascetic gaze of Rabbi Jacob Sasportas as painted by Isaack Luttichuijs. The minor figures, too, who appear in etchings and paintings of everyday life—outside or inside the synagogue, at the cemetery, at a wedding or a festival—are not, except for certain outer trappings, distinguishable from non-Jewish figures in similar scenes.

Nevertheless, the Low Countries had their own medieval heritage of anti-Jewish opinion, and here as elsewhere it often passed only slightly transmuted into Protestant opinion. Given this heritage, it was not obvious at the outset what place (if any) Dutch authorities would grant Jews in the social order. The regents could hardly have been ignorant of prevailing patterns in other European nations. By the early modern period, Jewry laws had become highly restrictive. In those western and central European lands where Jews were still allowed to reside—i.e., in some German states, northern and central Italy, Comtat Venaissin, and Alsace—Jews were extremely limited in the economic functions they were permitted to fill, and segregated both socially and physically from the Christian population. Jews could settle in some towns (in restricted numbers) but not in others. Those who lived in cities were often confined to ghettos. In some places they were required to wear a distinguishing badge. They paid special taxes, often onerous. And they were forced into marginal economic roles as moneylenders, second-hand clothes dealers, and the like. In short, late medieval European society viewed Jews not just as foreigners but as an outcast population which was to be carefully controlled and granted the minimal privileges required to perform certain economic tasks.

This was the prevailing pattern. That the Dutch regents would adopt it in the Netherlands in general and in Amsterdam in particular was, however, by no means a foregone conclusion.

Regents, Predikants, and Jews

Holland's magistrates tended to be cultured men who had inherited something of the Erasmian tradition. They were also international merchants, at home in the world of commerce and acutely aware of Holland's overall commercial interests. In the large towns, at least, economic motives inclined the magistrates to tolerate different religious sects. Moreover, by the 1560s, the growing realization that Dutch society was destined to remain denominationally divided gave ideas of toleration new force. To be sure, calls for the suppression of Catholicism or Anabaptism or (later) the

Remonstrant sect were not lacking. But they were not common within the ruling elite. William the Silent, who led the revolt against Spain and was far from rigid in religious matters (he was converted from Lutheranism to Calvinism in 1573 largely for political reasons), lobbied in 1578 for a *Religionsvrede* which would allow each person to "hold and possess his religion in peace and quiet, and serve God according to the light granted him."[15] And William, first among the regents, was not exceptional among members of the elite in his tolerant views (though he grew significantly less tolerant toward Catholics after 1580). It is noteworthy that one of the most influential magistrates in Amsterdam, Cornelis Pieterszoon Hooft, who served as burgomaster twelve times between 1588 and 1626, was also one of the most consistent and outspoken proponents of freedom of conscience.[16] Because of the regents' moderate views, and perhaps also because Jewry laws had not been enacted for generations in a Netherlands where there were no Jews, Dutch authorities seemed little disposed from the start to impose severe restrictions on "Portuguese" settlers. (A similar situation would develop in London in the 1660s.)

But counterpoised to the regents were the Calvinist clergy, to whom municipal leaders were at times forced or inclined to yield. It is true that members of the Reformed clergy varied greatly in their views as to whether to permit public non-Calvinist worship. In the long public debate beginning in 1572 on the issues of the toleration of religious nonconformists and the relationship between church and state, quite different ideas were expounded by the Calvinist rigorists and the active minority of liberal-minded Calvinists.[17] Most of the conservative-minded believed that nonconformist worship could (and must) be banned by the magistrates. But they were kept somewhat in check by the more liberal-minded clergy, and in any case the magistrates tended to turn a deaf ear to their demands.

The real issue, from the regents' point of view, was how to maintain civil peace. The Jews had no place in this debate. In the voluminous polemical literature produced on this matter, a uniformly Christian society was taken for granted, however splintered it might be. This can be sensed in such pronouncements as that of the liberal Calvinist minister Caspar Coolhaes that "we should not foster schism among those that are baptized in Christ."[18] But clergy who were zealous in their anti-Catholicism tended to react with similar zealotry where Jews were concerned. If Catholic "idolatry" could not be tolerated, how much less so Jewish blasphemies.

As early as the 1570s there were signs of the conflict to come between regents and Calvinist *predikants* over a Jewish presence. In 1577–78, William the Silent had been ready to reverse Habsburg exclusionary policies toward Jews when he sought to attract Ashkenazi Jews to the Netherlands; but the opposition of the Reformed clergy brought these early efforts to naught.[19] When "Portuguese" settlers arrived in Amsterdam in the last years of the sixteenth century, the fact that they were to all appearances Christian prevented alarms from sounding among the *predikants*. Amsterdam's magistrates (among whom the burgomasters held the real governing power) avoided conflict over the matter by ignoring it.

The magistrates' policy of evasiveness was evident as early as 1597. In March of that year, the burgomasters of Amsterdam allowed the Portuguese merchant Manuel Rodrigues Vega to purchase the *poortersrecht* (burghers' rights). The following year, the burgomasters passed a resolution permitting other "Portuguese" to purchase this privilege. The resolution contained two stipulations: "that [the purchasers] be Christians and live an honest life as good burghers," and "that before taking the [burgher's] oath they be warned that in this city no religion can or may be practiced other than that practiced publicly in the churches."[20] But these stipulations were not to be taken at face value. Although prohibited in public, Catholic worship was tolerated in Amsterdam if practiced privately, and Catholics could purchase the *poortersrecht*. Since the authorities probably knew of the judaizing inclinations of the "Portuguese,"[21] the stipulations were most likely intended to warn the emigres that their rights were restricted in the way Catholics' were. That is, while the *poortersrecht* did not grant them the right to worship in public synagogues, they might practice Judaism privately. This interpretation is supported by the fact that in subsequent years, when the "Portuguese" were openly acknowledged to be professing Jews, they continued to purchase burghers' rights, albeit with certain restrictions. (An ordinance of 1632 specifically prohibited Jewish *poorters* from carrying on retail trade or guild trades—that of the brokers' guild excepted.[22] They were also unable to serve in public office or to pass on the burghers' rights to their children as Christians did.[23])

By the time the policy of evasion became impracticable, the "Portuguese" had had ample time to size up both the weakness of the Reformed clergy vis-à-vis the regents, and the fractured structure of Dutch politics. Thus, when the clergy began to exert pressure on the authorities to prevent the open practice of Judaism in Amsterdam, the "Portuguese" were able to exert effective counterpressure by playing one town against another. As early as May 1604, Uri Halevi, who had already dealt with the Alkmaar authorities in arranging for the first cemetery near there in 1602, negotiated a charter with the Alkmaar city council for the admission of "Portuguese" and other Jews, with the right of public worship. This put pressure on the Amsterdam authorities to improve conditions for Jews there, lest they lose the ability to attract and keep "Portuguese" merchants.[24]

This was the first of several such attempts. In November 1605, a group of leading "Portuguese" merchants in Amsterdam, stressing their commercial ties with Peninsular conversos and Jews of the Levant, submitted a petition to the authorities of Haarlem. The Haarlem burgomasters were aware that they would have to offer excellent terms to persuade "Portuguese" merchants to choose their town rather than Amsterdam, and they did.[25] But in the end, these terms proved insufficient to lure Jews to Haarlem, where a regular community was organized only decades later. A quite similar attempt was made by Amsterdam "Portuguese" in 1610 to obtain favorable conditions of settlement in Rotterdam—with similar results.

Perhaps the most illuminating example of the way the "Portuguese" learned to maneuver for advantage amid the hostile demands of the Reformed clergy and the pragmatic proclivities of the regents is the manner in which the first synagogue was established. In 1612, presumably with some private assurances from high places, they drew up a contract for the building of a synagogue. (In order to comply with both Jewish and Christian law regarding the sabbath, the contract stipulated that the carpenter not work on the building between sunset on Friday and Sunday night.)[26] But a few months after the contract was signed, the city council of Amsterdam passed a resolution prohibiting anyone of the Portuguese Nation from living in the building then under construction or from practicing in it the ceremonies of their religion, "on penalty of having the said house or building razed."[27]

It seems clear that the Reformed clergy had pressed the city council to take this action. Among those who opposed the erection of the synagogue was the Reformed preacher Abraham Coster, who had written in his *History of the Jews* (Rotterdam, 1608) that these "unclean people" sought to establish a public synagogue "in which they can perform their evil and foolish ceremonies and spew forth their gross blasphemies against Christ and his holy Gospels, as well as their curses against the Christians and Christian authorities."[28] Yet despite the city council's resolution, the building was completed and used as a synagogue. To pacify the clergy and maintain appearances, it was arranged that the building would be owned by a Christian, who would rent it, in turn, to the Jews. Ownership was transferred to Nicolaes van Campen, a Catholic and, though Catholics were not supposed to hold office (many did), himself a member of the city council that had passed the resolution.[29] (A similar strategy was sometimes adopted by Catholics to help them maintain houses of worship—*schuilkerken*, as they were called: the Catholics, of course, rented from Protestants.)[30]

Generally, then, the position of the Amsterdam authorities was to hold the clergy at bay by imposing minimal restrictions on the "Portuguese." While the Reformed clergy periodically protested the granting of this or that right,[31] the burgomasters mostly ignored their demands, like those the clergy made in other areas of Dutch life (imposing restrictions on Remonstrants, introducing sumptuary laws, prohibiting tobacco, banning liquor on the sabbath, banning theater performances, closing shops and banning the loading of ships on the sabbath, and the like). When a Pastor Wachtendorp complained to the burgomasters in October 1645 that on his walks "he had noticed that streets and bridges were decorated with large branches in honor of the Jewish Feast of Tabernacles," he received the support of the Reformed church council (*Kerkeraad*) of Amsterdam. But the burgomasters merely promised to investigate and, in fact, did nothing until the festival was over.[32] As one scholar of Dutch Jewish history put it, "The [Reformed] church frequently meddled with the Jews, but more in theory, so to speak, than in practice."[33]

There was, then, a kind of unspoken agreement between the magistrates and the Portuguese Jews concerning their freedom to practice Judaism openly, whatever the opinions of the clergy. But the magistrates were more responsive to pressures from the guilds, who sought to prevent "Jewish competition" in their trades, than to pressures from the clergy. As mere "residents" (*ingezetenen*) in Amsterdam, not full burghers, the Portuguese Jews were denied the right to engage in most guild and retail occupations. (They were permitted to engage in some—wholesale trade obviously being one of them.)[34] But the classification of Jews as part of the larger category of "residents" was misleading. When the law concerning these trades was reformed in 1668 to allow Christian "residents" to engage in guild trades and crafts, it still excluded Jews.[35]

One might be tempted to conclude that were it not for the guilds and the *predikants*, the Portuguese Jews would have been free of special restrictions in Amsterdam. But this would be to ignore anxieties about socioreligious boundaries that were as alive among the regents as the *predikants*. Indeed, both the Jews and the Dutch were eager to maintain these boundaries.

For the Dutch, the most scandalous violation occurred when a Christian converted to Judaism. The most tolerant of minds recoiled at this unnatural event. And it did happen. The most spectacular case occurred in Hoorn, where a certain Hans Joostenszoon was arrested in 1614 along with two other "villains and murderers." Originally a Mennonite from Emmerich, he had met and taken up with a woman who was evidently also of Mennonite origin. Together they went to Damascus, where they were converted to Judaism and adopted the names Abraham and Sara. The couple returned to Holland, where Joostenszoon served briefly as a *shammes* (beadle of a synagogue), before moving to Grosthuizen, near Hoorn, where he made kosher cheese. There an elder of the Reformed church fell under his influence and went to Constantinople, where he was circumcised and converted to Judaism before returning to the Netherlands. In Hoorn the two men were sentenced to be burned at the stake and the wife to death by drowning (though eventually they were merely banned from the provinces and released).[36] The scandal brought unwanted attention to the Portuguese Jews, despite the fact that they had not been involved in the conversions.

At this point, with two Jewish congregations active and a Jewish cemetery established at Ouderkerk outside Amsterdam (the villagers of Ouderkerk protested its establishment, but the Amsterdam magistrates characteristically ignored them),[37] the need for a better-defined policy vis-à-vis the Jews was evident. The States of Holland therefore appointed a commission to draw up statutes for the Jewish nation, comprised of Adriaen van Pauw and the eminent jurist Hugo Grotius. No copy of Pauw's opinion has survived. Grotius's *Remonstrantie,* which has received detailed scholarly attention, is a confusing blend of Erasmian notions of toleration, Protestant conversionism, and medieval restrictionism.[38] For its time, however, it was notable for the generosity of its recommendations.

The statute drafts of Grotius and Pauw were considered by the States of Holland when in December 1619 they took action.[39] Or rather, when they decided not to take action, for they decided not to issue their own set of laws pertaining to the "Hebrew Nation" (*Hebreeusche Natie*). They thus placed the responsibility for determining Jewish status exclusively in the hands of the municipalities.[40]

This gave new authority to a set of regulations concerning the Jews that Amsterdam's burgomasters had issued in 1616. (This had been the first official document that explicitly acknowledged it was dealing with persons of the *Joodsche Natie*.) In characteristically evasive fashion, it neither granted nor denied Jews the right to public worship. (Indeed, no official statement was ever made on this matter.)[41] It warned the Jews on three matters: "not to speak or write anything (and to ensure that nothing be spoken or written) that may, in any way, tend to the disparagement of our Christian religion; not to attempt to seduce any Christian person away from our Christian religion or to circumcise one; and not to have any carnal relations, whether in or out of wedlock, with Christian women or girls, not even those of ill repute."[42]

These prohibitions were all standard in medieval Jewry law. While the first and second were regarded with some seriousness, the third (despite a warning to communal officials) was rarely enforced. Notarial deeds between 1600 and 1623 reveal many instances of sexual relations between Portuguese Jews and gentile women, few of which were prosecuted.[43] Fleeting liaisons of "Portuguese" merchants with gentile maidservants seem not to have been regarded as a serious breach of socioreligious boundaries.

As it turned out, the 1616 municipal provisions governed the Jews of Amsterdam for the better part of two centuries. Government regulation of Jewish affairs was thus minimal. No residential restrictions were enacted; no special taxes were imposed; no formal measures were taken to establish state supervision of Jewish affairs. Such a lack of interest in controlling the Jewish population was unknown in contemporary Europe, where the trend was, if anything, toward stricter regulation.[44]

Predictably, however, the *Kerkeraad* was not satisfied. A month after the decision of the States of Holland in 1619, the church council, distressed with the status granted the Jews in Amsterdam, sent a commission to the burgomasters to complain of the Jews' "great freedom" and "great nastiness." To this the burgomasters replied that the *Kerkeraad* should "let things be."[45] Their advice, however, went unheeded. The expansion of "Portuguese" communal institutions drew new responses from the *Kerkeraad,* which complained in 1620 and 1623, and once again in 1639 when the "Portuguese" expanded their synagogue. None of these complaints moved the burgomasters to act.[46]

This is not to say that the burgomasters turned a blind eye to all violations by "Portuguese" of the formal legal restrictions placed on them. As noted above, the cases most disturbing to the authorities were those involving conversion and intermarriage. The Portuguese-Jewish communal leadership, sensitive to Dutch fears about conversions to Judaism, prohibited in the community's statutes of 1639 the circumcision "of anyone not of our Hebrew Nation."[47] But when in 1649 a certain Jan Cardoso, a Christian who had been converted to Judaism, married a woman who had "become Jewish" in order to marry him, there was general consternation. In this case the burgomasters put pressure on the leadership of the Portuguese Nation to enforce existing policy among its members, that is, "to take steps [to ensure] that nothing be spoken or written which could be taken as showing disdain for our Christian religion, [and that nothing be done] to cause anyone to convert from our Christian religion or to be circumcised."[48]

The "Portuguese" also responded to Dutch sensitivities (and to the danger of provoking the *predikants*) by maintaining a low religious profile outside the synagogue. In 1639, for example, the *Mahamad* decreed that "bridegrooms or mourners must not travel in procession, to avoid the problems which can occur with crowds and to avoid being noticed [in an unfriendly way] by the inhabitants of the city."[49] Even toward the end of the period being considered, when relations were solidly established, the leadership of the Portuguese Jewish community took measures to keep the Reformed clergy at bay. In 1690, the *Mahamad* resolved that neither members of the community, their children nor their servants were allowed to appear in the streets during Purim, as was customary, in costumes or masks, "since some of our enemies use this [custom of] masquerading to demonstrate their ill intent toward us."[50] Similarly, in 1700, the *Mahamad* decided to abolish the custom of carrying Torah scrolls outside the synagogue on the exuberant holiday of Simhat Torah because of the resulting "grave troubles and commotion among the gentiles [*goyim*]."[51]

There was a need for discretion, then, and a recognition of the potential for gentile hostility. Still, the "Portuguese" in Amsterdam recognized quite early on that the conditions under which they lived were remarkable. The author of a rabbinic query sent to Salonica in 1616 (perhaps Joseph Pardo) reflects a kind of wonder about the stability enjoyed by the "Portuguese" in Amsterdam. By way of providing background, he wrote the following description:[52]

> Today a tranquil and secure people dwells in Amsterdam, and the officials of the city have sought to expand the settlement and to establish laws concerning it. Among these [laws] they have allowed every man to believe in divine matters as he chooses, and each lives according to his faith, as long as he does not go about the markets and streets displaying his opposition to the faith of the residents of the city. And since "this city is near to flee to" [Gen. 19:20], conversos of our time, great in number and prominence, have gone there and have entered under the wings of the Divine Presence.

For the author of this passage, what was important about conditions in Amsterdam was that they allowed conversos from the Peninsula to "enter under the wings of the Divine Presence" (that is, to be initiated into rabbinic life and practice) almost as if in a protective vacuum, untouched by the specific character of their surroundings. This, of course, was an idealized and greatly simplified conception. The way the emigres came to see themselves, their community, and their role within "the Nation" was profoundly affected by their finding themselves in a non-Iberian and non-Catholic environment.

Maintaining Boundaries

In this environment, the collective identity of the emigres was bound to change. In contrast to the Peninsula, the Dutch environment was relatively stigma free and almost entirely free of anti-Jewish paranoia of a racial nature. To be sure, the burghers of Amsterdam thought the Portuguese Jews had erroneous religious ideas. But this kind of disapproval could be confronted now by a "Portuguese" intelligentsia free to formulate its defense of Judaism and to reiterate classical rabbinic apologies. Moreover, most "Portuguese" were ready to be persuaded—if they were not already—that they belonged to a superior religion.

Also in contrast to the old environment was the clarity of cultural difference setting off the "Portuguese" from their surroundings. While in the Peninsula the Iberian cultural traits of New Christians were indistinguishable from those of Old Christians, in Amsterdam the linguistic and other Iberian traits of the "Portuguese" distinguished them sharply from others, making them dependent on one another for the kind of "old country" camaraderie immigrants typically seek.

The "Men of the Nation" certainly recognized that it was in their interest to cultivate their dual identity as "Portuguese" and as Jews in their relations with the Dutch. This is reflected in the by-no-means accidental "improvement" on the Yom Kippur incident in the founding lore, according to which the Dutch sheriffs believed they had come upon Iberian Catholics, only to discover to their relief that the worshipers were Jews. This story acknowledges in pithy form the advantages of making clear the Jewish as well as the Iberian nature of the community. As we have mentioned, "Portuguese" economic activity was heavily concentrated in commerce with Spain and Spanish territories, particularly with Portugal (which was annexed to Spain from 1580 to 1640). "Portuguese" merchants were thus pursuing trade with an enemy nation—one with which the Netherlands was, however, interested in maintaining trade. The emigres were thus custom-made for their role in Amsterdam's trade: their Iberian background gave them the necessary ties and knowledge for mercantile activity with Spain, while their Judaism (associated with hostility to the Spanish government) ensured that their activities with Spain would not include outright political subversion.

The Dutch thus had their own reasons for recognizing the emigres as both Portuguese and Jewish—reasons which dovetailed nicely with the desire of the "Portuguese" communal leaders to cultivate both aspects of affiliation (to be discussed in later chapters). This state of affairs did not change significantly even when the Jewish population of Amsterdam came to include significant numbers of Ashkenazim. It is true that after 1635, when Ashkenazi Jews founded their own community in Amsterdam, Dutch authorities began to use the term *Joodsche Natie* to refer to all the Jews of Amsterdam. But the communities were separate and were often dealt with separately, and the Dutch authorities continued to refer to the "Portuguese" as a separate "nation"—the *Portugeesche Joodsche Natie* or the *Joodsche Portugeesche Natie*. Official Dutch terminology continued to validate collective boundaries which the "Portuguese" leadership, as we shall see, sought to strengthen and even enforce.

While cultural and religious boundaries were clarified in the new surroundings, economic lines of division were somewhat obscured. In Amsterdam the "Portuguese" were far less distinctive economically than they had been in the Peninsula. One of the terms by which they had been known in Portugal was *homens de negócios* (Men of Commerce)—as if the world of commerce and the boundaries of "the Nation" were coextensive. While this was by no means true, in largely rural Spain and Portugal the conversos did stand out as a predominantly urban, commercial element, concentrated in cities like Madrid, Seville, Porto, and Lisbon. In a society in which commerce and banking were held in disdain, this not only set them apart but heightened their stigma.

In relatively urbanized Holland, in contrast, the "Portuguese" did not stand out in this way. It would have been the height of absurdity to refer to them there as *"the* Men of Commerce." Not only did Holland's upper echelons feel no disdain for commerce—they avidly pursued it. Over the course of the sixteenth century, the elite mercantile element had wrested power from members of the old nobility living on their estates.[53] (In fact few nobles remained by the seventeenth century, and their numbers continued to dwindle after the revolt, when no new titles were granted.) From an economic point of view, the "Portuguese" formed a routine part of Holland's landscape—or rather townscape.

While economic contacts were routine and frequent, there was little social interaction between the "Portuguese" merchants and their Dutch neighbors, nor did either side expect such interaction. Up to the emancipation in the late eighteenth century, Amsterdam's salons and welfare societies excluded Jews as a matter of course.[54] In the period which concerns us, this was of little consequence to the "Portuguese," who had developed a deep-rooted clannishness, partly as a response to the shared trauma of the Peninsular experience. Moreover, as with all immigrant groups, the experience of being uprooted intensified pre-existing social ties. This made them little inclined to mix with *anyone* outside their group. The emigres' own "ethnic" life, sustained by the bonds of language, kinship, memory, ritual life, and interpersonal style, made fraternization with Netherlanders unnecessary and even undesirable.

There was also a formal religious barrier to socializing with the Dutch, once the community and its leadership accepted rabbinic Judaism. Jewish law includes a large body of rabbinic precepts and prohibitions, developed over many centuries, which regulate and restrict relations between Jews and gentiles.[55] At least for the genuinely observant among the "Portuguese," the dietary laws, the laws of the sabbath and holidays, and the prohibition of participating in gentile religious ceremonies served to concretize and reinforce from within the socioreligious boundaries that separated, for example, a merchant-banking family like the Pintos from an entrepreneurial family like the Trips—who otherwise, in lifestyle and business interests, had much in common.[56] The prohibition of intermarriage with gentiles was probably of little practical significance, given the fact that Portuguese Jews had strong inhibitions about marriage outside their own ranks, even with other Jews.

There was one realm in which a number of "Portuguese" males seemed little inhibited by either Jewish or Dutch law: in their sexual behavior. Sexual relations between Portuguese merchants and lower-class gentile women, often maidservants, were fairly common, as we have mentioned. In the period between 1600 and 1623, thirteen such cases appear in published notarial records. Of course there must have been others since we learn of such cases only when something went wrong. (It was usually a pregnancy, though in one case there was a charge of rape, and in another a charge by the father of the offender that his son had stolen jewelry to give to his lover.)[57] Portuguese Jews also frequented gentile brothels, judging from police records. (When apprehended, they were merely fined.)[58]

Since these encounters did not involve marriage or the intent of producing offspring, they were not regarded within the community as a breach of the very powerful ethnic boundary the "Portuguese" drew about themselves. Indeed, such liaisons may be seen as a perpetuation of Iberian mores and social attitudes. They did, however, stand in conflict with Jewish law as well as with norms of acceptable behavior in traditional Jewish societies. But this belongs to another chapter. What is important to note here—perhaps it is obvious—is that these liaisons were not indicative of social openness to Dutch society, any more than an aristocrat's roll in the hay signified a wish to invite peasants into his social life.

Relations between the Dutch and the "Portuguese," then, remained at a fairly superficial level. But at that level a kind of normality prevailed in Dutch-"Portuguese" relations that was unusual in Jewish-gentile relations in seventeenth-century Europe. True, the cultural style of the "Portuguese" was different from that of the Dutch. "Portuguese" merchant families entertained aristocratic notions about themselves which must have left them somewhat puzzled by the Dutch elite, whose most respected members did not belong to the nobility and sometimes lived quite simply. While the domestic, unpretentious image of the Dutch upper classes in the seventeenth century is something of a stereotype, it has a basis in reality. The Dutch upper classes *were* relatively unpretentious. A regent of the early seventeenth century was hardly distinguishable from passersby in the street. In 1587, a visitor was astounded to encounter a Leiden magistrate "sitting on the steps in front of his door." It was even said that some deputies to the States General attended in their slippers![59]

The ethos of simplicity did change, however, in the course of the century, and perhaps the "Portuguese" felt a growing affinity for the Dutch upper classes as the latter began purchasing seigneurial rights and titles, building grand houses on the canals, wearing periwigs, calling themselves *"Heer van"* so-and-so, and dressing in French fashion. Moreover, elite tastes in the second half of the century were becoming less regional and more receptive to European trends, first toward Renaissance and classical style and then toward French classicism, so that "Portuguese" and Dutch tastes were brought into increasing harmony.

In any case, the Europeanization of the "Portuguese" over the decades they had lived as New Christians in the Peninsula permitted them to feel at ease among the Dutch in a way other Jews would not have. They did not, like most Ashkenazi Jews, regard the synagogue and the home as a haven from an alien world. Mixing with the Dutch and other Europeans at the stock exchange or in the market place, they were not, in contrast to Ashkenazim, distinguishably Jewish. "Portuguese" men generally wore quite small, trim beards like their European contemporaries; both men and women dressed in the fashions of their neighbors. While the "Portuguese" did not ordinarily know Dutch well, many knew French or Latin. Some "Portuguese" rabbis—Isaac Aboab da Fonseca was one—possessed libraries that contained numerous classical and Renaissance texts in the original or in Spanish translation. Aboab's collection contained works of all the major classical authors except Plato, as well as works by much later authors such as Jean Bodin, Lope de Vega, Machiavelli, Montaigne, and Thomas Hobbes (in French translation).[60] And it was not only the Jewish intelligentsia—rabbis, physicians, and misfits like De Barrios and Uriel da Costa—who were interested in classical and contemporary European letters. There was a high estimation of letters among the merchants as well. Shared cultural attitudes did, at least, contribute to a certain level of mutual comfort between "Portuguese" and Dutch.

To Dutch culture in its "golden age," however, the Portuguese Jews remained rather apathetic. This is reflected in the linguistic sphere. The official language of the community remained Portuguese. At the opening ceremonies of the new Portuguese synagogue in 1675, all the orations were in Portuguese.[61] This was not merely a matter of convenience for the speakers. Given the occasion, it was also a clear statement about identity.

It is understandable that the "Men of the Nation" continued to speak and cultivate Portuguese and, to a lesser extent, Castilian. True, their Portuguese was peppered with isolated Iberianized Dutch words, such as *pacuz* for the Dutch *pakhuis* (warehouse), *escotete* for *schout* (sheriff), and *vira* for *bier* (beer).[62] They also adopted loan words from Hebrew and French. And over time, given their isolation from a Portuguese- and Castilian-speaking environment, their Iberian languages became impoverished and corrupted.[63] But it is remarkable that before their emancipation in the late eighteenth century, they rarely used Dutch among themselves.[64] (Of course, the "Portuguese" were not alone among immigrants in their indifference to Dutch. Many French exiles, including Descartes, did not bother to learn Dutch; Pierre Bayle spent a quarter of a century in Rotterdam without learning Dutch. "Portuguese" merchants, brokers, and printers did however learn the language and used it when necessary.) It stands to reason that the "Portuguese," cultured as they might be, were not great consumers of Dutch literary productions. Spinoza, though he often referred to Holland as *mea patria* (and he had good cause to feel that way) possessed very few Dutch books in his library.[65] In this respect at least, he appears to have been typically "Portuguese."[66]

What the "Portuguese" did cultivate with the Dutch were good relations at the formal public level. One of the most notable public relations events was the official visit to the synagogue in 1642 of Prince Frederick Hendrik (the stadholder), his son William II, and the queen of England. (It was probably not a coincidence that the visit took place at a time when the queen was in need of Jewish financial aid.) With this visit, the Portuguese Jews were formally recognized as subjects of the commonwealth. In his welcoming pamphlet to the visitors, Menasseh ben Israel spoke of the Jews' liberties in the United Provinces, contrasting them to the cruel treatment they had received in Spain. Further, he wrote, "We no longer hold Spain and Portugal, but Holland, to be our fatherland; we no longer recognize as our masters the Castilian or Lusitanian kings, but rather the most noble States [General] and your Highness."[67] Such expressions were not entirely cynical, but they served political ends and should not be understood as reflecting genuine convictions about affiliation.

In summary, the boundaries between the Dutch and the Portuguese Jews were quite clear—linguistically, religiously, and culturally. There existed little of the entanglement, intensity, and intimacy that had characterized New Christian/Old Christian relations in the Peninsula. Certainly religious tensions existed. But the policies of the Dutch regents kept potential problems in check. What this state of affairs meant for the "Portuguese," among other things, was that they enjoyed space for the task of reconstructing their own ruptured notions of self and community.

Confronting Calvinism

It would be a mistake, however, to ignore one area in which the Portuguese Jewish leadership was intensely sensitive to currents in Dutch society. This was in the sphere of Calvinist teaching and preaching. On the one hand, the largely Calvinist regime in Holland was responsible for providing the conditions which permitted the free practice of Judaism, and this aroused gratitude. On the other hand, a missionizing Reformed church, operating in a climate free of Iberian racialism, offered the Portuguese Jews, who were already familiar with Christianity and not necessarily comfortable with Judaism, the tempting promise of genuine assimilation into Christian society, and this aroused trepidation among communal leaders. At one moment Dutch Calvinists might appear to the "rejudaized" in a positive light, as heroic rebels against a familiar Spanish tyranny; at another, their churches might spark hostile feelings, reminding one that their religion had a great deal in common with Catholicism. In short, for a Portuguese-Jewish leadership eager to maintain a strong community, Calvinism was a matter of considerable concern. Within the wider Jewish world, this placed the "Portuguese" in a novel position.

By the sixteenth century, Jews had been engaging in polemics with Latin Christianity for more than fourteen centuries. While these polemics varied with changed circumstances, the essential arguments had changed little.

Even with the great upheaval of the Reformation, the vast majority of European Jews in the sixteenth and seventeenth centuries had scant interest in the Christian world and felt little need to differentiate between Catholicism and the new Protestant creeds.[68] Given these circumstances, the early encounter of a group of ex-conversos with the Reformed (Calvinist) Church in seventeenth-century Amsterdam merits close attention.

As elsewhere in Europe, the Reformed clergy in the Netherlands believed that if the Jews would only grasp the great difference between the Reformed church and the Catholic church, they would willingly embrace the message of the Gospels.[69] One of Hugo Grotius's reasons for permitting Jewish settlement in Holland (in his *Remonstrantie* of 1615) was his belief that with the reform of the Christian church Jews would be less resistant to conversion. Indeed, he was heartened by the fact that "conversion of individual Jews to the true religion [i.e., Protestantism] takes place regularly."[70]

This, then, in broad terms, was the environment in which the Dutch Portuguese Jews' attitudes about Calvinism took shape. Two questions immediately present themselves. To what degree did the emigres transfer their hostile attitudes regarding Christianity, as they had known it in the Peninsula, to Calvinism? Or did they, at least to some extent, consider Calvinism a new phenomenon, distinct from and more acceptable than Catholicism?

Oddly, no study has been devoted to this subject, despite the relevant material in the rich polemical literature produced by the Portuguese Jews in Amsterdam. To be sure, the need to produce such a literature had more to do with the Catholic Iberian experience than that of Calvinist Amsterdam. The emigres might at last be free of inquisitorial threats and coerced conformity to Catholic life, but they were not free of the psychic legacy of Catholic piety, on the one hand, and Catholic persecution, on the other. In their efforts to liberate themselves from the only fully elaborated religious system they had known—one which had impressed itself on them in countless subtle and not-so-subtle ways—they needed not only to assert the superiority of Judaism but also to repudiate the basic teachings of Christianity. But the polemical and apologetic literature of Amsterdam's Portuguese Jews was not written in a vacuum. It was written within the context of a proselytizing and potentially attractive Protestant world.

As early as 1606, Portuguese Jews in Amsterdam became targets of Protestant conversionist efforts when Hugh Broughton, a friend of Hugo Grotius and pastor of the English congregation of Middelburg, published in Amsterdam a conversionist tract in Hebrew (*Parshegan ha-nishtevan ish ivri* [Copy of a Letter to a Hebrew Man]) with a Latin translation, supposedly a reply to a Jew in Constantinople.[71] In response, David Farar— a Portuguese-Jewish physician, merchant, and communal leader—challenged Broughton to a public disputation, where Farar was bold enough to challenge the divine character of the New Testament.[72]

Nevertheless, there were limits to what Jews could say in public. As we have noted, when laws regulating the governance of the Jews were drawn up in 1616, the Amsterdam authorities stipulated that Jews were "not to speak or write anything (and to ensure that nothing be spoken or written) that may, in any way, tend to the disparagement of our Christian religion."[73] The Portuguese-Jewish leadership, too, was fully aware of the need for caution in public discussions of religious matters. The communal statutes of 1639 prohibited religious disputations with gentiles, undoubtedly a reiteration of prohibitions mentioned in earlier statutes which have been lost.[74] Again, in 1677, the Portuguese-Jewish communal leaders prohibited members of the community from engaging in disputations—public or private—with Christians, for fear of "arousing the hostility of the gentiles."[75]

Yet these statutes were not rigidly enforced by either side. In the years following 1644, at least three members of the Portuguese-Jewish community—the merchant Isaac (Lopo de Luna) Montalto,[76] Menasseh ben Israel, and the learned merchant Jacob Judah Leon—debated with Jan Pieterszoon Beelthouwer, a self-taught polemicist with Mennonite and Socinian leanings. Beelthouwer appealed in a new way to Jewish sensibilities when he expressed his heterodox view that Scripture contained no allusions to the Trinity.[77] At a more sophisticated level, there were polemics between the financier Abraham Senior Coronel (Diego Teixeira de Sampayo) and Jacob Alting, professor of theology at Groningen,[78] and between Rabbi Jacob Abendana and Antonius Hulsius, at the time a preacher in Breda and after 1668 an instructor in Hebrew at the University of Leiden.[79] An unidentified Sephardi Jew also carried on a correspondence in 1642 with the Hebraist and Christian kabbalist Johann Stephan Rittangel. The correspondence initially focused on the old issue of the interpretation of Gen. 49:10 ("The scepter shall not depart from Judah . . ."), but degenerated, on Rittangel's part, into an abusive and routine harangue.[80]

If there was one disputation which had, theoretically, the potential to produce some rethinking of positions, it was the protracted debate in the 1680s between the Portuguese-Jewish polemicist and physician Isaac Orobio de Castro and the proto-Enlightenment Remonstrant theologian Philip van Limborch.[81] Limborch struck out on a new path of argumentation, one which reflected his exposure to new currents of biblical criticism: he argued that the text of the Old Testament was unreliable. But Orobio (who in any case was not inclined to think in Limborch's terms) was limited in his freedom to challenge the reliability of the New Testament and was cautious to avoid key issues such as the Trinity and the messiahship of Jesus. The debate has been characterized as a somewhat odd contest between a

Remonstrant theologian who argued in radical seventeenth-century terms and an old-fashioned Aristotelian Jewish rationalist.[82]

These debates were not intellectual exercises. The Portuguese Jews who engaged in them were on the defensive. The conversionist rhetoric of most of the Protestant polemicists—sometimes quite blunt, as in the case of Jacob Alting—expressed underlying hostility and represented a dangerous encroachment into Jewish psychoreligious and even linguistic territory. Under these circumstances, it is understandable that, notwithstanding the communal prohibition on religious debate, communal leaders permitted qualified persons to defend their collective turf.

In the 1670s, efforts to convert Jews in the Netherlands became more organized. In earlier decades, the Reformed synods had pressed mainly for restrictions on Jews.[83] But at the Calvinist synod of Dordrecht in 1676, a different attitude was adopted when the representatives of Gouda proposed a plan to disseminate Christianity among the Jews. A year later at the synod of Delft some participants expressed the by then conventional Protestant idea that Catholicism, with its vain beliefs and rituals, had had an ill effect on the Jews, preventing their conversion to Christianity. They proposed to invite rabbis and other Jewish scholars to engage in "amicable discussions" (*minnelijke conferentiën*) on Moses and the prophets. *Predikants* were urged to study Hebrew so as to be able to examine Jewish anti-Christian polemical literature. Converts from Judaism were to be given financial support. (A minority opinion supported even more radical measures, such as requiring Jews to hear *predikants* preach in their synagogues or requiring that Jewish books be censored by Reformed ecclesiastics.)[84]

It was undoubtedly the conversionary efforts of the Calvinists that spurred Portuguese-Jewish polemicists to refute specifically Calvinist doctrines. They recognized the special danger to a community of neophytes to Judaism (or their offspring) of Calvinist claims that the practitioners of "true" Christianity rejected the "idolatry" of the "papists," that they did not worship crucifixes or images of the saints, and that their loathing of "idolatry" and the abuses of the Catholic church had led them to take up arms to free themselves from the Spanish yoke.

Such arguments were likely to touch deep chords of converso anti-Catholic feeling. Indeed, there are interesting parallels between "Portuguese" and Protestant anti-Catholic rhetoric and mockeries of Catholic ritual.[85] For the conversos, the Iberian Peninsula was the land of "false idols," "superstition," "pagan abominations," and so on. Protestant anti-idolatry rhetoric resonated, then, and might well have produced a sense of identification.

But the alleged affinity between Judaism and Calvinism was both dangerous and spurious in the eyes of the theological spokesmen of the Amsterdam community, and they responded accordingly. They could not, however, respond directly in public. Like much of the Portuguese-Jewish anti-Christian polemic on sensitive issues, the anti-Calvinist polemic was conducted quietly by circulating manuscript treatises in Spanish and Portuguese.[86] The most notable of these works were by the rabbinic scholar Saul Levi Mortera and the physician Isaac Orobio de Castro. They were not impartial or evenhanded. If Calvinist proselytizers sought to obscure the fundamental differences between Calvinist and Jewish doctrines, these Jewish apologists sought to highlight them, to shore up threatened barriers.

The most highly elaborated attack on Calvinist teachings was composed in Portuguese in 1659 by one of the major rabbis in Amsterdam, Saul Levi Mortera, who has been discussed earlier.[87] At the outset Mortera announced that with this treatise he was mounting a battle against the "so-called reformed churches," which, having successfully defended their consciences, defeated their enemy, and rejected "the great idolatry of the Host, the worship of the crucifix and other images," were nevertheless deeply in error. He intended, he wrote, to refute the doctrines even of *"os reformados de noso tempo"* (the reformed of our time), by which he meant the Socinians, with whose antitrinitarian doctrines he was acquainted. True, the latter had succeeded in freeing themselves from the doctrines of the Trinity and the Incarnation, but they continued to adhere to the false notions that the Gospels were divinely revealed, that Jesus was the messiah, and that the Law of Moses had been abrogated.[88]

Interestingly, Mortera chose as the key issue in his work neither the doctrine of predestination nor the doctrine of grace (though he touched on those too), but the highly charged issue (for Portuguese Jews) of idolatry. Calvinists turned to Jews with the claim that they had purified the church of "idolatry." Not so, argued Mortera. While the Calvinists had indeed rid themselves of "material idolatry"—crucifixes and statues of the saints—they remained ensnared by what Mortera called "mental idolatry"—their belief in the plurality of God (i.e., the Trinity) and the corporeality of the Son. To underscore his point, Mortera cited what he viewed as the dual message in Zechariah's description of the messianic era: "On that day the Lord shall be One" (i.e., there would be no material images beside Him) "and his *name* One" (i.e., he would no longer be called Father, Son, and Holy Spirit).[89] According to this reasoning, the Calvinists had taken only the first of two steps required to eliminate idolatry.[90] It was only the *"novos reformados,"* as he called the antitrinitarians, who had totally eliminated this error.[91]

It is clear not only from Mortera's long chapters dealing with the distinction between "material" and "mental" idolatry, but also from the catalogue of errors he attributes to Calvin's teaching (e.g., the retention of Sunday as the day of the sabbath[92] or the teaching that grace rather than works is needed for salvation[93]), that Mortera wished to create in his reader's mind a strongly negative image of the Calvinist church. To be sure, he implied that in a hierarchy of Christian creeds, Calvinism was an improvement over Catholicism (and Socinianism over Calvinism), but, sensitive to the power of converso anti-Catholic imagery, he drummed home the message that the Calvinists indulged in idolatry—even if it was "invisible."

Similar views, less thoroughly explored, were expressed in another widely circulated treatise by the ex-converso physician Isaac Orobio de Castro.[94] Even more sharply than Mortera, but in the same vein, Orobio rejected Calvinist claims of having eliminated idolatry in their faith. "Those who 'carry their wooden idol' [Isaiah 45:20] are the papists," he asserted, "and those who 'pray to a god that cannot save' [continuation of same verse] are the reformers who, although they have repudiated the external trappings of idolatry, offer prayer to a dead man as if he were God—one who could not save himself, let alone them."[95]

It would seem that Calvinism was hardly better than Catholicism, and that the Portuguese-Jewish community of Amsterdam had been established in the heart of a new Babylon. But it is important to keep in mind the polemical nature of such works. Their aim was to establish the superiority of Judaism to all forms of Christianity, not to deny the important differences between Amsterdam and Seville.

Unfortunately, evidence is scarce concerning everyday attitudes to the Protestant world. But it is not altogether absent. The most telling evidence that the Portuguese Jews—regardless of what their theologians told them—felt at ease in a new way in a Calvinist world lies in the realm of everyday language. In the rich collection of surviving communal documents, letters, poetry, and other material concerning the Portuguese Jews of Amsterdam, the unique terminology adopted by these Jews reflects a great deal about how they viewed the outside world. One of the terms that appears with considerable frequency in these documents is *terras de idolatria* (lands of idolatry). When Portuguese Jews spoke of "lands of idolatry," they were invariably referring to Catholic lands. Attitudes grounded in theology could not easily be separated from attitudes grounded in experience. The Reformed clergy were argumentative and aggressive, but they did not propose inquisitorial prosecution, forced baptism, or the expulsion of the Jews. "Idolatry," for the Portuguese Jews, remained closely associated with the use of religious coercion, with the *requirement* that they (or their forebears) worship idols. In this respect, the "reformados" *were* different. Unlike the Spanish, the Portuguese, and the French (the Italians were an exception in the Catholic world), the Dutch allowed the Portuguese Jews to live (and defend) a religious life of their own, purified of whatever they themselves considered "idolatry." However much the polemicists might fulminate against Protestant "idolatry," no one would ever refer to the Netherlands as a *terra de idolatria*.

Indeed, a view quite contrary to Mortera's is presented in a biblical-mythical fantasy Daniel Levi de Barrios developed in his *Triumpho del govierno popular*, suggesting a profound spiritual (and even ethnic!) tie between the "Portuguese" and the Dutch.[96] This work, aimed at pleasing the *parnasim*, may reflect something of the merchant elite's general attitude about the Dutch (though not their thinking).

De Barrios based his myth on a Hellenistic-Jewish story in which the biblical figure Yoqtan, a descendant of Shem, intervened heroically to rescue Abram and other dissenters who refused to cooperate in the plan to build the tower of Babel. Yoqtan was ultimately unable to prevent Abram from being thrown into a brick kiln, but Abram was saved by a miracle, and it was the evil Nimrod and his followers who suffered death by fire.[97] (A puzzled reader should not be overly concerned with biblical chronology.)

According to De Barrios, the heroic Yoqtan's father, Eber, was the ancestor of the Dutch people, who migrated from Spain and inhabited the Netherlands.[98] Having established that the Dutch were Semites with roots in Spain (and not, as Dutch mythmaking would have it, descendants of the ancient Batavians of Roman times),[99] De Barrios went on to analyze the similar paths taken by the descendants of Eber and the sons of Abraham. Just as the ancestral figures had rebelled against Nimrod's tyranny and idolatry, so their descendants were haters of despotism, as they had shown in their rebellion against Spain and the idolatry of the Church of Rome.

De Barrios even maintained that there was a positive religious historical bond between the Dutch and the Jews. Yoqtan's wife was, he claimed, the legendary Jewish woman Moso, said to have written the Torah—a figure who is mentioned by the first-century Greek scholar Alexander Poly-histor.[100] According to De Barrios, Moso expounded the seven Noachide Laws (the laws held by rabbinic tradition to be incumbent on gentiles) to the sons of Eber.[101] The nonidolatrous "Noachide" beliefs of the sons of Eber, De Barrios suggested, could be found in the Calvinist doctrines of their seventeenth-century descendants. It was the strength of these beliefs that permitted the descendants of Yoqtan in the Spanish Netherlands to rise up and overthrow the tyrannical rule of an idolatrous monarch, and afterward it was they who offered the sons of Abraham a refuge from the flames of the autos-da-fé. Wrote De Barrios:[102]

> The Babylonians burned to death those who did not worship the statue they raised to King Nebuchadnezzar. In the same way the Inquisitors burn to death those who do not worship images. But the States of the United Provinces [the governing body of the Dutch republic] show favor to them [who do not worship images], just as the prince Yoqtan did to the patriarch Abraham and his companions.

The extreme, one-sided views of Mortera and De Barrios about the Dutch Reformed Church surely do not reflect common attitudes among the merchant elite. They do suggest an unavoidable ambivalence the "Portuguese" leadership felt toward a world of *goyim*—a term used by communal officials in their records to refer to the Dutch—that included both tolerant regents and offensive preachers. But in the fragmented, tolerant, particularistic world of seventeenth-century Amsterdam, Portuguese Jews felt no pressure to prove that they "belonged" to the majority society, as Jews later would in modern European states, so that their attitude to Dutch society was not a key issue. The kind of kinship De Barrios suggested was purely fanciful, desired neither by Dutch nor "Portuguese." True, the founding myths of both groups involved oppression by, and liberation from, the Spaniards. Both groups invoked biblical images to describe their historical dramas, especially the image of escape from Egyptian bondage and idolatry. But here the similarities ended. The founding dramas and myths of the two groups were profoundly different,[103] and the cultural, ethnic, and religious barriers between them enormous.

In various ways, Dutch society actually encouraged (or at least did nothing to inhibit) the cultivation of a distinct Portuguese-Jewish identity among the emigres. Moreover, it provided the conditions that allowed the community to develop its own "expansionist" role as a nerve center for the entire Atlantic "Portuguese" diaspora. And, given its utter acceptance of the emigres' self-definition as "Portuguese" as well as Jews, it in no way challenged the identification of the emigres with the Iberian past. In ways we shall explore in the next chapter, it was the impalpable world of Iberian memories that dominated "Portuguese" self-consciousness, even among those born outside the Peninsula.

4

⭐

Iberian Memory and Its Perpetuation

Constructing a Converso Past

One of the difficulties the "Portuguese" in Amsterdam faced was the need to affirm a past that had been lived within the Catholic orbit. In public discourse, they promoted certain attitudes toward the past while discouraging others. This is a feature of all societies. But it was complicated for Amsterdam's "Portuguese" by the fact that their "past" was still being lived, so to speak, by those who remained in the Peninsula. And their experience was not a coherent, consistently uplifting one: much of it was chaotic, bewildering, and painful. Conversos demonstrated the full range of human responses to oppression and persecution, including not only courageous defiance, but also identification with the oppressor, pragmatic or unthinking adaptation to given conditions, and ashamed concealment of origins.

Inquisitorial documents often bring into striking focus the difficulties of everyday life for "those of the Nation." Strife, betrayal, and fear of betrayal were part of the fabric of that life. Those who collaborated with the "enemy," however passively, could arouse deep hostility among those who resisted coercion. This is eloquently revealed in reports of witnesses for the Inquisition. In the 1580s, for example, the conversa Brites Alvares, while in the home of neighbors, let it be known she intended to go to mass, whereupon a visitor violently reproached her, saying, "If you were my daughter, I would break your legs: first, because you eat blood sausages, and second, because you go to mass so often." As she left, the mistress of the house said about her, "Why tell her anything, she's a saint-sucker [*uma papa santos*]."[1]

"Assimilating" conversos could also display hostility toward "judaizers." In Rouen in 1632, conflict between a group of judaizing conversos and a group of New Christians (and some Old Christians) who adhered to Catholicism resulted in the latter denouncing the judaizers to the French authorities.[2] There were heroes but there was also a dark, unpleasant side to converso life.[3]

The fact that some New Christians sought to sever themselves from "the Nation" was another blot on collective memory. Escaping association with "the Nation" was achieved in various ways. It was sometimes possible, for example, to buy certificates of *limpieza*. One might move, change one's name, marry into an Old Christian family, or leave the Peninsula and join a Catholic community elsewhere (as in Rouen). One might even, at least under the regime of the Count-Duke of Olivares, buy an Inquisition office as a means of gaining recognition of one's spurious claim to *limpieza*.[4] The merchant Isaac de Pinto, who fled Antwerp for Rotterdam in 1647 and whose valuable memoirs are cited frequently in these pages, made clear what he thought of those in his family who tried to assimilate into Old Christian society. Pinto did not perceive this kind of escape as a denial of identity (a modern construct) but as a failure of loyalty and an act of opportunism.[5]

Even the unwillingness of conversos to flee the Peninsula despite opportunities to do so was deplorable in the eyes of some emigres. The language of official communal documents reinforced such feelings with their references to *terras de idolatria*. The communal rhetoric of "idolatry" concerning Spain and Portugal, while setting sharp, clear boundaries, also obscured the ambivalence in the heart of many emigres concerning the places they had left behind.[6] In fact, quite a few emigres returned permanently to the Peninsula (including the poet Antonio Enríquez Gómez, who during his years in France had written some of the most moving poetry dealing with converso martyrdom). This was disheartening in the extreme to those stirred by the idea of restoration. The ex-converso polemicist Immanuel Aboab lamented in 1626 or 1627: "From letters that have arrived from this land [France] it can be seen how many persons of our nation return to Spain."[7] To be sure, many left Jewish life only temporarily. Daniel de Barrios himself, a key shaper of the mythology of return, spent time in the Spanish Netherlands after having settled in Amsterdam, and like other such persons was required upon his return to ask forgiveness in the synagogue.[8] The frequent crossings into *terras de idolatria* show that the boundaries were porous and the break with the Iberian-Catholic past not so clear as communal mythology would have it.[9]

One of the ugliest aspects of life under the Inquisition was its use by its victims to take revenge on other victims. Every converso must have heard stories of "Men of the Nation" who had taken advantage of the Holy Office to denounce an enemy who was of his own "lineage." Since the accused was not told who had denounced him or her, the best he or she could do was to tell the tribunal who all his or her enemies or suspected enemies were. The lists by accused persons of potential denouncers are fascinating but tragic: they include business partners, spouses, and even their own children.

Some denunciations were made out of sheer desperation by conversos under interrogation who sought to "prove" the sincerity of their repentance. Denunciations of persons who were dead or outside the grasp of the Inquisition were not convincing. This lesson was brought home to the notorious Hector Mendes Bravo, who appeared before the Lisbon Inquisition in 1617 after spending years as a Jew in Venice, Amsterdam, and Hamburg. He readily denounced as many ex-conversos living as Jews in those places as he could remember (including over a hundred in Amsterdam). But when the sincerity of his repentence was questioned, he gave evidence against a converso whom the Inquisition had arrested and was holding.[10] According to Cecil Roth, during a case in Toledo in 1669–70 against Fernando Gil de Espinosa in Madrid, information elicited from him led to the issue of arrest warrants for 213 persons still in Spain, as well as others abroad.[11]

Even those whom the Inquisition punished severely were not necessarily the heroes many emigres would have liked to believe. Evidence indicates that the Inquisition condemned a significant number of conversos who faithfully conformed to Catholic norms—sometimes because torture produced false confessions, sometimes because "innocent" actions were interpreted as judaizing, and sometimes because the Inquisition was interested in the property of the accused. Converso complaints of unfounded inquisitorial arrests and convictions were quite common. The Amsterdam merchant and memoirist Isaac de Pinto alluded to the frequency of such cases when he wrote that his in-law António Enriques was condemned to death as a *negativo*—a person who refused to confess—because he was not "able to make up lies," adding somewhat ambiguously, "which is what their confessions consisted of."[12] In a similar vein, the ex-converso Abraham Idaña, who fled Spain and settled in Amsterdam in 1660, wrote vehemently of "the many imprisoned for observing the Law of Moses who had never done so—who though of the Jewish nation had always lived in blindness, worshiping wood and stone." Such persons, tried and threatened by the Inquisition, "confessed to things they had never done," and the inquisitors eagerly confiscated their possessions. This caused some to change heart and even to become "perfect Jews." Others remained indifferent to Judaism but were burned at the stake because they refused to say what the inquisitors wanted them to say.[13] An anonymous rhymester in early seventeenth-century Amsterdam summed it up thus:[14]

> The upright soul becomes a criminal here,
> Swearing to words and deeds that never were.

Here such tricks are played, and clever abuse,
That Christians are converted into Jews.

This is an eloquent acknowledgment of the fact that while the Inquisition was always black, its victims were sometimes gray.

The ambiguities of converso life in the Peninsula—the deceptions, the strife, the internal and external conflicts—were familiar to all emigres. But this is not the stuff of which collective memory is fashioned. As in all societies, the history of the group, as fashioned and celebrated in the public sphere, was a creation in which fact and fantasy merged. Stories of genuine heroism were remembered and repeated, and the heroism of the few was allowed to flow over and grace the group as a whole.

What made this projection compelling was the fact that while not everyone was a martyr, everyone had suffered and could identify with the martyrs. If any one experience united the emigres, it was suffering at the hands of the Inquisition. Collective memory among the "Portuguese" in Amsterdam was virtually knit together by the theme of the Inquisition— not the Spanish or Portuguese Inquisition, but simply "the Inquisition." The term was not merely the name of an institution. It evoked a universe of painful human experience, of anxiety, trials, confiscations of goods, torture chambers, prisons, separation from loved ones, autos-da-fé, and so on. Few emigre families were completely sheltered from this experience; for many it was the immediate precipitant for flight.

It should thus come as no surprise that the Inquisition is mentioned with great frequency in the records and literature of the Dutch "Portuguese."[15] This had to do partly with the need of the survivors to recall and share memories of a collective nightmare. But oppression is also an important catalyst of self-consciousness. The cruelties and injustices of the Inquisition, and the heroism of conversos who defied it, were important components of converso identity and pride.

In the case of the conversos, suffering also had an atoning aspect. Those who "returned" to Judaism were well aware that in the Peninsula they had been isolated from the institutions and rituals of Jewish life—which meant, more deeply, that they had not participated in perpetuating the covenantal relationship between the Jewish people and God. But what redeemed the past, indeed elevated it, were memories of sacrifices made and dangers endured by the defiant, whether or not they were actually cryptojudaizers or suffered merely because of their Jewish blood.

The most exalted of those who were remembered were the martyrs, those who gave up their lives because they had "judaized." (To be sure, some perished who had never "judaized.") Even among the ranks of the martyrs there was a hierarchy. The highest place of honor was reserved for those who had chosen to be burned alive—an excruciating death—rather than "repent" at the last moment in order to merit an easier death. (The "penitents" were strangled with an iron collar tightened by a screw—the *garrote*—before being burned at the stake.)

The remembrance of martyrs was not an emigre innovation, but had roots in the Peninsula. There, however, reverence for martyrs was expressed clandestinely, and little remains of such peninsular traditions. Two cases stand out for their brazenness (which may be why they came to light)—both attempts (though perhaps, in the second case, merely an accusation of an attempt) to establish a confraternity, ostensibly no different from thousands of other Catholic confraternities in the Peninsula, but in fact a memorial to a converso martyr.[16] If such efforts were made, surely narratives of martyrdom were an important part of the secret and unrecorded lore of crypto-Judaism.

Occasionally, such lore surfaces in Inquisition records. An accused converso at a trial in Bahía in 1618 was reported to have said to a witness who testified against him that the New Christians burned at the stake in the Peninsula died as martyrs for the Law of Moses and as such were "better Jews than those who received the Law at Mount Sinai."[17] (This is a reweaving of a theme we have noted elsewhere in the form of the assertion that the trials of the New Christians were greater than those of the Israelites in Egypt.)

What was new in Amsterdam was the public, even institutional, role that "Portuguese" leadership gave to the memorialization of converso martyrs. Even without special initiative, the act of adopting traditional Jewish liturgy in the synagogue would have achieved this, since remembrance of martyrs is a routine aspect of synagogue worship. But at least one prayer book printed in Amsterdam included a special *hashkavah,* or memorial prayer, for individual conversos who refused to repent and were burned alive at an auto-da-fé.[18] The prayer, printed in both Hebrew and Spanish, reflects anger and bitterness toward the Inquisition as well as love and respect for the martyred:[19]

> May the great, mighty, and terrible God avenge his holy servant [so-and-so][20] who was burned alive for the sanctity of His name. May He avenge his/her blood from His enemies with His mighty arm and repay His foes as they deserve . . . as it is written: "Rejoice, O nations, with His people, for He will avenge the blood of His servants, and will render vengeance to His adversaries, and will forgive His land and His people." (Deut. 32:43)

This memorialization of a converso living "outside Judaism" was a strict exception in synagogue practice and attests to the special status of those burned alive. In the matter of memorial prayers in the synagogue, the communal and rabbinic leadership saw a need to draw a line and to check the natural tendency among ex-conversos to view all Peninsular conversos as fully accepted Jews. In 1645 the *Mahamad* took action against indiscriminate memorialization of converso dead, presumably under the guidance of the rabbinic leadership. They issued an ordinance prohibiting the custom of giving a Hebrew name to a relative who died *fora da judesmo* ("outside Judaism") and saying a *hashkavah* prayer for him or her.[21] Thus, in synagogal matters, where rabbinic norms prevailed, *post facto* acceptance of Iberian conversos as full members of the Jewish people was limited to those who had made the ultimate sacrifice. In other cases, a boundary was to be maintained excluding those who lived outside the discipline of rabbinic Judaism, however painful that might be to their relatives.

A certain tension between rabbinic and "converso" ideas can be found even in the understanding of the significance of martyrdom. One idea, consistent with traditional Jewish thinking, was expressed by the Amsterdam apologete and physician Isaac Orobio de Castro. Orobio wrote that those who insisted on being burned alive were following in the footsteps of Jews through the ages, "sanctifying His holy name"—an ancient rabbinic expression. Their martyrdom was a purely religious act, an expression of love of God. Interestingly, Orobio noted the universality of such martyrdom. Among those who had demonstrated their love for God in this manner were "many Papists in China, Japan and the West Indies" and "many Protestants [*Reformados*] in France, Germany, and Italy." But he spoke with the greatest emotion of those "many Jews [i.e., conversos] over the years of [the activity of] the Inquisition of Portugal and Spain, who offered their lives and sacrificed great well-being to convert themselves to their religion, despising all things human in order to sanctify the name of God in the flames, dying while acknowledging the Divine Law."[22]

For Orobio, the story of condemned converso martyrs was an integral part of the long history of Jewish martyrdom. It did not entirely reflect reality. It is quite certain that not all who refused to "repent" did so to sanctify God's name and to purify their souls. But this aim was projected onto all converso martyrs, at least implicitly, by those inclined to evaluate converso experience through the lens of traditional Jewish historical memory.

A more idiosyncratic idea about martyrdom also circulated among the Amsterdam "Portuguese": martyrdom as an act affirming "Portuguese" honor. The ex-converso rabbi Jacob Abendana in a speech in memory of Abraham Núñez Bernal and Isaac d'Almeida, victims of the Cordova auto of 1655,[23] did not deny the victims' religious heroism. "These men demonstrated," he wrote, "that in their hearts there reigned the perfect love of God, in paying to Him the tribute of the greatest courtesy [*finesa*] of which men are capable, in offering their own lives for the honor of His holy name." But he went on to express sentiments of a different kind: "By such an act, they have brought glory to God and luster to their stock [*linaje*], and have increased the treasury of merit of the chosen people."[24] There is an appeal here to the sense of "ethnic" honor among the conversos, an appeal that might strike a chord even among those apathetic to the Law of Moses.

The idea of martyrdom as an act of honor independent of religious belief was reiterated by others. It was expressed in the most succinct terms by the converso poet Antonio Enríquez Gómez, who in his period of Jewish enthusiasm prior to 1649 wrote:[25]

> Who would suffer the loss of one's liberty,
> save for the law of honor, which ever was
> the loftier part of the man of honor?

Love of God is not the point of sacrifice in this passage; it is the defense of self-esteem.

Likewise, Manoel Dias Espinosa of Brazil, tried in Lisbon in 1622, held that "many of those who were burned died as martyrs because they were honorable men and maintained their honor, refusing to confess." Those who capitulated and confessed, he said, were common people with no honor.[26] Implicit here is the ascription of martyrdom even to those conversos who were *falsely* accused of judaizing and refused to save their lives by "confessing."

What added to the galvanizing power of martyrdom in the converso diaspora was its periodic resurfacing. It was not an event that occurred in a distant past; it was also part of the present. Its power was felt in Amsterdam most electrifyingly when someone known there was martyred. One of the most stirring of these cases was that of Isaac de Castro Tartas, a young ex-converso from Portugal who had come to Amsterdam in his youth with his family. At the age of sixteen, in 1641, he left for Dutch Brazil, where a Jewish community flourished in Recife. In 1644 he left for Bahía in Portuguese Brazil—according to some, to proselytize among New Christian relatives, according to others, to flee Dutch justice, or perhaps for commercial reasons. There he claimed to be an unbaptized Jew who wished to be baptized, but witnesses were produced who testified otherwise, and he had apparently brought phylacteries (*tefilin*) with him. He was extradited to Portugal, where the Inquisition imprisoned and tried him. When he saw that he would not be freed he confessed to being a scrupulously observant Jew, repeatedly stating his intention to sacrifice his life for the Law of Moses. He was burned alive at the stake in Lisbon in 1647.[27]

His death sent shock waves through the entire northern "Portuguese" diaspora. But Isaac de Castro Tartas was most intensely mourned in Amsterdam, where he had been known and where his parents and brothers lived. The now mature *hakham* Saul Levi Mortera delivered a funeral oration, and Menasseh ben Israel praised him in his *Esperança de Israel*.[28] Salomon de Oliveyra interpreted and idealized the event in a Hebrew poem which employed some of the standard imagery of converso martyrology:[29]

> Go worship the cross! said they [the inquisitors],
> Smoothing their deceitful tongue to swallow [him],
> Not knowing, like beasts, their folly,
> The work of men's hands, wood and stone.
>
> He answered in a pleasant voice and with joyful heart,
> Why do you torment and confuse me?
> I shall rise and take courage—I am triumphant;
> You will bow down to nothingness and fall.

Thus was Isaac de Castro Tartas transformed into an icon, a figure who could inspire and encourage those who were caught up in the travails of everyday living.

Less than a decade later, in 1655 and 1656, news that three members of the Bernal family had died at the hands of the Inquisition, two in Cordova and one in Santiago de Compostela, rocked the Amsterdam community. Various members of the community contributed elegies to a collection printed in honor of two of them who had refused to recant and were burned alive.[30] A decade later, the past once again became immediate when Jorge Mendez de Castro (Abraham Athias), father of the Amsterdam printer Joseph Athias, was burned at the stake in Cordova in one of the most famous autos of that city. (It was said to have lasted from seven in the morning until nine at night, at which time the 75-year-old Athias was burned alive.)[31]

For relatives of the victim, martyrdom became a badge of family honor. Abraham Athias's son Joseph used his status as a kind of title, identifying himself as "Joseph, son of the martyr Abraham Athias" on the title page of the Hebrew Bible and Ashkenazi prayer book he printed. His role as son of a martyr became part of his self-definition. He also ensured that the martyrdom of his father would be incorporated into communal ritual; he donated 250 guilders on condition that his father be specifically mentioned in the prayers on behalf of martyrs that were recited on the first sabbath after the seventeenth of the Hebrew month of Tammuz and on Yom Kippur. A generation later Joseph's son Immanuel recalled the martyrdom of his grandfather in the colophon of the last part of his edition of the *Mishneh Torah*—further evidence of the centrality of this kind of event in family identity.[32]

Evidence of the special status of relatives of inquisitorial victims appears strikingly in the records of the *Dotar* society established to provide dowries for poor orphans and other girls throughout the "Portuguese" diaspora. Each year the officers drew up a list of approved candidates, and winners of a dowry were chosen by a combination of election and lottery. The lists of candidates usually identified a girl by name and/or the name of a parent, as well as (usually) her place of residence. They offer additional information only in a few cases—those cases in which candidates' fathers had been seized by or died at the hands of the Inquisition. In the spring of 1616, for example, the list included a "daughter of Antonio Rodrigues, a native of Trancoso, who is in [the hands of] the Inquisition [*que esta na inquicissam*]." At the time, the girl was with her mother in St. Jean de Luz close to the French-Spanish border, a place of refuge for fleeing conversos. The next entry mentioning her, a year later, tells a poignant story: this time she was listed as "a daughter of Isabel Rodrigues, widow of Antonio Rodrigues Madouro who suffered in this auto-da-fé in Coimbra [*que padesco nesta auto de Coimbra*]."[33]

Lower, perhaps, in the "Portuguese" hierarchy of suffering, but still part of the historical drama that bound members of "the Nation" together, were the more common—but by no means trivial—sufferings of those who spent years in inquisitorial prisons (some died there), were humiliated publicly at autos, or had their property confiscated. These were the rank and file of sufferers, so to speak, and were not singled out individually on public occasions or in literary works. Their sufferings were, however, acknowledged in a general way in polemical writings that excoriated the Inquisition, and individually (as Pinto's memoirs suggest) in family lore.

From an emotional point of view, there is nothing exceptional about the emigres' tendency, in public life, to focus on the martyrs and heroes. This seems to be a typical collective response to oppression. But in the construction of a "Portuguese" past there was a more specific need to emphasize martyrdom and suffering. Doing so allowed the emigres to view their experience not as an aberration in Jewish history, but as part of its mainstream. The "Portuguese" poetry of martyrdom, in its repeated recourse to the imagery of idolatry and capitivity (Babylonian and Egyptian), the Exodus, and the story of Esther, served to weave the converso experience into the larger cloth of Jewish history.[34] In the Spanish verse version of Psalm 30 by the Amsterdam merchant David Abenatar Melo, for example, Melo boldly transformed the psalmist into a converso ("doomed in the depths to dwell / Of the Inquisition's hell") who laments how, "when in cruel torture / They had me bound tight. . . . / There I saw them burnt." Aware of the liberties he was taking, Melo concluded this psalm with a prose comment: "I adjusted the above psalm to my situation—I, whom the blessed Lord delivered from the Inquisition . . . where I saw eleven *negativos* burned—may their blood be avenged."[35] In "adjusting the psalm" to his situation, Melo underscored the point that, isolated as he had been from rabbinic culture, he had played his part in the ongoing drama of Jewish survival and suffering in exile.

On the Importance of Being Iberian

While converso suffering in the Peninsula constituted an emotionally powerful element of "Portuguese" collective identity, it was only one of various materials the emigres used to build an elaborate structure. Although the practice of Judaism among the emigres did not define the boundaries of "the Nation," it did become a part of the ethos that sustained "Portuguese" identity. But paradoxical as it may seem, an equally important aspect of the old/new structure was the cultivation of Iberian cultural and mental habits. To the extent that these were ingrained and unconscious, there was a vestigial character to them. But vestigial traits soon die out. It was the conscious, systematic efforts of the emigres to sustain and even institutionalize Iberian habits which reveal the profound importance of "Iberianness" to their collective identity.

Given the elements of persecution, resistance, and liberation in the "Portuguese" emigre experience, one might expect to find in the liberation phase, as has so often been the case in modern nationalist movements, an intent to reject the culture of the oppressor. But there was never any effort on the part of the communal leadership in Amsterdam to eliminate the cultural imprint of Spain and Portugal, nor was there a feeling that what remained of this imprint could be tolerated only out of necessity. Iberian values and culture continued to be an integral part of "Portuguese" identity, one in which the emigres and their descendants took pride. Their hatred of the Catholic church and the Inquisition did not preclude their avid consumption of Iberian (especially Spanish) culture. Most emigres felt entitled to enjoy their share of Iberian *grandeza* and experienced little conflict between Iberian cultural habits and a commitment to rabbinic Judaism. Yet, as we shall see, feelings of ambivalence did surface at times.

One aspect of the Iberian legacy transplanted with apparent ease was an unshakable belief in the importance of social rank. Scholars have discussed in detail the Spanish obsession with honor and nobility,[36] an obsession which conversos naturally shared. But converso aristocratic pride may have had some less obvious sources. Long before the Expulsion, Spanish Jews had developed a collective image of themselves as aristocrats, priding themselves on their purported descent from the tribe of Judah, that is, from the royal tribe. This conviction was confirmed in their minds by the figure of the Spanish-Jewish courtier—physician, advisor, tax collector, diplomat, or astronomer to the king, and defender of Jewish interests at court—a figure without parallel in other Jewries.[37] Even as late as the seventeenth century conversos may have incorporated something of medieval Jewish aristocratic traditions into their self-image.

Whatever the source of aristocratic notions of self, the experience of conversion and discrimination inevitably altered them. In some cases

Jewish descent was rendered noble in a christianized form. Descendants of Jews who had once boasted of belonging to the royal tribe of Judah, for example, now claimed that their lineage went back to the family of Mary. Such an idea took root in the distinguished Santa María family. A Bohemian traveler in Spain in the 1460s reported that outside the city of Burgos there was "a new and elegant monastery founded by a bishop [Pablo de Santa María, né Solomon Halevi] who was descended from the family of the Mother of God." When Pablo de Santa María's brother, also a convert and a member of the Order of Caballería, learned the traveler was from Bohemia, he noted "that he too had been in Bohemia, and that he had acquired the title of equestrian there when King Albert conquered the city of Taborense."[38] The idea of descent from Mary was probably not perceived as unrelated to membership in a military order or a title bestowed by royalty. While contemporary tokens of status had value in themselves, they were far more valued in the Hispanic mind if they could be associated with ancient noble lineage.

With time, as "purity of blood" statutes spread and concern about "purity" seized Iberian society, converso interest in noble status intersected with this new issue. Since conversos were by definition tainted (*maculados, notados, manchados*—the variety of terms reflects the persuasiveness of the concept), the numerous marriages of conversos into the "old" Spanish nobility created confusion and anxiety among Spaniards. This confusion led to the following effort at resolution by a certain Josef Luyendo in the early sixteenth century:[39]

> In Spain there are two types of nobility. The principal one is based on noble lineage [*hidalguía*], the other is based on purity of blood [*limpieza*], [found in those] whom we call Old Christians. Even if the first type—nobility of lineage—is more honorable to achieve, yet it is far more degrading to be without the second; for in Spain we esteem a common person who is *limpio* much more than a hidalgo who is not *limpio*.

Popular thinking was not so well defined. Still, widespread obsession with "purity of blood" did jeopardize the perceived social worth of conversos, regardless of titles they had acquired. Some conversos responded by inverting Iberian values. In 1492, a converso from the environs of Cuenca was reported to have said "that the blood of the Jews was good and pure, and that they were of royal blood. . . . And moreover, because the Jews were of such pure blood, God has chosen Our Lady for his incarnation."[40] Similarly, in 1672, an Old Christian complained that some *chuetas* (conversos) in Mallorca boasted that "they came from a better lineage [*casta*] than Old Christians because the Mother of God was a Jew, and that they descended from her line [*casta*]."[41] Such ideas, evidently sincere, represent a radical transfiguration of contemporary Iberian notions of lineage.

An interesting case of the "christianization" of a form of status conferred within the Jewish ritual sphere is found in the writings of the Jewish courtier Solomon Halevi of Burgos, mentioned above, who was baptized, apparently out of genuine conviction, in 1390 or 1391 and was thenceforth known as Pablo de Santa María. In a work written late in his life, he advised his son that his levitic ancestry made him suited for a priestly (i.e., clerical) role.[42] In the first half of the fifteenth century, such efforts to integrate aspects of Jewish identity into a new Christian gestalt were acceptable. But such traditions of priestly lineage might also reflect Jewish loyalties, and though they continued to be transmitted privately in converso families, they could not be used openly to enhance one's social status. Indeed, they became prima facie evidence of judaizing.[43]

But lineage also had a clearly ethnic aspect for conversos, some of whom must have wondered whether social status conferred on Jews in the medieval Spanish-Jewish world remained valid for their descendants who had joined the Christian world. A chronicler of converso descent attempted quite early—in the 1440s—to answer this question, that is, whether "those converted to the Christian faith who had been nobles while still holding their former Law or Sect retain the nobility of their lineage after becoming Christians." His reply was that "not only do such [converted] retain the nobility and dignity of nobleness [*fidalguía*] after having converted, but, moreover, they increase it. . . . And there are nobles among the Jews and Moors in the same manner as among the Christians."[44] Again, such ideas would soon be associated with heretical efforts to cling to a Jewish identity, and went underground.

But once a "Portuguese" emigre society emerged, such ideas resurfaced with renewed power. Spanish-Jewish ideas of hierarchy and Iberian ideas of purity of blood—sometimes the two were conflated—continued to determine status. De Barrios knew well how to mobilize them. He wrote, for example, that among the first members of the Portuguese Jewish community of Amsterdam were "the noble Sosas [Sousas], the pure [*limpios*] Sarfatines, and the fortunate Curieles who resemble those [of the tribe] of Menasseh in trying not to mix themselves in marriage except with those of their own stock."[45] The *infectados*, as New Christians were sometimes called, had indeed been infected.

Others responded to the denial of secure social status with a heightened effort to acquire the external signs of status. The acquisition of titles of nobility came to serve a defensive function, affirming, in the face of the attitudes of Old Christian society, that those who possessed them were of "good lineage." Those who could not pay for titles of nobility and coats of arms, or perform services to rulers in exchange for them, might try to achieve the luster of nobility by adopting aristocratic Spanish names, leading an aristocratic lifestyle, or rubbing shoulders with figures at court.

It is telling that in his autobiography, written long after he had left the Peninsula, Isaac de Pinto went out of his way to mention the noble status attained by members of his family (despite his disapproval of marriages with Old Christians, which was one way to attain it). His great-grandfather married a lady [*senhora*] from a family of "very escutcheoned people [*gente muy escudeirada*]."[46] A daughter of this union married into an Old Christian family (*gente grave*—"important people"). One of this daughter's grandsons married "an escutcheoned lady" and became a member of a military order [*cavaleiro de habito*], a highly prestigious position.[47] His mother's sister Isabel married "a nephew of the postmaster general, people who had been raised to the nobility [*gente afidalgada*]."[48] Similarly, he listed the several titles acquired by his grandfather Manuel Alvares Pinto and added that "all of this is confirmed by letters patent [*hua alvaro autentica*]" in his possession.[49] He even noted that the people with whom his grandfather lodged when he first arrived in Antwerp were the parents of Thomas Lopez Ulhoa, "who later became Baron of Limale and Count and Marquis of the Empire."[50] Many years after his flight to the Netherlands, these old connections to the nobility still enhanced Pinto's image of his family.

So internalized had Hispanic values become that even outside the Peninsula "purity of blood" served a role among the emigres. The intellectual elite of the diaspora communities—either because they had come to hold and value ideas of ethnic purity or because they intuitively grasped their polemical value—enunciated notions of Jewish "purity of blood" that were, however unconventional from a rabbinic point of view,[51] a means of mobilizing Iberian preconceptions to bolster Jewish pride and the notion of Jewish chosenness. This was clearly the intent of Isaac Cardoso when he emphasized the purity of lineage of the Jews in comparison with other peoples:[52]

> The gentile peoples do not proceed from one father, nor do they follow one law. Since in their lineage all are intermingled with one another, none can say that he is an Italian, Frenchman, Spaniard, German, or Greek, and so with the other peoples, because all are confused and mixed. There came to Italy and Spain Tyrians, Phoenicians, Chaldeans, Egyptians, Arabs, Goths, Iberians, Vandals, Carthaginians, Alemani, and many others who intermingled, so that they cannot trace their ancestry, and since the gentile nations do not separate themselves in matters of food or women, they cannot attain the same separation and distinction as the sons of Israel, who are apart from all.

In this passage, Cardoso implicitly expresses contempt for Iberian claims to purity of lineage and paranoia about Jewish blood. But there is a certain irony in his insistence on Jewish separateness, given the fact that Cardoso's readers were well aware of converso intermarriages with Old Christians. The Amsterdam merchant and writer David Abenatar Melo, too, (of whom more will be said) wrote of the "noble and clean blood from which we descend."[53] It was a rhetorical counterclaim believed by those who wished to believe it.

Some merchant emigres, in their own less articulate way, revealed an impulse to express their *hidalguísmo* within the Jewish sphere. The wealthy merchant Diogo Texeira made every effort while in the Peninsula to identify with the Portuguese aristocracy, claiming descent from the Old Christian aristocratic family Texeira de Sampayo. Indeed, in 1643 he succeeded in obtaining certification that he belonged to this family, as well as permission to use its coat of arms. After he and his son reverted to Judaism in Hamburg in 1647, Texeira continued to use his Iberian coat of arms. It was, however, significantly altered: the cross that had once graced it was replaced by a tree.[54] Texeira also took a step that would have delighted Old Christians who made converso behavior the butt of their jokes: Diogo took the Hebrew name Abraham Senior, claiming direct descent from the last Castilian "chief rabbi" and courtier of that name who chose to convert rather than leave Spain in 1492.[55]

Another strategy for expressing Iberian-rooted social impulses in the Jewish sphere was to claim descent from a Jewish warrior clan, i.e., the Maccabees. A converso family in Brazil asserted that one of its members possessed a deed of nobility proving such descent;[56] and a similar claim existed in the family of Joseph Salvador, an eccentric thinker of converso origin who lived in nineteenth-century France.[57] A more common way of "judaizing" one's *hidalguísmo* was to claim descent from the priestly caste, the *kohanim*, who in ancient times constituted the Jewish aristocratic class, or, alternatively, from the Levites, a somewhat lesser distinction. The Azevedo family, some of whose members were prominent in the Amsterdam community, embellished its Peninsular coat of arms by placing the symbol of the priesthood—two hands opened in the configuration made when performing the priestly blessing—above the black wolf of the Azevedos.[58] Other Dutch-Sephardic families also displayed both the family coat of arms and the symbol of the priesthood, especially on tombstones.[59] To possess both of these was perhaps the ultimate in Portuguese-Jewish status.

There is no way to verify the truth of claims to priestly status in these families, but it is noteworthy that the rabbis of Amsterdam did not automatically accept them. The Pinto family, for example, claimed priestly status, which would have entitled its male members to pronounce the priestly blessing in the synagogue. But the rabbis regarded their claim as spurious and denied them the privilege.[60] This did not prevent them, however, from insisting on their priestly lineage. The marriage contract of Isaac de Pinto's son David is decorated with, among other images, the two hands symbolizing the priesthood.[61] Their tombstones also display the symbol of priesthood, along with the coat of arms. So insulted were the Pintos that the rabbinate did not recognize their claim to priestly status that they habitually left the synagogue when the priestly blessing was being recited by recognized *kohanim*.[62]

The adoption of Jewish tokens of nobility did not, however, displace the drive to obtain social recognition where it really counted—that is, in Christian-European society. There were those who sought, acquired, and flaunted European titles of nobility even after they "returned" to Judaism. These titles were sometimes Iberian, odd as that may seem: outcast conversos, hounded from their native land where they failed to find acceptance, holding and valuing titles of nobility from Portugal or Spain. But the psyche is ingenious. Human beings do not easily relinquish marks of status, whatever their source.

The usual way to acquire these titles was to lend large sums to needy rulers.[63] In 1672, the great Amsterdam merchant-banker Antonio Lopes Suasso (who incidentally had married into the Pinto family) lent generously to the Spanish crown during the French invasion of the northern and southern Netherlands. For this, Carlos II of Spain granted him the title of Baron d'Avernas-le-Gras, a small barony in the Spanish Netherlands.[64] Antonio's son Francisco, the second Baron d'Avernas-le-Gras, who was rumored to have lent William III of Orange the astronomical sum of two million guilders, was as comfortable in the court life of The Hague as he was in his role as banker. When he posed for an oil portrait, he did so in a flowing wig, an embroidered coat set off by an abundance of red ruffles, a sheathed sword at his knee, an orange in his hand—indistinguishable from any late eighteenth-century courtier of Christian stock.[65] The European-aristocratic aspect of self-image remained thoroughly unjudaized. Yet the Suassos, like the Pintos, Belmontes, Curiels, Texeiras, and others, did not question the appropriateness of such an image in the context of Jewish life, with its synagogue rituals, circumcision ceremonies, and Passover *seders*. On the contrary.

There were those, however, who felt some tension between the social norms of Iberian society and those of rabbinically ordained Jewish life. This is evident in a discussion of nobility in the preface to a sermon delivered at the inauguration of the new Portuguese-Jewish synagogue in Amsterdam in 1675. The author, David de Castro Tartas, in dedicating his sermon to Isaac Gabay Henriques, wrote:[66]

> There is an ancient debate about [the value of] inherited nobility versus [the value of] virtue obtained by one's own merits, attributed to one's character [*natureza*]. . . . But without deciding [between the two], well-ordered reason would conclude that a person in whom the two coincide—both nobility inherited from one's ancestors and the personal virtue appropriate to such illustrious birth—is truly perfect.

Iberian Memory and Its Perpetuation

Dedication of the new Portuguese synagogue, 1675. Etching by Romeyn de Hooghe. The inscription at upper center reads, *Libertas conscientia incrementum republicae* (Freedom of worship is the mainspring of the Republic). Inscription upper left shows plan, upper right shows exterior view. *Courtesy of the Library of the Jewish Theological Seminary of America.*

The author of the sermon attributed such "perfect" nobility to the ex-converso Gabay Henriques, to whom he dedicated the sermon. As far as inherited nobility was concerned, he maintained that his addressee's deportment and training were "those of the nobility alone" in Portugal. As for virtue, Gabay Henriques had demonstrated this by his "judaizing" in the Peninsula:

> But what is more worthy of consideration and esteem is that worldly honors did not interfere with his recognition and observance of the Divine Law, insofar as this was possible in that captivity; [and he did so] fearless of the cruel dangers perpetrated by our adversaries' malice.

And he had proved his nobility yet further, "since he has abandoned the ambitious vanity of the gentiles to pursue perfectly, in the congregation of Israelites, the true honor and nobility of the Divine Law."

This bombastic discourse on honor does, as its author states, focus on issues debated elsewhere—especially in Spain—about the relationship between nobility and virtue. The author's sense that there *should* be a correlation was a common one. What distinguished his position was the identification of the virtue appropriate to nobility *with the practice of Judaism*. Given the criteria for granting titles to conversos (and others) in early modern Spain—primarily financial services to extravagant courts—David de Castro's position is less than convincing; but it does reflect a need to justify in Jewish terms the alien trappings of nobility that the elite of Portuguese-Jewish society, with few exceptions, valued highly.

Easier to grasp from a twentieth-century point of view is the enduring attachment the emigres felt to the culture in which they had been raised and whose greatness they recognized. This was above all true in the linguistic sphere. Since Portuguese was the native tongue of the overwhelming majority of the emigres, it became the language in which communal records were kept, sermons delivered, gossip exchanged. But even among native Portuguese speakers, Spanish was the language of literary expression. Works aimed at transmitting rabbinic tradition to the emigres were frequently published in Spanish translation, although Portuguese translations also appeared.[67] (This will be more fully elaborated in chapter five.) Even the later descendants of emigres whose most comfortable language was Dutch were taught Portuguese in school. As late as 1816, the "Portuguese" teacher Moses Cohen Belinfante published in Amsterdam two teaching guides to Portuguese, a *Portugeesch leesboekje* and a *Gronden der Portugeesch spelkunst, ten gebruike der Armenschool van de Nederlandsche Portugeesche Israëliten te Amsterdam*. In his introduction to the latter, the author acknowledged that Portuguese was still commonly spoken by members of the community, but that isolated from its roots in the Peninsula it had become a "bastardized language [*bastaardtaal*]."[68]

It is not enough to say that the emigres spoke in Portuguese and Spanish. These languages, and the literature produced in them, spoke to them. The affection the "Portuguese" harbored for Iberian culture is reflected, among other things, by the establishment in Amsterdam of two literary academies in imitation of the Spanish *tertulias literarias*[69]—the *Academia de los Sitibundos* (Academy of the Thirsty), founded in 1676, and the *Academia de los Floridos* (Academy of the Select) founded in 1685.[70] De Barrios devoted several pages of hyperbole to the latter,[71] but in fact they were short-lived affairs. There is no mention of the first after its second year, and none of the second after the year of its establishment.

This raises the question whether the impulse to continue Iberian socio-intellectual patterns was always sustainable. Perhaps it proved difficult to maintain in exile an institution that was deteriorating even in the Peninsula. Or perhaps too few of the members were able to breathe life into these societies. The academy about which we are best informed, the *Academia de los Floridos,* had thirty-nine members, but was largely a platform for De Barrios and the wealthy, highly cultivated merchant José Penso de la Vega.[72] This state of affairs may have become wearisome for all involved.

One scholar has speculated that the academies expressed an impulse to break with the organized community.[73] However, there is no evidence that communal leaders acted to curb their activity; indeed, some were members. It is true that no communal rabbi participated in the gatherings.[74] But this is not surprising, given their frivolous side. Although at the meetings of the *Academia de los Floridos* serious theological issues were occasionally discussed, more frequently such issues were debated as which of the different senses was noblest, or which was the worse vice, being a spendthrift or a miser. At one meeting a beaver hat was awarded to the member who best explained a complex *enigma* in prose and verse.[75] It is impossible to imagine any of Amsterdam's *hakhamim* sitting comfortably at such proceedings. More significantly, the fact that material resulting from the academies' meetings was published in Amsterdam—that it passed the scrutiny of communal censors—indicates that the leadership found it essentially harmless.

A more lasting expression of Iberian tastes was the interest in Spanish theater among Amsterdam's "Portuguese." It seemed perfectly natural to Isaac de Pinto when he married his cousin Rachel de Pinto Henriques in July, 1648, a short time after his arrival in the Netherlands, to entertain the wedding guests with one of the most popular plays of the seventeenth-century Spanish stage. "My wedding," he wrote, "was celebrated with great festivity and attended by many guests who came from Amsterdam, as well as many from the city, all of whom had a marvelous time at the various parties. On the second day a play was put on, *La Vida es sueño,* well performed."[76] This *comedia* by Calderón de la Barca may have seemed appropriate because it ends with the celebration of two marriages. It is also conspicuously lacking in Christian themes and material.[77] But the play was chosen in large part because its presentation of the issues and idiom of early modern Madrid resonated with the audience.

The importance of the Spanish stage to the emigres reveals itself eloquently in their dogged efforts to keep it alive in Amsterdam, despite the obstacles facing them. In 1667, Aron de la Faya, Benjamin Henriques, Jacob Navarro, Abraham Israel, Daniel Levi de Barrios, and Samuel Rosa performed a play before an audience of more than thirty persons in a warehouse rented from Samuel Pereira.[78] In 1696, Francisco Rodrigues Henriques rented a warehouse for theatrical performances.[79] In 1708, "devotees of Spanish comedies" among the "Portuguese" applied for official permission to stage performances at least once a week—on Wednesdays, when the municipal theater was closed—adding that the society had been doing so for the past nine years.[80] One would like to have a glimpse of these amateurish performances and the responses of the audiences. The *hakhamim* of the community, immersed in rabbinic traditions as they were, could not have been delighted with such diversions. It is a reflection of their realism and humanity that they did not prohibit the staging of Spanish dramas by their congregants. But it is significant that in 1632 the communal umbrella organization, the *Imposta* board, prohibited the use of the synagogue for theatrical performances or other amusements.[81] This became the basis for a similar prohibition in the 1639 statutes of the united community: "There shall be neither feasts nor enigmas in the synagogue, neither on Simhat Torah nor at any other time."[82] Frivolous leisure habits of Iberian origin that had become deeply ingrained in the "Portuguese" were to be tolerated, but not within Jewish sacred space.

The depth of interest in Spanish forms of expression is most vividly demonstrated by the impulse to create new literary works in an Iberian vein. De Barrios was the most prolific author of such literature.[83] But he was certainly not alone. In the seventeenth century, it was not at all unusual for "Portuguese" merchants to try their hand at poetry or prose—in Spanish, of course. Among Amsterdam's merchants the outstanding "secular" author was José Penso de la Vega. In fact, writing appears to have been his first passion. "I have robbed some hours from sleep," he wrote, "and usurped some time from commerce in order to publish eight books [of mine] which have piled up."[84] To be sure, much of what was produced was very bad, and much has been lost. One may wonder, too, whether poetry writing was not yet another manifestation of the protean pretensions of the "Portuguese" elite. Yet the sheer volume of the surviving literature attests to a genuine love of play with language—the Spanish language.

The interest in Iberian literature, though mainly diversionary, was not entirely divorced from the enterprise of rejudaization. The "Portuguese" not only amused themselves with the language they knew best, they also used it to produce an impressive literature dealing with Jewish issues, a literature which will be explored in the next chapter. The literary value of this corpus derives in large part from its reliance on Spanish traditions. Without the emigres' active interest in Calderón, Góngora, Quevedo—and even the Jesuit theologian António Vieira—they could not have created such a literature.

This is wonderfully illustrated by a discovery made by the late poet and scholar Dan Pagis.[85] In a manuscript from seventeenth- or early eighteenth-century Holland, he found, among other scribblings, the Hebrew line *"afar ashan avak va-zel va-ain,"* and in the margin two Spanish words, *"en nada."* The Spanish words served as a clue to the origin of the Hebrew line, which proved to be a verbatim translation of the last line of a sonnet by Góngora: *"en tierra, en humo, en polvo, en sombra, en nada"* (to earth, to smoke, to dust, to shadow, to nothing). There is no way to know the intention of the person who jotted down these fragments. His words seem to convey his wish to possess in Hebrew a thought he had been struck by in its original Spanish. It is, in any case, a poignant example of a mind that did not hesitate to test one cherished language against another.

There is, overall, a peculiar, polarized quality to the set of attitudes the "Portuguese" held about Iberian society. The great majority of them were able, it seems, to divorce the experience of converso persecution from the world of Iberian values and culture, demonizing the former and holding fast to the latter.

From the perspective of collective history as cultivated by the communal elite, Spain and Portugal were *terras de idolatria.* The memory (and continuing reality) of converso life in the Peninsula was distilled into an image of converso heroism and inquisitorial evil, of a struggle between helpless but steadfast conversos and "the Inquisition," frequently depicted in brutally bestial terms. In terms of pure power relations, the image conveyed an inescapable reality. But it eliminated some of the most powerful aspects of converso experience—the doubts, guilt, and ambivalence felt by so many. Perhaps the communal elite hoped that purging the recollected past of these feelings would help purge them from the present.

In contrast, where Iberian culture and values were concerned, the "Portuguese" in Amsterdam were intent on perpetuating their close affiliation to the Peninsula. They manifested a striking fixation on Iberian aristocratic social values, which found expression (sometimes in "judaized" form and sometimes not) in various contexts—including the synagogue and cemetery. The Iberian legacy was even drawn upon to provide a semisacred language. While Portuguese remained the language of everyday life, Castilian early on became the language of biblical, liturgical, and rabbinic translations, and to a large extent of theological discourse. The elevation of Castilian to such a role has its paradoxical side. But, given the continuing respect the "Portuguese" felt for Spanish intellectual and literary achievement, it was a natural step in the process of "rejudaization." It is to that process, promoted by "converso" memories but not, apparently, impeded by the retention of an Iberian cultural style, that we will now turn.

5

⊰◈⊱

The Rejudaization of "the Nation"

Reeducation

Members of virtually all immigrant groups seek to preserve and share among themselves deeply ingrained linguistic and cultural patterns from the "old country." What differentiates the "Portuguese" in Amsterdam was the need to integrate the Iberian experience into their new lives while at the same time taking on quite a different project: that of rejudaization.

Reclaiming rabbinic Judaism was a collective enterprise, but it required individual effort. Some emigres were more willing and eager than others to invest that effort. But all emigres from the Peninsula needed instruction in the basics of Jewish observance if they were to participate in the life of the community. For adults, this could be exhilarating but difficult. There was a language barrier to overcome—and psychocultural ones as well.

Isaac de Pinto's memoirs offer vivid insight into the process. When Pinto and members of his family arrived in Rotterdam from Antwerp, they immediately set about, as Pinto recalled, "instructing ourselves about Judaism and learning to read Hebrew." A month or so later, when his father and uncle arrived safely from Antwerp, the males of the family sent to Amsterdam for a *mohel,* or circumciser, and underwent circumcision. At the ceremony three of Pinto's brothers and his uncle, who had not hitherto done so, adopted Hebrew names. A fortnight later, Pinto and his father, both of them first-born sons, underwent the festive ritual of "redemption of the first-born" (*pidyon ha-ben*), usually performed a month after birth.[1] (This is an interesting detail, given the family's claim to priestly status, since *kohanim* do not redeem their first-born.) These ceremonies, so closely linked to birth, were individual manifestations of the rebirth of the community, and were experienced in that way.

Judging from his memoirs, the early days of Pinto's life in the Netherlands were thrilling and liberating. "We were willing to believe anything," he wrote of being persuaded to settle in Rotterdam rather than Amsterdam, "so happy we were to have become Jews in the service of God."[2] Like many emigres, he seems to have been prepared by the family's converso legacy and the religio-ethnic defiance sparked by inquisitorial persecution to accept the discipline of rabbinic life. Having the means to reattach themselves to Jewish life in grand style, the Pintos rented a house to be used as a synagogue and sent to Amsterdam for a *hakham*. (They were able to hire Yoshiahu Pardo, a grandson of Joseph Pardo.)[3] It is not entirely clear why the family first settled in Rotterdam and only later in Amsterdam, but it is abundantly clear that they at once established themselves as practicing Jews. Though settled for the time being in Rotterdam, Pinto was aware of the excitement surrounding the growth of the community in Amsterdam, and the rapid development of its administrative, welfare, and educational institutions. All of this must have seemed a vindication of his family's decision to leave the Iberian realm.

Entering the rabbinic realm, however, was not without its problems. Neither Pinto nor his father ever achieved facility in studying rabbinic texts. But they were able to compensate for this by supporting talmudic scholars, as wealthy Jews had traditionally done. Pinto's father took his role of patronage quite seriously. Until his death in 1668 he lived "removed and secluded from worldly matters, betaking himself every day to the *Midrash* [house of study] which he had instituted there for twelve scholars to study throughout the morning and afternoon."[4] This is poignant testimony to the often uninformed yet impassioned attachment of emigres to a tradition the access to which they felt they had been denied.

Most emigres could not build private synagogues or support a dozen talmudic scholars. But otherwise the initiation into Jewish life Pinto describes must have been similar to that of others. The act of circumcision was a particularly crucial rite of passage—not merely an act of compliance with Jewish law, but a ritual replete with powerful symbolic meanings. In the converso imagination, circumcision took on a transcendental transitional significance, perhaps akin to that of a Christian sacrament. The ex-converso apologete Isaac Cardoso spoke of it as a "mysterious sacrifice," an act that compensated for the original sin of Adam, and one without which a Jew could not be saved.[5] (Unfortunately, women left no record of what they thought of such an idea.)[6] Notions like this existed in the Peninsula and outside it as an integral part of converso folklore. A rejudaized converso who later returned to Spain related to the Madrid Inquisition in 1635 that after coming to Bordeaux, before departing for Amsterdam, several conversos in Bordeaux "tried to persuade him that he be circumcised before departing, because if he should die at sea without doing so he would not qualify for salvation, and it would be better if he would bear the mark of the Lord."[7] Perhaps this converso was only concocting a story to try to absolve himself of responsibility for having later been circumcised in Amsterdam.[8] But if so, he was echoing notions that would have been familiar and perhaps persuasive to the inquisitors.

From a rabbinic point of view, the idea of the salvific power of circumcision was both bizarre and misguided. Still, such an idea did serve to impel the male converso being initiated into Jewish life to endure the pain of adult circumcision. Less helpful in the transition, however, was another common converso idea about circumcision—one that apparently *inhibited* emigres' willingness to be circumcised. This was the notion that without circumcision a Jew was not obligated to observe the Law. To the rabbinic leadership, it was important to dispel this misconception, and the Venetian Sephardi rabbi Samuel Aboab condemned it roundly. The emigres must be disabused, he wrote, of

> the vain idea which has spread among almost all the sons of our people who come from the servitude of the soul [i.e., the Peninsula] . . . , that so long as a man is not circumcised *he is not part of Israel* [my emphasis] [and] his sins are not sins. . . . And some claim that the day of their circumcision is the first day on which their sins begin to count.

All of this, Aboab stressed, was contrary to Jewish law, which holds that "circumcision is [merely] a commandment like all the rest of the Torah" and anyone of the "seed of Israel" is bound by all the precepts, whether circumcised or not.[9] This was an eloquent insistence on rabbinic standards by someone deeply sympathetic to converso needs.

The belief in the religio-ethnic defining power of circumcision, like many "converso" beliefs, was not an arbitrary aberration. It had served an important function in the Peninsula, assuaging the conscience of conversos who were unable to observe Jewish law, allowing them to believe they were not strictly bound to observe it. It made the "Egyptian condition" more bearable. Among the emigres, one of the effects of placing so high a value on circumcision was that the circumcision ceremony evolved into a much-needed rite of passage.

The centrality of circumcision in the ritual of "return" is vividly reflected in the inquisitorial case of Cristóbal Méndez, a converso who settled in Venice in 1643, but was arrested in Madrid in 1661 while on a business or personal mission. Under interrogation he revealed the story, step by step, of how he had been inducted as a "returning" Jew into the Ponentine (largely "Portuguese") community of Venice. His uncle and an ex-converso rabbi urged him to undergo circumcision, which despite his hesitations he agreed to do. For a month before the circumcision ceremony, the rabbi gave him some rudimentary instruction, using a Bible in Spanish translation. Immediately after the circumcision, he was given a prayer shawl and phylacteries. Presumably it was at this time that Méndez adopted the name Abraham Franco de Silveira. When he had recovered from the surgery, he made his debut at the Sephardi synagogue, where he put on the prayer shawl and phylacteries and was called to the ark to recite the blessing of deliverance, which he repeated word for word in Hebrew after the cantor.

The Rejudaization of "the Nation"

This cluster of ceremonies became a life-cycle event for the male ex-converso. Even if Méndez was already a Jew, as Aboab argued, these ceremonies served to mark his "return."[10]

In the period after his or her induction into Jewish life, emigres began to learn not only how the Law of Moses was understood by rabbinic authorities in the seventeenth century, but also the rhetoric of the community, the nature of its institutions, and its expectations of him or her. The doting attention of the "old-timers" no doubt eased the transition. But the emigres also faced the difficulties of overcoming their considerable ignorance of traditional Jewish life. Converso cryptojudaizing undoubtedly provided a certain preparation for a rabbinically regulated life, exposing conversos to concepts and focal rituals which would strike them as familiar with their entry into Jewish communities. But by the seventeenth century, the gap between normative Jewish observance and converso judaizing was enormous. By this time "judaizing" had largely been reduced to the relatively safe undertaking of holding a set of attitudes and ideas. It will be helpful to examine some of these, to grasp something of the crypto-Jewish culture the emigres brought with them.

Crypto-Jewish ideas often took the form of attacks on Catholicism rather than direct affirmations of Jewish belief. Indeed, such is the prominence of anti-Catholic motifs in converso belief that Stephen Gilman was led to characterize cryptojudaizing as "a kind of worship in reverse."[11] But in doing so Gilman overlooked the fundamentally Jewish character of "converso" refutations of Catholicism. When conversos scorned images of the saints and the Holy Family—for example, when the Portuguese conversa Isabel Lopes stated in 1583 that "the painted saints were nothing more than pictures that somebody had painted"[12]—they were affirming Jewish belief by attacking an aspect of Catholic worship that Jews regarded as idolatrous.

Denials of Catholic belief were expressed in a variety of colorful ways, often in statements that were pithy and barbed, primed to stick in the memory and, given their rhetorical power, easily disseminated among conversos. Such were the countless witticisms conversos produced about the virgin conception and birth. Characteristic were the remarks of João Lopes, "You can't make cheese without curds [i.e., male seed]"[13] and Garcia Mendes d'Abreu, "How can you draw a yolk out of an egg without breaking the shell?"[14] Another converso conveyed the message by referring to Mary as "our stork."[15] Important also in the converso repertoire were denials of the divinity of Jesus. The taboo-like nature of ascribing divinity to a man of flesh and blood reportedly caused the converso family of Isabel Núñez to avoid saying the name *Jesucristo*, referring to him rather as "Christóbal Sánchez."[16] Less cautiously, Simão Vaz of Lisbon reportedly stated that God "had no need of putting himself into the womb of a woman and that the messiah was not God."[17] However these ideas were put, they tended to deflate Catholicism from a generally Jewish point of view and implied a counterview.

Not surprisingly, judaizers also produced formulas to nullify the Catholic rituals they were required to perform. We have already seen this with Isaac de Pinto, who in childhood was taught to say the *Shema* when he entered a church. Similarly, the Portuguese New Christian Gonçalo Vaz was reported in 1543 to have said (under his breath) at the moment the host was elevated by the priest, "Old bread and wine—I believe in the Law of Moses."[18] Yet more trenchant was the formula taught to Marina de Avila by her half-sister in the late sixteenth century. When the priest raised the host, she would say, "I see a piece of bread; I worship you, Lord, instead [*Una torta de pan veo, en ti Señor adoro y creo*]."[19]

But crypto-Jews like these were also likely to hold a few central affirmative Jewish convictions. As we have noted, an important historian of the conversos cited three crypto-Jewish notions that seem ubiquitous in judaizing circles: a) the rejection of Catholicism as a form of idolatry, b) the conviction of belonging to the Jewish people which worships the only true God and which will be redeemed by the Messiah, and c) the belief—a Jewish counterclaim to a central Catholic doctrine—that personal salvation is achieved only through the Law of Moses.[20]

Of these, only the last was truly problematic. Belief in the salvific power of the Law of Moses was indeed widespread among crypto-Jews. In the testimony of conversos accused of judaizing, the "Law of Moses" was invoked in an almost abstract way, like the Zion imagined by the medieval Jew—a notion to cling to rather than an intrinsic aspect of everyday life. A natural result of this situation was the emergence of the idea among judaizers, quite alien to rabbinic Judaism, that the actual observance of precepts was not necessary—that it was sufficient to "believe in one's heart." This conviction appeared surprisingly early. It was suggested as early as 1503 by a rabbinic scholar—one who, forcibly converted in Portugal, had escaped to Salonica. God would view the forced converts in Portugal, he said, "by their thoughts, not by their deeds." (It is noteworthy that at a later time this same scholar would thoroughly condemn such a view.)[21] In subsequent generations, the belief in the sufficiency of inner allegiance to the Law of Moses became a persistent theme in crypto-Jewish thinking. One converso related that when his father initiated him into crypto-Judaism, he told him "that one must perform many ceremonies and rituals, but that one could not perform them in this realm because of the danger of being discovered." But he assured the boy that "for now it was enough to fix his heart on one single God and be aided in this by the Great Fast which falls on the tenth day of the new moon of September [i.e., Yom Kippur]."[22] Similarly António Homem, a passionate judaizer and professor of canon law at the University of Coimbra, who was burned at the stake in

1624, was said to have preached in a Yom Kippur sermon in 1615 that "while living in persecution it was sufficient to have in mind the intention of performing the precepts of the Law."[23] The idea became so entrenched that it took on a life of its own. The conversa Catarina Fernandes reported that "because she was blind and could not control the use of her hands," she "only lit the sabbath candles in her heart."[24] Such ideas reflected a reverence—not without its own power—for a way of life that had become alien. But believing in the Law of Moses was not, obviously, the same as observing it.

Moreover, conversos often expressed their allegiance to the Law of Moses within a conceptual theological framework that was Catholic. Their religious thinking was permeated with an anxiety about personal salvation which they had absorbed from their environment—a goal which virtually eclipsed the sense of everyday purposefulness inculcated by rabbinic Judaism through the notion of covenantal obligation. Numerous judaizers stated that they were driven to choose Judaism over Christianity because they were convinced that the Law of Moses was the only law through which one could be saved. The concern for salvation was internalized so thoroughly that, astonishingly, a conversa of Trancoso told the Coimbra Inquisition in 1574 that it was "for the salvation of her soul" that she baked unleavened bread for Passover![25] There is here an echo of a more general phenomenon in the history (not mystique) of resistance: a determined rejection of a repressive social order accompanied by an unwitting embrace of some of its deepest impulses.

And even its liturgy. Crypto-Jews naturally longed for time-honored vehicles of religious expression such as those they observed in church. Given the absence of Jewish devotional material, it is not surprising that some conversos improvised, using readily available Catholic texts and developing syncretistic "Jewish" liturgical practices. A converso tried in Évora in 1637 was said to have taught local conversas "to recite two Pater Nosters and two Ave Marias *and offer them to Moses*" (my italics).[26] Another converso told the same Inquisition in 1591 that he said the Pater Noster because he did not know any Jewish prayers.[27] To be sure, such testimony cannot always be relied upon. But judging from the Christian sources cited in works written outside the Peninsula by ex-conversos *to support their own positions*, including the works of contemporary Spanish theologians, it appears that crypto-Jews drew heavily from the only body of spiritual and theological literature at their disposal to give content to their "Jewish" spirituality.[28]

But expressions of Jewish allegiance varied enormously among judaizers. It may be recalled that the prayer composed by Jacob Israel Belmonte, while devoid of specifically Jewish content, was influenced by Catholic formulations. At the other extreme were converso prayers that are extraordinarily rich in material drawn from the rabbinic liturgy. The most easily obtained material was that found in the Bible: psalms in particular and, in at least one case, the story of the sacrifice of Isaac from Genesis.[29] But, remarkably, rabbinic formulations were sometimes preserved and transmitted as late as the second half of the sixteenth century. In 1583 a conversa who appeared before the Coimbra tribunal recited most of the first benediction said before the *Shema* in the evening prayers, in an almost verbatim Portuguese translation.[30] And in 1584 another conversa recited a version of the morning benedictions (*birkhot ha-shahar*).[31] To see these texts in sixteenth-century inquisitorial documents is truly astonishing, and clear testimony to the careful preservation and transmission of rabbinic liturgical formulations in some converso circles.

Thus, while "converso" Judaism was always impoverished relative to Judaism practiced outside the Peninsula, the degree of its remoteness from rabbinic Judaism varied greatly. For those who sought it out, information about postbiblical Judaism was available. Ironically, Iberian society sometimes freely offered conversos information of which they might otherwise have been ignorant. The "Edicts of Faith," for example—proclamations calling for judaizers to come forth and confess their crimes, and for the faithful to denounce judaizers—provided detailed lists of Jewish rituals in order to inform potential denouncers what to look for. Ironically, such lists also furnished valuable information to judaizers to whom the Inquisition had systematically denied access to such knowledge. Autos-da-fé were also a source of information. In Coimbra in 1574 Belchior Fernandes was accused of having said that "if he knew about them [the Laws of Moses], it was from having heard them read in the copies of the sentences that the students from the village of Sea wrote down from the autos-da-fé and read to them."[32]

The more educated the judaizer, the greater access he and members of his family had to knowledge of rabbinic practices. Those who knew Latin were especially equipped to acquire postbiblical Jewish knowledge, piecing together a conception of rabbinic Judaism, however shadowy, from references to rabbinic ideas and practices in writings of the Church Fathers as well as contemporary anti-Jewish sermons and polemical writings. Y. H. Yerushalmi has shown how the converso physician Isaac Cardoso, and presumably others as well, were able to accomplish this.[33] Such figures, needless to say, did not keep their findings to themselves. We have already noted in chapter two how the learned physician Eliahu Montalto became a mentor to members of his immediate and extended family, virtually head of a network of judaizers. We also know that the university-educated physician Juan de Prado, who was disciplined for disseminating heterodox ideas in Amsterdam, had earlier proselytized in the Peninsula among members of his family and others, urging them to adhere to Judaism.[34] At least some judaizers, then, were able to catch a glimpse of the great edifice of postbiblical rabbinic reasoning which the Inquisition sought so systematically to suppress.

Still, what emerged from even the most sophisticated of such efforts was a seriously skewed picture. As new information was acquired, it was inevitably assimilated into a theological framework that was heavily influenced by Catholicism. That is, rejudaization, in the true sense of the word, required more than absorbing new information. It entailed a transformation of religious experience—an understanding of the experiential characteristics of Jewish worship and practice, a conditioning to the rhythms of the synagogue and the Jewish year, a grasp of how *halakhah* (Jewish law), in all its minutiae, was integrated into everyday activity.

No book teaches such things. In these matters, a crucial role was played by the *hakhamim*, as well as by emigres who had spent time in other Jewish communities and by a few "old" Sephardim—descendants of Spanish exiles—who settled in the Netherlands. Especially in the early years of the community, the *hakhamim* had to muster all their skills of tact, firmness, and human understanding to alter ingrained ideas and patterns of behavior. We have caught a glimpse of this in the anecdote (mentioned in chapter two) about the intervention of the *hakham* Joseph Pardo to abolish the custom of mourning the destruction of the Temple in the synagogue on the three sabbaths preceding the Ninth of Ab (a major fast day).[35]

Unfortunately, few anecdotes such as this survive. The considerable literature of rejudaization available to the emigres provides the best material for understanding the approach adopted to aid the neophyte emigres' entry into the world of rabbinics. As Yerushalmi put it, "The returning Marrano was essentially an autodidact and, like all autodidacts, he needed books to read."[36] In response to the demand, there was a burst of activity in the printing of Jewish books in Portuguese and Spanish: apologetic and ethical works, guides to Jewish practice, and translations of classic Jewish texts. By the mid-seventeenth century, a sizable library of such works had been produced. While in the early years of the seventeenth century Venice turned out most of these books, Amsterdam soon took the leading role.[37]

The works most needed in translation were the Hebrew Bible and the prayer book. As we have noted, Spanish—a language with which native-born Portuguese were acquainted—rather than Portuguese was the language used for all editions of these texts. Spanish was also the language of instruction in the schools. Perhaps because the literary status of Spanish was superior to that of Portuguese, it was felt that Spanish would better convey the sanctity of Scripture and the liturgy, or perhaps Spanish was used because it was the language that united the Sephardi diaspora as a whole.[38] Since the prayer service and Torah reading in the synagogue were in Hebrew—a language the adult newcomers could not easily acquire—some important prayers were transliterated, that is, printed in Hebrew in Latin characters. Italian printers and booksellers did a brisk business

מחזור

ORDEN
DE ROSHASANAH Y KIPVR, TRASLADADO
en Eſpañol, y de nueuo cmẽda-
do: Yañadido elSelihoth,el qual
ſe dize quarẽta dias ãtes del dia
de Kipur en las madrugadas.
Talmud Torah bet Yaahkob.

Eſtampado por induſtria y deſpeſa de
Dauid Abenatar mello .A. primero
de ſiuan, de 5377. En Amſtradama.

Title page of a prayer book for the High Holidays in Spanish published by David
Abenatar Melo (Amsterdam, 1617). *Courtesy of the Library of the Jewish Theological
Seminary of America.*

supplying the Amsterdam community with Spanish prayer books and Bibles until local presses began producing their own editions.

It was not long before Amsterdam became a center for the printing of such works. As early as 1612, the merchant and devoted communal leader Isaac Franco financed the publication of a three-volume festival prayer book in Spanish translation.[39] Numerous editions of liturgical works in translation (or in Hebrew with accompanying translation) followed.[40] Among them are a prayer book for the High Holidays (1617) and a Passover Haggadah (1622), both in Spanish translation, printed by the merchant David Abenatar Melo, whose religious conversion experience we have discussed. (The books were printed at a press he himself set up in Amsterdam in 1616.)[41] Amsterdam presses also produced many editions of the Hebrew Bible in Spanish translation (all based on the famous Ferrara Bible of 1553), the first appearing in 1611.[42]

Essential as these texts were for a grasp of Judaism, they became the foundation of a living tradition only when the themes that spoke most immediately to the "Portuguese" public were drawn from them and elucidated. The Bible was interpreted to the "Portuguese" in sermons and through an extensive polemical and apologetic literature produced largely in Venice and Amsterdam by figures like Saul Levi Mortera, Menasseh ben Israel, Immanuel Aboab, Isaac Aboab da Fonseca, Isaac Orobio de Castro, Isaac Cardoso, and others. These polemicists and exegetes drew from centuries of Jewish interpretation but, consonant with their own needs and those of their readers, they tended to read the biblical text from an uncommonly anti-Christian point of view. While such polemical interpretations were no doubt intended to win over the unconvinced, they also served to enhance "Portuguese" solidarity by giving expression to shared hostility to Catholicism.[43]

"Portuguese" presses also turned out numerous translations of the classics of medieval Jewish thought. The texts chosen were invariably of *Spanish*-Jewish origin. In part, this reflected the special interest of the "Portuguese" in a Sephardi legacy they wished to reclaim. But this was not the only reason for a partiality to Sephardi works. The great philosophical and ethical works of eleventh- and twelfth-century Spanish Jewry were interpretations of rabbinic tradition by Jews living in a highly sophisticated Greco-Arabic culture. For the "Portuguese," with their experience of what might be called a Greco-Christian culture, these texts resonated in a way that Ashkenazi works, with their more alien rabbinic style, did not. Moses Maimonides, however remote in time, was much closer to them than Moses Isserles.

Many of the translations of these works were produced and published in Amsterdam. Among them were the eleventh-century ethical treatise *Duties of the Heart (Hovot ha-levavot)*, published in Spanish translation in 1610 and in Portuguese in 1670;[44] Judah Halevi's *Kuzari* (1663);[45] Maimonides' "Laws of Repentence" from his *Mishneh Torah* (1613); and the latter's enumeration of the 613 precepts, *Sefer ha-mizvot* (1652).[46] With these and other works available in translation, emigres with little knowledge of Hebrew could discover a Jewish legacy no less sophisticated than the Catholic culture they had known in the Peninsula.

At a more mundane level, the emigres needed help learning the details of Jewish practice. This was important for the overall character the community was to assume, but it was also important for assuring the status of the community in the wider Jewish world. The proud merchants who dominated *K.K. Talmud Torah* were not likely to accept a less than honorable place in that world. With the cooperation of the rank and file of the community, they were able to achieve it. Even so, bringing norms of practice in Amsterdam into relative harmony with practice in older Jewish communities like Salonica or Venice—not to mention Prague or Cracow—was a huge task.

Much of what occurred in effecting this transformation is hidden from the view of the historian. Judging from behavior in similar circumstances—the initiation of newcomers into Jewish circles in Moscow in the 1970s, for example, or the "rabbinization" of Ethiopian Jews in Israel in recent years—nothing would have been more important in encouraging the successful adaptation of the new emigres than the welcoming embrace of those already conditioned to observing some of the finer points of Jewish law in the home, synagogue, and workplace.

The only concrete remains of this effort are the many manuals of Jewish practice published in Spanish and Portuguese, many in Amsterdam. At the time they were published, the accepted basis for practice throughout most of the Jewish diaspora was Joseph Karo's code, the *Shulhan arukh,* which first appeared in 1564. Even in translation, this work was too demanding (and overwhelming) for the "Portuguese" emigres. An abridgment in Ladino (Judeo-Spanish written in Hebrew characters, prevalent among Balkan Sephardim) appeared in 1568, shortly after publication of the original work. But there was some reluctance to produce a translation into Spanish or any other language in Latin characters since this would make the work readily accessible to gentiles. An abridged version of the *Shulhan arukh* appeared in Spanish only in 1609, with the publication in Venice of Moses Altaras's *Libro de Mantenimiento de la Alma.*[47] Other works with a similar purpose appeared subsequently, most notably Isaac Athias's *Tesoro de Preceptos* (Venice 1627, Amsterdam 1649) and Menasseh ben Israel's *Thesouro dos Dinim* (Amsterdam 1645–47), written in Portuguese "for the use of our Portuguese nation."[48]

Somewhat different from these manuals, because it presented Jewish law within a larger and more theoretical framework, was the work of the

Amsterdam physician and merchant Abraham Farar, *Declaração das seis-centas e treze Encomendanças da nossa Sancta Ley* (Amsterdam 1627), a description of the traditionally accepted 613 Jewish precepts, including those no longer of practical significance, presented in the order prescribed by Maimonides in his *Sefer ha-mizvot*, a work which, as mentioned, was published in translation by an Amsterdam press in 1652. Those who wanted more direct contact with talmudic texts could consult a Spanish translation of the *Mishnah*, with the classic commentaries of Maimonides and Ovadiah Bertinoro (Venice 1606, Amsterdam 1663).

These works reflect an interest in thorough, not minimal, practice, and—in the case of Farar's book and the translation of the *Mishnah*—even in the complex halakhic structure underlying practice. This does not mean that they offer an accurate reflection of the interests of the emigres. As in all societies, there was a wide spectrum of interest and commitment. But these works would not have appeared if there were no demand for them, nor would they occupy so much space in present-day collections of Sephardica if they had not been bought.

For those emigres and their descendants who took to heart the obligation of the adult male Jew to study Torah at appointed times (and who had achieved sufficient facility with rabbinic texts to do so), it was natural to seek out companions for study, and eventually this led to the organization of societies for the study of Torah. This in itself was hardly novel in a Jewish community. What may have distinguished these associations (aside from the language in which discussions took place) is hidden from our view, since we are largely dependent on De Barrios for information about them, and cannot glean much about their character from his discussion.[49] It is worth noting, however, that according to De Barrios the members of one such society, Torah Or, founded in 1656 and initially headed by Isaac Aboab da Fonseca, met six days a week for half an hour to study "the book by Maimonides" (presumably the *Mishneh Torah*).[50] The choice of a quintessentially Sephardi rabbinic text for study was altogether in keeping with "Portuguese" inclinations, and educated members of the community would no doubt have appreciated Maimonides' systematic distillation of Jewish law from its unruly rabbinic sources.

More basic in the effort of the Amsterdam "Portuguese" elite to perpetuate its ideals were the steps it took in educating its children (to be more precise, its boys). In this area of communal life as in others, the *Mahamad* did not hesitate to deviate from time-honored patterns in Jewish society. Its organizational and pedagogical innovations were keenly noted by two Ashkenazi visitors to Amsterdam. The first, the rabbinic scholar Shabbetai Sheftel Horowitz, son of the renowned Polish talmudist and kabbalist Isaiah ben Abraham Horowitz, spent time in Amsterdam in the early 1640s,

Title page of Abraham Farar's *Declaração das 613 Encomendanças de Nossa Sancta Ley*, a description of the traditional 613 biblical commandments (1627). Farar or (Pharar), who was aided by Saul Levi Mortera, describes himself as "a Jew of the Portuguese exile." *Courtesy of the Library of the Jewish Theological Seminary of America.*

and described, like a traveler in a strange country, how the school for the "Portuguese" children was divided into grades to meet the needs of children of different ages, each grade studying subjects suited to its age group.[51] This was indeed a striking feature of the community's educational policies. In Ashkenazi communities, as Jacob Katz has put it, education was typified by "the lack of systematization and comprehensiveness in educational goals."[52] Children of different ages would attend a school or *heder* under the tutelage of one teacher or *melamed,* and would study the Pentateuch or *halakhah* in a haphazard manner determined not by pedagogical common sense, but by the weekly order of synagogue Torah readings or the need to learn certain aspects of *halakhah* for practice. In contrast, the Amsterdam community's merger agreement of 1639 lays out a well-ordered course of study for seven grades, each with its own teacher or *rubi* and its own curriculum. A child would advance from the study of the alphabet and addition in first grade, to the study of the Pentateuch from beginning to end ("from 'in the beginning' [Gen. 1:1] to 'in the sight of all Israel' [the last verse of Deuteronomy]," as Sheftel Horowitz put it approvingly), to the study of *halakhah* and finally to the study of Talmud under the *hakham* Saul Levi Mortera in the seventh grade.[53] Having described this curriculum, Sheftel Horowitz penned a little cry of distress: "Why don't we do thus in our land? Would that this custom would spread through the entire Jewish diaspora!"

The second visitor, the rabbinic scholar Shabbetai Bass of Prague, who visited Amsterdam in 1680, echoed Horowitz's admiration for the system of graded education but gave a more thorough overview of its organization.[54] The *Mahamad,* he noted, assumed the role of supervising the education of all children, wealthy and poor alike, appointing teachers and paying their salaries. (In fact, the details of administration were handled by the directors of the *Talmud Torah* society, who were, however, subordinate to the *Mahamad.*)[55] This stood in stark contrast to the norm elsewhere in Jewish society, where communal government took responsibility only for the education of the poor, leaving the wealthy to hire tutors for their children.[56] Given the marginality of the poor, in such a system communal leaders had a limited interest in the quality of education it provided, while the tutors to the wealthy, unsupervised by the community, were totally dependent on the parents who hired them. In contrast, Shabbetai Bass observed, in Amsterdam the teachers had a measure of dignity and independence.[57]

The *Mahamad*'s insistence on supervising education seems to have been a policy pursued consistently at least from 1639. Well before the unification of the congregations, perhaps as early as 1616, a society known as *Ets Haim* was established to provide financial assistance to needy students who might otherwise be forced to drop their studies. With the unification of 1639, this society became an integral part of the communal apparatus, its treasurer being one of the *parnasim* of the *Talmud Torah* society.[58] But the communal leadership also insisted on supervising the education of the affluent. This is vividly illustrated by the steps the *Mahamad* took in 1659 to prevent dissatisfied parents of means, unhappy with a certain teacher hired by the community, from establishing a separate school. After more than twenty students had been withdrawn from the *Talmud Torah* school to study privately with the learned Moses d'Aguilar—leaving the teacher hired by the community with "only those boys who receive stipends (*aspacha*—Heb. *haspakah*) and a few others"—the *Mahamad* decided to act. Jealous of its authority to supervise education, it offered a high salary to Moses d'Aguilar to persuade him (successfully) to replace the teacher who had caused the exodus.[59]

Shabbetai Bass was also impressed by the fact that most of the "Portuguese" schoolchildren in Amsterdam were "expert . . . in the science of grammar, in writing verses and poetry in meter, and in speaking correct Hebrew." Even if the "Portuguese" curriculum did not produce the educational miracles he reported, it was, as he recognized, a pedagogically effective curriculum, and unlike the Ashkenazi institution of the *heder* included in its goals the child's aesthetic development.

In general, innovation was a necessity in the rejudaization of the Amsterdam community. An educational system was required that would be consistent both with rabbinic tradition and with "Portuguese" intellectual tastes. And there was a need to introduce adults to the basics of Judaism, including the Hebrew alphabet, without offending their mature sensibilities. Given the demands of adult life, it is remarkable how many men born and raised in the Peninsula (and perhaps women, though they left little evidence) maintained a steady course in their effort to repossess Judaism. It is just as remarkable that this neophyte community was able, by the 1630s, to produce its own rabbis—personalities of the stature of Menasseh ben Israel and Isaac Aboab da Fonseca. More importantly, collectively speaking, is the fact that for every rabbi and theological thinker produced there were many members of the community who were willing and able to participate actively in its life, whose knowledge of Jewish tradition was adequate, if not brilliant.

The Ambivalent and the Heterodox

In such a community there were also bound to be persons who would not adapt to or comply with the enterprise of rejudaization. Not everyone responded to the rhetoric of "restoration" or accepted the authority invested in the *parnasim*. What happened when persuasion failed to bring cooperation? And given the difficulties of the transition the emigres were expected to make, what could reasonably be expected of them and their children? For the early communal leaders, a crucial task was that of establishing their authority, defining the boundaries of acceptable behavior, and dealing with deviance.

Theoretically, the powers of the *parnasim*, like those of the leaders of every Jewish community (*kehilah* or *kahal*), derived from Jewish law and centuries-old patterns.[60] Jewish law did not prescribe a particular system of governance but did recognize the constituted authorities, however chosen, as representing the entire community and granted them full juridical and disciplinary powers. The Amsterdam merger agreement of 1639 and other evidence suggest that the particular model for the governance of the new community was the "Ponentine" ("Portuguese") community in Venice.[61] Indeed, its name, *K.K. Talmud Torah*, was borrowed from that community. Unfortunately, the degree to which the Amsterdam community borrowed from "Ponentine" patterns of organization cannot be fully established, since the statutes of the Venetian community have not been preserved.

The basic principle behind the community's organization was concentration of authority in the hands of a few. The *Mahamad* dominated every aspect of community life. The matter was put bluntly in the very first article of the 1639 communal statutes (called *haskamot*, a Hebrew term used in Sephardi communities),[62] which stated that "the *Mahamad* shall have authority over everything."[63] The *Mahamad* was a self-perpetuating body in which the outgoing members chose the incoming ones, so that a group of "insiders" shared power among themselves. The oligarchical character of the community's government reflected the trend in Jewish communities everywhere in the early modern period, a result of the emergence of a stratum of extremely wealthy families which paid a large portion of the communal taxes. But the power of the *Mahamad* also represented deeply ingrained patriarchal patterns in "Portuguese" society. Given the highly corporate structure of Dutch society, it is not surprising that Dutch authorities were willing to recognize the wide powers of the *Mahamad*. They did not, though, regard its authority as absolute, and on occasion the magistrates chose to interfere in internal communal matters.[64]

The members of the *Mahamad* (*parnasim*, or *senhores do Mahamad*, as they were known) were entrusted, along with other tasks, with maintaining rabbinic norms. The major instruments they possessed to impose discipline were censorship, denial of synagogue or burial privileges, and ultimately the *herem*, or ban. But using these measures required a certain delicacy. On the one hand, communal officials did not wish to alienate the ambivalent, especially since one of their goals was to bring into the sphere of Jewish communal life all "Jews of the Portuguese exile." On the other hand, they were committed to establishing a community that would be recognized as legitimate within the wider Jewish world, a goal that required adherence to rabbinic norms.

There were various degrees and types of resistance to the program and authority of the *Mahamad*. There were those who lived at the fringes of communal life and declined to pay the communal *finta* tax assessed by communal leaders, as well as the voluntary taxes or *promesas*.[65] Such marginal persons who otherwise possessed social status did not exist in most Jewish communities, where social status required communal participation. Moreover, the marginal "Portuguese" knew they had the option of living, as they long had, in Christian society, and they sometimes chose that option, joining one or another of the Christian sects in the Netherlands.

For all its formal power, then, the *Mahamad* suffered from inherent weakness. This can be seen in a case from 1646 when a member of the community, Samuel Marques, was faced with excommunication for adultery. He was offered the alternative of leaving Amsterdam, but he spurned it, saying outspokenly that he did not recognize the members of the *Mahamad* as his leaders.[66] He was apparently not threatened by banishment from the community since he had never really lived within it. A similar case was recorded in 1622, when the *Mahamad* gave a certain Francisco Lopez Capadosse an ultimatum to have himself and his sons circumcised and join the community by a certain time or be put under *herem* (a ban). Unmoved, Capadosse replied that members of the community could "do whatever they please."[67]

The ultimatum given to Capadosse is worth closer consideration. We have discussed the great importance the ex-converso initiates placed on the act of circumcision and the need rabbis felt to dispel misconceptions about it. Nevertheless, rabbis frequently cooperated in making circumcision a precondition for full acceptance in "Portuguese" communities. *Some* criterion was clearly needed to draw a line between those who attached themselves to the community, however superficially, and those who arrived in a place of freedom yet lingered "outside Judaism." Interesting in this respect is the decision of a rabbinic court in Livorno in the seventeenth century as to whether a Portuguese Jew who had not been circumcised—because, it was explained, he had assets in the Peninsula and might want to return there—might hold a Torah scroll. A rabbinic scholar in Pisa (Jacob Seneor) ruled that it was entirely permissible for him to do so. The Livorno court did not disagree with this ruling in principle, but taking into consideration the particular circumstances of the "Portuguese" decided to make a contrary ruling:[68]

> We rule that although the law is thus [i.e., permits this], the times are such as to make this inappropriate. So you must not give them [the uncircumcised] equal status with fully practising Jews [*yisra'elim gemurim*] by allowing them to touch sacred objects. . . . This would result in ruin, for they would put off entering the Covenant of Abraham if they saw that although uncircumcised they are denied nothing and may touch sacred objects just like fully

practising Jews. Such an unacceptable situation will not develop if an explicit distinction is made.

Rulings that drew barriers between circumcised and uncircumcised became common in the "Portuguese" diaspora. In 1620, the Bet Israel congregation in Amsterdam ruled that persons who had not undergone circumcision by the upcoming sabbath prior to Rosh Hashanah would not be permitted to enter the synagogue, and that newcomers would be given two months to be circumcised.[69] One of the earliest ordinances of the London community barred any uncircumcised male, as well as members of his family, from burial in the communal cemetery.[70] Among the "Portuguese" of Amsterdam this was apparently not the case, since at least two persons buried at Ouderkerk were circumcised after death.[71] But as the Capadosse case of 1622 shows, this does not mean that circumcision was not viewed in Amsterdam as a key criterion for belonging to the community.

Denial of the right of burial *was* used by the *Mahamad* in Amsterdam, if not to encourage circumcision, to pressure a few of the emigres to undergo formal conversion to Judaism. These were persons who unquestionably belonged to "the Nation" but, because of known female Old Christian ancestors on their mother's side, were not Jewish according to rabbinic law, which held that Jewishness was transmitted through the mother. These persons were required to undergo ritual immersion (as well as circumcision, in the case of males) in order to be recognized as Jews. To encourage compliance, a ruling of April 1624 denied Jewish burial to any person "who was of the gentile race [*que tenha raca de goy*]" in the "feminine line."[72]

It is interesting that the few cases recorded in which such persons were denied Jewish burial involved marginal members of the community: an illegitimate son of a "Portuguese" man, a mulatto woman, and a daughter of a person identified only as "the English Jew."[73] Partly, this was a result of the very strong endogamous marriage patterns among the "Portuguese" in the Peninsula. Most of the emigres did not have Old Christian maternal figures in their genealogies. But it may also reflect a "don't ask, don't tell" policy on the part of the *Mahamad*. Communal leaders probably hesitated to act on such matters unless, as in the cases mentioned, the problematic female relative was a very recent ancestor and a person whose gentile status was well known. Given "Portuguese" ideas about the purity of Jewish blood, members of the *Mahamad* would not have been eager to uncover gentile blood in respected families.

For figures like Francisco Lopez Capadosse, who scorned the community's threats, the available sanctions had little significance. But these were the exception. Most emigres, whatever their degree of commitment to Judaism, wished to live among their own, belong to the community and participate fully in its social and ritual life. This powerful social need was an important bulwark of the *Mahamad's* authority.

It was precisely this social need that made the *herem*, or ban, an effective sanction. It was not a measure of last resort, nor was it necessarily a severe measure. Indeed, for certain violations of communal norms it was used quite routinely—and lifted just as routinely. It is thus often quite misleading to translate the term *herem* as "excommunication."[74] Persons who committed relatively minor infractions, like publicly insulting other members of the community or buying meat from an Ashkenazi butcher, could incur the *herem*.[75] Menasseh ben Israel was banned for a period of one day for verbally attacking the *Mahamad* in the synagogue over a measure he found personally insulting.[76] Sometimes the *herem* meant only that a person would be denied a particular privilege. In 1656, for example, the *Mahamad* declared that Abraham Gabay Mendez would not receive the honor of being called to the Torah or any other synagogue honor for two years because when he was in London he did not worship in a *minyan* with the Jews there (or even identify himself as a Jew), although he had been circumcised.[77] While the offenses that were punished by *herem* differed (in some cases they were not even stated), the most frequent were journeys (usually for business) to "lands of idolatry" where Judaism could not be observed;[78] overt challenges to the *Mahamad's* authority; and violations of sexual norms.[79]

Members of the *Mahamad* clearly understood that the sanctions they wielded to punish such behavior derived from rabbinic law. But their actions sometimes betray a penchant to follow norms with roots in the Peninsula. A look at violations of sexual norms in the community and their punishment (or nonpunishment) is revealing in this respect. Jewish law, as well as civil law in most Christian states, prohibited sexual relations between Jews and gentiles; and in Ashkenazi communities attitudes strongly reinforced these prohibitions among upstanding members of the community. But as mentioned in chapter three, it was not unusual for "Portuguese" merchants to have sexual relations with Dutch or other gentile women, often maidservants. In the period between 1600 and 1623, thirteen such cases appear in published notarial records—and of course we learn of such cases only when something went wrong, usually a pregnancy.[80] Some of the men involved in these affairs were pillars of the Portuguese-Jewish community. One of them—Duarte Fernandes (Joshua Habilho), accused of fathering a child by a nineteen-year-old Dutch girl in 1600—later went on to become an important figure in the community, a founding member of the *Dotar* and one of the three persons who drafted the 1639 *Haskamot*.[81] Another who admitted a liaison ending in pregnancy was Jeronimo Henriques (Joseph Cohen), a member of the Bet Jacob congregation as well as one of the founders of the *Dotar* (and twice an officer of that institution after the birth of an illegimate child by his Norwegian maidservant).[82] The children of such unions were often recognized by their fathers, who made some monetary compensation to the mother, sometimes considerable. In the case of Jeronimo Henriques's illegitimate child, the girl actually lived in Henriques's house for seven years. Antonio Lopes Suasso (Isaac Israel Suasso), the enormously wealthy financier who married a Pinto in 1653, and his son Francisco Lopes Suasso (Abraham Israel Suasso) both maintained gentile mistresses (in addition to "Portuguese" wives) who bore them illegitimate children, for whom they took some responsibility.[83] Such behavior was undoubtedly regarded with disapproval by the *hakhamim* and more pious members of the community. But no action was taken to punish it.

However, communal officials did impose the *herem* in cases in which other sexual norms were breached: adultery (or even suspected adultery) within the community, the marriage of youths without the knowledge of parents or communal leaders, and bigamy. Concerning adultery, relations between a "Portuguese" man and a "Portuguese" married woman were regarded with special severity. To be sure, this was consistent with Jewish law. But such relations also brought into play the issue of "Portuguese" honor. This can be seen in a case from 1654, when the *Mahamad* placed Jacob Moreno, Moreno's wife, and Daniel Castiel under the ban because, despite repeated warnings that Daniel Castiel refrain from entering Moreno's home in the husband's absence, Castiel continued to do so.[84] The *herem* was not imposed for adultery per se—nothing had been proved—but rather defiance of the *Mahamad*. What is significant is that this was not the kind of offense the *Mahamad* could overlook.

The allegiance of communal leaders to Iberian sociosexual norms is displayed most unambiguously in the policies of that quintessentially "Portuguese" institution, the *Dotar*. According to its statutes, illegitimate girls of "Portuguese" fathers were allowed to enter the *Dotar* dowry lottery, despite the fact that Jewish law did not recognize them as Jews. (Presumably they converted to Judaism to receive a dowry.) However, illegitimate daughters of "Portuguese" *mothers*, who were Jewish from birth according to Jewish law, were not permitted to apply for a dowry "under any circumstances."[85] The reinforcement of Iberian sociosexual attitudes, even when these were at odds with rabbinic principles, is particularly conspicuous in this stipulation. Its clear message was that extramarital relations between a "Portuguese" man and a gentile woman (presumably of inferior class) did not constitute a blemish on "Portuguese" honor, while extramarital relations involving a "Portuguese" woman were a scandal and a disgrace.

Whether supporting "Portuguese" or rabbinic norms, the members of the *Mahamad* showed themselves to be deeply conservative in spirit. They worked to create a traditional, ethnically tight-knit society that was both an enclave of Iberian social values and a bastion of traditional Jewish thinking. They cultivated an ideal with roots in Iberian converso society, but adapted it in a way which must have seemed natural to them in the new conditions of the diaspora. The ideal cultural type that emerged was very complex indeed, yet coherent and reproducible. In Amsterdam and Hamburg, there were many who seemed to represent this ideal. They were, of course, men. Each was an important figure in a far-flung family-cum-commercial network, possessed a coat of arms or even an aristocratic title, was a regular synagogue-goer with a prestigiously located seat, and played an active role in communal affairs. Such a person, be his name Belmonte, Texeira, Pinto, Curiel, Azevedo, Senior Coronel, or any number of others, had achieved the pinnacle of social success in the "Portuguese" diaspora.

The conservative character of Amsterdam's Portuguese-Jewish communal elite has sometimes been masked by its cultural cosmopolitanism. In comparison to Ashkenazi communal leaders, the "Portuguese" were better able to absorb new trends in European society because of their command of European languages and their interest in European culture. And, indeed, the libraries of the "Portuguese" reflected intellectual interests that extended well beyond the rabbinic world. However, what is significant is not the fact of "European" interests among the Portuguese Jews—this was entirely natural—but the conservative nature of these interests. Their libraries reflect a pursuit of the safe and the comfortable—classics, "histories," travel literature, and the like.[86] Even the erudite physician Orobio de Castro, a spokesman for the communal elite in the 1660s and, unlike his fellows, a man unusually well acquainted with new philosophical trends, adhered to quintessentially conservative ideas about both Judaism and medicine.

Yet even the somewhat antiquated cosmopolitanism of the "Portuguese" posed a threat to the ethos the communal leadership wished to promote. The themes and images of European belles lettres which had taken root in the New Christian imagination naturally continued to thrive in ex-converso minds despite the rites of passage of rejudaization. The *Mahamad,* as we have noted elsewhere, did not attempt to eliminate all expressions of Iberian culture from communal life. It banned theater productions from the sacred sphere of the synagogue, but did not otherwise interfere with the freedom of community members to indulge their appetite for European, and especially Iberian, literary works.

The *Mahamad* did, however, claim the right to censor the literary output of members of the community. This was stated unequivocally in clause 37 of the 1639 statutes, which stipulated that no member of the community might print—either in Amsterdam or outside it—books in Spanish or Portuguese (*livros ladinos*), or in Hebrew, without the *Mahamad*'s approval.[87] The *Mahamad*'s authority in this matter was less than it laid claim to, though, since it had no power to enforce its ruling outside Amsterdam, and members of the community could (and did) publish offensive or potentially offensive books in Antwerp or Brussels.[88] Some Amsterdam "Portuguese" authors even managed to print books in Amsterdam under the *Mahamad*'s nose by citing a false place of publication.[89] The *Mahamad* did have the power to prevent such books from circulating in the community, however, and could thus limit their sales.

What kind of material did the *Mahamad* seek to repress? The books it censored tended to fall into three categories: 1) works with openly erotic content, 2) works emphasizing pagan mythological motifs, and 3) literary works which presented scriptural narratives in a "profane" manner.

One document that reveals much about the leadership's conception of its role as censor is a memorandum drawn up by a board of rabbis reviewing Daniel Levi de Barrios's *Coro de las Musas*, which the author had had printed in Brussels in 1672. Before detailing the reasons for condemning the book, the rabbis pointed to two general aspects of its contents which disturbed them: matters that jeopardized the "honor of our Jewish faith" and "lascivious [matters]." They did not invoke *halakhah*. Indeed they opened with a list of three features of the book which, "while not totally prohibited, were somewhat scandalous." These were a) the author's way of referring to planets and other creatures by the names of pagan gods; b) the author's use of the title "saint" for "idolatrous and impure Christians"; and c) the author's readiness to grant Christians and idolators a place in heaven. There follows an enumeration of a number of even more obviously insincere (many of them trivial) passages in the book that were deemed offensive.[90] The members of the board were well aware that De Barrios was not championing pagan practices or endorsing the Church's dogma on saints. He was courting and flattering Christian readers and patrons, for pecuniary reasons. But in succumbing to the all-too-easy posturing of the converso (and not for the first time)[91]—in playing the admirer of both pagan and Christian Rome—De Barrios was violating important taboos.

In censorship cases in which books, not their authors, were banned—most notably those of De Barrios and Jacob (Manuel) de Pina[92]—the communal leaders were not facing a frontal attack on the community's values, but rather a threat to its image (or, as they would put it, its "honor"). Erotic verses and pagan imagery were deplored, their authors chastised and resocialized, and the little storm passed.

The greatest threat to the community was part of a far broader phenomenon in European culture, namely the criticism of religious tradition. A few generations later, the attack on clerical authority would begin to pose a challenge to all traditional European Jewish societies. But in the seventeenth century, the northern European communities of ex-conversos were unique among European Jewries as crucibles for sweeping, ideologically anchored attacks on rabbinic Judaism. There is a paradoxical aspect to this. Most of the emigres responded to the traumatic Iberian experience by embracing a self-affirming ancient religious tradition and a secure "Portuguese" collective existence. But others were driven by the same experience to reject vehemently this new orthodoxy. To the consternation and concern of the leadership, anticlerical and deistic ideas similar to those being cultivated in small intellectual circles throughout Europe surfaced fairly early. From 1616 to 1657, several searching and provocative souls openly challenged the very premise on which the community was built, namely the obligation of Jews to observe the Law of Moses as interpreted by the rabbis.

It is difficult to characterize the response of the members of the *Mahamad* to these subversive ideas, since they left little record of their thoughts. With the exception of Orobio de Castro they probably did not grasp the import of new philosophical currents. What is perhaps most profoundly reflected in their behavior is not their piety or stringency, but their rejection of the principle of individual freedom of conscience. They led a profoundly collective existence anchored in belief in the divine scheme of things. They had built a community that successfully integrated large numbers of emigres, educating their children, supporting the poor, attracting (and eventually producing) important rabbinic figures. This community had presses that were renowned throughout the Jewish world; it was a nerve center second to none for "the Nation"; it had worked out a uniquely favorable modus vivendi with the Dutch authorities. All of this had been achieved painstakingly, for the sake of "the Nation" and the service of God and, of course, for the ego rewards communal leadership offered. These leaders were not likely to tolerate repeated public statements by persons who challenged the foundations and significance of this enterprise (as well as their own authority).

Sensitivity to potential challenges appeared early, in an episode discussed briefly in chapter two. A person in Amsterdam (probably the physician David Farar) insisted in 1615 that the Torah could be interpreted properly only according to the plain meaning of the text (*peshat*). This represented a rejection of the large and highly revered body of traditional homiletic commentary. Members of the communal elite were troubled, and one of them—presumably one of the *hakhamim*—turned to an eminent rabbinic authority in Venice, Leon de Modena. Modena held that the position the nonconformist had adopted was legitimate and indeed implicitly criticized those who questioned it.[93] Modena, who was not a Sephardi Jew[94] and spoke from the firmly established Venice community, may not have appreciated the fears awakened in a community of neophytes by a person who openly criticized any aspect of tradition.

The following year witnessed a far more threatening challenge to rabbinic tradition by a member of "the Nation" then living in Hamburg. The
rebellious spirit was Uriel da Costa, an ex-converso from Porto and a
former student of canon law at the university of Coimbra. Da Costa threw
down the gauntlet when he sent a written statement to communal leaders
in Venice attacking the rabbinic tradition (the so-called Oral Law) as a gross
distortion of the Law of Moses. No copy of his written attack has been
preserved, but its contents are described at length in a Hebrew refutation,
Magen ve-zinnah, by Leon de Modena.[95] According to Modena's summary,
Da Costa argued that the Oral Law was not an integral part of the Torah but
rather a "new Torah" contradicting the old.[96] Modena became involved
when the Venetian leaders referred Da Costa's composition to him.[97] He
must have seen at once that, unschooled as Da Costa was in rabbinics, his
arguments had a powerful and persuasive aspect—especially among ex-
conversos, who were more likely to be struck by Da Costa's view than Jews
educated from childhood to accept traditional teachings justifying rabbinic
innovation. Modena wrote to the Hamburg community demanding that
Da Costa be excommunicated if he persisted in his views. When he did
persist, the Venetian community, in August 1618, formally imposed a ban
on him and his followers, and this ban was promulgated in Hamburg as
well.[98]

The *Mahamad* in Amsterdam was not involved in this episode, although
it was surely aware of it. It took action only when Da Costa arrived in
Amsterdam in May 1623 with the intention of publishing a book there
elucidating his heretical views. The *Mahamad* imposed a *herem* on him in
February 1623.[99] This did not prevent Da Costa from having his book
published in that city in the spring of 1624 by a Christian printer.[100] The first
part of the book is simply a revised version of Da Costa's earlier attack on
the Oral Law. But in the second part Da Costa attacked another teaching of
Jewish tradition, the doctrine of the immortality of the soul: he argued that
it was an innovation with no basis in Scripture. With heavy-handed sar-
casm, Da Costa argued that "the saintly Pharisees"—the talmudic sages—
were "the real renegades and heretics who are accursed."[101] As if intent on
offending his readers, he went on to declare converso martyrdom (and
Jewish martyrdom in general) a futile act since, according to his reading of
Scripture, God did not require (or want) such a sacrifice.[102] He moreover
mocked persons he had encountered who deluded themselves that mere
lip service to "the Law" ensured their salvation. Likewise, he scorned those
who cited a certain rabbinic saying—"All Israel have a share in the world
to come"—as proof that salvation was assured for anyone of Jewish blood.
Ridiculing this convenient conviction, he wrote:

> Except for a wretch like me—heretic, excommunicated, excluded from
> your midst—all the rest of you, in one pack [*fornada*] or another, by means of

a prayer or some other measure, will find yourselves in the world-to-come, because you are the children of Israel and as such you possess that privilege and so can sleep in peace.[103]

Da Costa's attack was not just on rabbinic Judaism, but on the ex-converso establishment in general, with its entrenched belief in salvation through the Law of Moses. At this point he was clearly enraged, and struck at the most sensitive and charged areas of Portuguese-Jewish belief. There is no better guide to the collective ideology of this community than Da Costa's assault on it.

It has been argued that Da Costa was disciplined for publishing this book because he was jeopardizing the community in Christian eyes. In repudiating in print the doctrine of the immortality of the soul, he was repudiating a basic doctrine not only of Judaism but of Christianity as well. The "Portuguese" were already suspected—not without reason—of harboring skeptics among them. Only a few years before the Da Costa episode, Hugo Grotius had addressed the issue of "unbelief" among the Jews in his recommendations concerning the terms of Jewish settlement in Holland. One of the three beliefs he insisted each Jew must hold in order to be tolerated was that "after death there shall be another life in which the just will be rewarded and the evil punished"—precisely what Da Costa denied. Even more pointedly, Grotius noted that "among the Jews as well as among those of other religious convictions, there are often some atheists and impious people who should not be tolerated in any good republic."[104] While Grotius's recommendations never became law, they do indicate what was undoubtedly the opinion of most Dutch magistrates. By publishing his ideas, Da Costa was threatening the well-being of the community.

It would be a mistake, however, to conclude that Da Costa was excommunicated primarily because he endangered relations between the Portuguese-Jewish community and the Dutch authorities. No doubt the *Mahamad* was concerned about the opinion of the authorities in this matter. But this was only one aspect of the problem. Da Costa's opponent Samuel da Silva, who published a rebuttal of Da Costa's opinions on the immortality of the soul, articulated the deeper concerns of the "Portuguese" when he spoke of the need of the community to protect itself from "this hypocrite, or any others of his type who, excellent as their stock may be [!], do in some rare instances degenerate into monsters."[105] That is, Da Costa was a kind of mutant who threatened the community's arduously achieved Jewish gestalt. The *Mahamad* banned him—as Modena had earlier insisted he be banned—primarily because he had overstepped the boundaries of tolerable dissent within the Jewish world.

Da Costa formally recanted in 1628 and rejoined the Amsterdam community. But according to his autobiography which, however unreliable (and partly spurious) it may be,[106] has been shown to be based on historical fact,[107] he was banned once more in 1632 or 1633 and ended his life as a deist, denying not only the Oral Law but also the revealed character of Scripture and the providential nature of God. He committed suicide in 1640[108] after undergoing a second and, by his account, exceedingly humiliating ceremony of penance in the synagogue.

Da Costa must have been bitterly amused during his second period of excommunication by a debate that broke out in the community in the mid–1630s. A group of enthusiasts around the young *hakham* Isaac Aboab da Fonseca insisted that regardless of his or her sins no Jew would suffer eternal punishment, justifying this belief with the saying of the Sages, "All Israel have a share in the world to come." Da Costa had already, it may be recalled, ridiculed persons with such complacent views. But these views apparently played a special function in a community of ex-conversos. As the scholar who analyzed the episode suggested,[109] such a community had particular anxieties which were relieved by assurance that all Jews were, so to speak, automatically saved. While the emigres and their children living "in Judaism" believed they had hope for salvation through the Law of Moses, they would have been tormented by the thought that their forefathers and other loved ones who had lived (or were living) "in idolatry" would suffer eternal punishment. An idea of blanket salvation connected with Jewish identity offered a vision of a people who were scattered and divided in this world but united in the world to come.

Comforting as it was, the belief that any Jew, regardless of his or her sins, would enjoy a "portion in the world to come" contradicted traditional Jewish teaching. The "orthodox" rallied around Saul Levi Mortera, who insisted that only righteous Jews would be rewarded and that evil Jews would be punished for all eternity.[110] The strife between the two parties threatened to disrupt the community. Once again a sensitive issue of collective boundaries (this time in the afterlife) was referred to Venice.

In this case, the Venetian rabbinic authorities made explicit their concern about the reactions of the gentile world to this debate. The idea that sinners, as long as they were Jewish, would be saved was not only bad theology, it was offensive and heretical in the eyes of Christians. The rabbis therefore asked that the dispute not be brought formally before a Jewish court:[111]

> We know for certain that if knowledge of the dispute spreads among the gentiles, immense damage will arise for us from having suggested that such matters could be in doubt among us, the more so if they hear [that there is a belief among the Jews] that even the soul that has sinned will attain eternal salvation.

But gentile anger was not the only issue. The dispute was a clear case of "converso" innovation confronting rabbinic orthodoxy, and ultimately rabbinic orthodoxy won the day. The Venetian authorities chastised and silenced the young Aboab—who was to emerge in years to come, older and wiser, as a major rabbinic figure in the Amsterdam community.

Thus in the cases of both Da Costa and Aboab—the skeptic and the kabbalistic enthusiast—the Amsterdam leadership cooperated with the more established Venetian leadership to suppress manifestations of converso extremism. Both types of extremists resurfaced, however, in subsequent years.

The kabbalistic enthusiasts were important in fanning the flames of excitement during the messianic movement around the figure of Shabbetai Zvi in 1665–66. This convulsive episode has been discussed in great detail by scholars, most exhaustively by Gershom Scholem in his monumental work on the movement.[112] It is true that the Jews of Amsterdam, both Ashkenazi and "Portuguese," played an important role in the spread of the movement among European Jews after news arrived from Palestine in November 1665 about a curious figure who soon became known as the King Messiah and about his "prophet" Nathan of Gaza. Many of the major figures in the Amsterdam community, merchants and rabbis alike (including Isaac Aboab da Fonseca), were gripped by messianic fervor. But this was not particular to Amsterdam or to "Portuguese" communities. On the contrary, pillars of Jewish communities throughout the Jewish diaspora joined in the excited anticipatory activity. It is difficult to say whether this relatively brief episode and its denouement (Shabbetai Zvi converted to Islam under coercion in September 1666) were handled by the "Portuguese" elite in Amsterdam differently because of the particular characteristics of the community. To determine this would require a detailed comparative study that lies beyond the scope of this book.[113]

In any case, what is known about the episode throws little light on the issues of self-definition and boundary maintenance that concern us. The roots of the movement lay elsewhere in the Jewish world, in the Ottoman Empire. The communal elite of Amsterdam was faced by a complex situation, but not with a challenge to its authority, since it shared in the enthusiasm. Nor did its behavior raise eyebrows in the wider Jewish world, since members of Jewish elites of all backgrounds were behaving similarly, from Tunisia to Palestine, Poland to Yemen. And while aspects of sabbatianism *after* Shabbetai Zvi's conversion do have a "converso" dimension,[114] the rabbinic leadership in Amsterdam did not view it as a major threat. Indeed, the vehemently antisabbatian rabbi Jacob Sasportas treated one of the post-conversion "believers" (none other than Daniel Levi de Barrios) with considerable indulgence.[115] Thus, in my view, the sabbatian movement did not play a significant role in the development of "Portuguese" identity in Amsterdam, and we will focus here on more specifically "Portuguese" issues of skepticism and heterodoxy.

The Rejudaization of "the Nation"

The greatest crisis involving militant unbelievers in the community arose in 1656, when three articulate, vocal, and provocative persons with somewhat similar deistic views began teaching their ideas, primarily to the young.[116] Two of them, Juan de Prado and Daniel Ribera, were emigres from the Peninsula. Prado had flirted with deistic ideas even before he left Spain.[117] The third, Baruch Spinoza, was a young man of twenty-four, born and raised in a merchant family in the Amsterdam Portuguese-Jewish community.

Of the three figures, the one whose ideas at this time are least-known is, ironically, Spinoza, about whose later ideas we know so much. He was excommunicated in July 1656. But the *herem* imposed on him, severe as it was, was extremely vague, speaking only of his "abominable heresies [*horrendas heregias*]" and "monstrous deeds [*ynormes obres*]."[118] Unfortunately his *Apologia para justificarse de su abdicación de la Synagoga*, said to have been written after his excommunication, either has not been preserved or was never written. The most revealing description of Spinoza's views in this period is a brief statement given to the Madrid Inquisition by an Augustinian friar who met Spinoza and Prado together in Amsterdam in late 1658 or early 1659. The friar reported that the two said they had come to hold three key beliefs antithetical to rabbinic Judaism—that "the Law was not true, and that the soul dies along with the body, and that God exists only philosophically"—and that they had been expelled "from the synagogue" for these beliefs.[119] If, as seems to be the case, Spinoza and Prado insisted on disseminating such ideas, the *Mahamad* could hardly have ignored them. In early February 1657, after Spinoza's excommunication, the *Mahamad* launched an investigation into the teachings of Prado and Ribera (though the latter had apparently left Amsterdam). The relatively abundant testimony about the two men indicates that they denied the election of Israel and the divine origin of the Law of Moses. Ribera was even said to reject the existence of God. They were far from quiet about their beliefs and, moreover, openly vented their hostility toward the *hakhamim* and the *Mahamad*.[120] It is not surprising that when the investigation was completed Prado was excommunicated.

Scholars have debated to what degree the *Mahamad*, in banning Spinoza and Prado, was acting to placate Amsterdam's civil and ecclesiastical authorities. There is no way to know. Certainly one could be severely disciplined in Dutch society at this time for disseminating such ideas, as Spinoza understood clearly when he later published (or decided not to publish) his works.[121] Moreover, the Portuguese Jews still felt their position was precarious, as a minority in a Christian state. However tolerant the Dutch authorities had become regarding philosophical ideas that did not conform to the basic tenets of the churches, the *Mahamad* did not wish to jeopardize the image of the Portuguese Jews as good citizens who adhered to the principles of an ancient religion.[122]

Nevertheless, the *Mahamad* seems to have been concerned first and foremost with internal issues. This is reflected in the role assumed in the Prado affair by the newly arrived emigre Isaac Orobio de Castro. Technically, Orobio was not permitted to correspond with the banned Prado, then living in Antwerp, even though Orobio had known Prado in Spain and felt an obligation to try to bring him back to Judaism.[123] But the *Mahamad*, while carefully regulating (and even censoring) the correspondence between the two, not only did nothing to punish Orobio but even allowed Orobio's first letter to circulate in manuscript.[124] Orobio thus became a spokesman for the community and its ideals and an important ideologue in the conflict.

He was particularly well suited for this role. He was soon himself a member of the communal elite, playing a significant role in communal affairs in the years after his arrival.[125] But unlike other members of this elite, Orobio had academic training and the theological sophistication to rebut Prado's arguments. What is striking, however, is that in many ways he was not far from the habits of mind of the Pintos and Belmontes. However intellectualized his position vis-à-vis Prado was, it resonated with the ideology and instincts of the merchant elite. The central argument in his correspondence with Prado was that an individual's reasoning can easily lead him astray, whereas an ancient tradition about which learned men agree, as long as it does not directly contradict reason, should be accepted as the basis for faith.[126] It was an argument for perpetuating the ancestral faith that deeply harmonized with crypto-Jewish ways of thinking. Ultimately, truth was validated by collective ethnic consent.

In general, Orobio regarded novel ideas as suspect. In a revised version of the prologue to his first letter, his *Epístola invectiva contra Prado*,[127] he denounced the search for novelty as a moral vice. He depicted those who invented new notions as self-promoting, even malicious, while those who submitted to tradition demonstrated their dignity and reason. To attack Scriptures which had been preserved uncorrupted for centuries was a sign of moral weakness. "The unworthy and frivolous claims that malicious innovation [*la innovadora malicia*] produces against this inalterable truth," he wrote of those who attacked the divinity of Scripture, "are worthy neither to be recorded nor discussed."[128] Speaking primarily of Prado, he asserted that this man, "who loves his [own] opinion so much," should "submit himself to a judgment . . . which our ancestors have possessed for three thousand five hundred years without interruption and which, rather than declining, is continually being enhanced."[129]

While Orobio's intellectual instincts may have been related to his experience as a converso, he perhaps found support for them in contemporary European society. Orobio's biographer has pointed out the similarity between some of his arguments and those of certain contemporary Christians who were battling skepticism, especially the Jansenists and those whom

Richard Popkin has referred to as "fideistic skeptics."[130] These defenders of faith argued—to simplify and generalize their beliefs greatly—that while human reason was important for evaluating beliefs, it could easily lead one astray if used alone, without reliance on authority. Whether or not Orobio was familiar with these ideas, he anchored his defense of rabbinic Judaism in similar arguments, arguments that spoke to wider questions about faith in early modern European society.

But Orobio's emphasis on antiquity and collective ancestral judgment as the foundations of authority seems to draw at least as much from "Portuguese" sources as from Christian polemics against skepticism, of which Orobio, as far as we know, knew nothing.[131] Orobio's line of thinking resonated quite naturally among the "Portuguese," with their drama (as they conceived of it) of repression in the Peninsula and "restoration" on free soil, of heroism at the stake and stubborn adherence to ancestral beliefs. In contrast, the individualistic, universalistic, and mercilessly unsentimental notions of Da Costa, Prado, and Spinoza ran deeply against the grain of their own religio-ethnic intuitions as well as their idealized conception of the community. If the converso experience had contributed to the conviction of a few rugged souls that they could rely on no truths except those arrived at through their own powers of reasoning, it seems to have persuaded other conversos—indeed most of the emigres—that in turning away from the Church they could rely only on an ancient countervailing tradition.

Relations with Other Jews: Tudescos, Polacos, Italianos

That ancient tradition had at its core an ethnic, collective conception of religious responsibility, of which the ex-conversos were well aware. Being a Jew meant being a part of the Jewish people; and the "return" to Judaism implied a "return" to the Jewish people as well—an entity that had hitherto been mainly an abstraction. For a group with so complex and tenuous an identity, this aspect of restoration was fraught with problems.

For early converso settlers in southwest France, Holland, Hamburg, and London, the "Jewish people" remained mainly an abstraction even after emigration, since there were few Jews in these places who did not have Iberian origins. Before long, however, this situation changed dramatically. As conditions for Jews in central and eastern Europe deteriorated, and as the governments of the developing Atlantic states began to readmit Jews, Ashkenazi Jews began to trickle—and then flood—westward, settling among other places in the centers of the northern "Portuguese" diaspora. For the conversos, the encounter with these alien Jews was highly problematic. The first to arrive were German Jews fleeing the Thirty Years War, arriving in

Amsterdam from the 1620s onward. They were not only culturally foreign to the "Portuguese," but tended to be poor and uneducated as well. Most were from the lowest social strata—butchers, peddlars, beggars, and the like. Often they became menial employees of Portuguese Jews. They did not conform to the self-image of the Portuguese Jews in any way, and were regarded by the latter with distaste from the start. Initially they were permitted to worship with the "Portuguese" and to bury their dead in Ouderkerk (in a separate plot, for those not of "the Nation"),[132] but they were not accepted as members of the congregations.

The term used to identify the German Ashkenazim was borrowed from Venetian usage, where the Italian *tedesco* (German) was used to refer to Jews of German-Ashkenazi origin. This term was adopted into the Portuguese language of the ex-conversos in Amsterdam, where it became *tudesco* and was given an Iberian plural ending—that is, *tudescos* (or *todescos*) rather than the Italian *tedeschi*.[133] Ashkenazi Jews were referred to as *tudescos* in some of the earliest records of the Amsterdam community, the first mentioned being a "Mahir [Meir] Tudesqo" who was buried in the Ouderkerk cemetery in March 1618.[134] As this instance illustrates, among the "Portuguese," Ashkenazi origins became part of one's name, a key identifier.

The exclusivist tendency of the "Portuguese" became more pronounced as the number of Ashkenazim increased. The *tudescos* formed their own congregation in 1635; and though for several years they remained somewhat dependent on the Portuguese-Jewish community, they soon had their own synagogue and rabbis.[135] In 1642, the "Portuguese" helped the Ashkenazim finance the purchase of their own cemetery in Muiderberg, which made it possible, among other things, to deny them the right to bury their dead in Ouderkerk.[136] The two groups also tended to live in different streets or neighborhoods. In the first decades of the seventeenth century, most of the *tudescos* lived near the Turfsteeg and in Ververstraat. Later, the poorer Ashkenazim lived in the crowded, shabby district of Marken and Uilenberg, while the poor of the Portuguese Jews lived in the Nieuwe Kerkstraat.[137]

The Ashkenazim were generally persons for whom poverty had become a way of life, while in contrast many of the "Portuguese" poor (though not all) were recently impoverished or did not feel themselves to be part of a permanent culture of poverty. These were the "shame-faced poor," the *vergonzantes*, as they were known in Spain. The *Dotar* records offer a glimpse of the pride and humiliation of such persons. A certain Daniel Campos, despite his genuine poverty,[138] refused to allow his daughter to accept the dowry she won in 1631. He insisted that he had not even known of his daughter's application.[139] Likewise, the winner of a dowry living in Venice requested that the dowry be sent to her before the wedding (contrary to the *Dotar*'s practice), because if the groom found out that she was marrying with the help of the dowry society—"which he views as charity"—the wedding would not take place.[140] It appears that for many of the poor among the "Portuguese," poverty was an affliction, not a way of life; and it can be understood why even those who lived off communal charity shunned contact with their Yiddish-speaking Ashkenazi counterparts, who were accustomed to begging door-to-door or at the gates of the synagogue, and were repeatedly berated for their begging, idleness, and "vices" by the *Mahamad*.[141]

As unattractive as these Ashkenazim seemed to the "Portuguese," however, they were unquestionably Jews. From the point of view of Jewish law, it was impossible to refrain from establishing ties of solidarity with them. Like other Jews, the "Portuguese" were obligated to relate to the wider Jewish world both conceptually (as reflected in liturgy and rabbinic literature) and in practice (in the areas of welfare and intercommunal cooperation).

In practice, the policies of the communal leaders toward the wider Jewish world made sense, given the discomfort they felt in actual contact with other Jewish ethnic groups. In matters concerning Jews in danger or distress, the community cooperated with Ashkenazi communities, sending aid to those in distress in Poland and in the German states. The community also granted aid to poor Ashkenazim who arrived in Amsterdam. However, it was not interested in encouraging such refugees to settle in Amsterdam. An episode from 1656 reflects this attitude. That year, when about three hundred Ashkenazi refugees arrived in Amsterdam from Poland and Lithuania, members of the "Portuguese" community received them, providing them with food, clothing, and shelter. But they also took pains to help many of the refugees continue on to destinations outside the Dutch Republic.[142]

The farther away the needy Ashkenazim were, the friendlier the attitude to them. When distant Ashkenazi communities suffered in times of war, the *Mahamad* was willing to offer substantial assistance. It granted a large sum, for example, to the Jews of Kremzier in Moravia in 1643 after that community had been destroyed by the Swedish army.[143] Similarly, in 1677 it contributed to the redemption of Polish Jews taken captive and held in Constantinople.[144] These are but two examples of the routine role the community assumed in offering aid and relief to Ashkenazi communities in distress.

There is no reason to doubt the sincerity of the expressions of solidarity that sometimes accompanied the decisions to grant such aid. In 1642, the community contributed a considerable sum to assist Ashkenazim in German lands who suffered from the ravages of the Thirty Years War. More interesting than the decision itself is the entry in the minute-book justifying it:

> The natural mercy and compassion of the Jewish people [*povo de Ysrael*], and especially of those belonging to this holy community, have stirred the

View of the Ashkenazi synagogue dedicated in 1671. Anonymous etching, 1675. Note the contrast in appearance between the foreground figures here and the figures in the companion etching of the Portuguese synagogue (see next page). *From the collection of J. van Velzen. Photograph from the Jewish Historical Museum, Amsterdam.*

men of their *Mahamad* to find a remedy for the great sufferings of the poor of our Hebrew nation, especially the Ashkenazim who have been expelled from Germany . . . and at the same time to bring an end to the great injury which has resulted from the desecration of the blessed name of God due to violations of His holy Torah, bringing loss of honor upon His people.[145]

Taking action in such a case was without doubt a religious obligation. Indeed, the solidarity expressed is couched in religious terms. The Jewish people is depicted as an ideal religious body, the collectivity of believers and observers of Torah law. The very fact that it was felt necessary to justify the decision in this way seems noteworthy, and the justifications themselves are interesting: 1) the natural compassion of the "Portuguese" Jews and 2) the honor of the Torah, which could not be properly observed by homeless and hungry refugees. In the archival documents I have studied,

Exterior view of the Portuguese synagogue dedicated in 1675. Anonymous etching, 1675. *Courtesy of the Library of the Jewish Theological Seminary of America.*

I have not seen—and would not expect to see—a decision to aid "Portuguese" Jews accompanied by such a justification.

Closer to home, such sentiments were not to be found. Although as we have seen, in the early years *tudescos* participated in the ritual life of the "Portuguese," this situation was short-lived. In 1639, the merger agreement of the united Portuguese-Jewish community stated that *K.K. Talmud Torah* was established for "Jews of the Portuguese and Spanish Nation," and that Jews of other "nations" would require permission from the *Mahamad* to participate in its services.[146]

Thus, in everything that concerned actual social contact, the communal leadership acted to maintain as great a distance as possible between the "Men of the Nation" and Jews of other ethnic background. This policy became more harsh and rigid with time. It is true that with the change in the character of Ashkenazi immigration in the period after 1648—when large numbers of Polish and Lithuanian refugees began arriving in Amsterdam—

"Portuguese" attitudes changed somewhat. They showed higher regard for these emigres than for the earlier refugees from German lands: the *polacos* were better educated and among them were respected scholars.[147] Indeed, the Lithuanian scholar Moses Rivkes, who arrived as a refugee in the Netherlands in 1655, was given the unusual honor of being admitted to the yeshiva of the De Pinto family in Rotterdam.

Around 1660 the Polish and Lithuanian Jews were able to break away from the German-Jewish congregation and organize themselves in a separate congregation, further emphasizing their difference. But the "Portuguese" soon viewed the *polacos* as having *tudesco* qualities, and by the time the German and Polish congregations united, in 1673, the willingness of the "Portuguese" to differentiate between the two groups of Ashkenazim seems to have disappeared.[148] Still, as late as 1683, one of the very few non-"Portuguese" to participate in any aspect of the life of *K.K. Talmud Torah* was the Polish rabbi Joseph bar Eliezer, who pursued rabbinic learning at the De Pinto yeshiva.[149]

Eventually, even the time-honored custom according to which the descendants of Uri Halevi, the rabbi from Emden, were accepted as members of *K.K. Talmud Torah* was challenged. It is not clear how many persons took advantage of this privilege over the years. In adulthood, Uri Halevi's grandson (Uri Phoebus Halevi) belonged for a time to the Polish-Jewish congregation and then the German-Jewish congregation of Amsterdam; apparently it was only in 1673 that he made use of his privilege and became a paying member of *K.K. Talmud Torah*.[150] A few other members of his family also joined the Portuguese-Jewish community. But even this concession to the family of the founding rabbi of the community galled members as time passed. In a ruling of 1700, communal leaders made a strikingly harsh ruling. It declared that the right to inherited membership claimed by Uri Halevi's descendants was "imaginary." True, Uri Phoebus Halevi and other members of the family had been admitted in the mistaken belief that their claim was valid, but an investigation by communal leaders showed that

> nothing is on record of any obligation on our part to extend to the . . . descendants [of Uri Halevi and his son Aron] the right to membership which they claim our congregation owes them; and even if this were the case (which it clearly is not), the communal officials of that period ought to have realized that it was not appropriate that these people continue on in our congregation, for they should have recognized that these people did not harmonize with our own people, as far as their customs are concerned.[151]

Those who had already been admitted as members were allowed to remain—Uri Phoebus Halevi was buried at Ouderkerk in 1715, with a tombstone inscribed in Portuguese[152]—but the ruling stipulated that "henceforth absolutely no other be admitted under any pretext."[153]

The strong inclination of the "Portuguese" to exclusivity had multiple causes—and functions. There can be little doubt that Iberian concepts of blood were internalized and adapted by the ex-conversos in a way that permitted them to retain in the diaspora a kind of ethnic segregation that had been forced on them in the Peninsula. But the impulse was also a response to the experience of being uprooted and undergoing a self-transformation that entailed many strains. The need to maintain a distance from Ashkenazim reflected in part the need to perpetuate a self-image of social superiority, and eventually became part of a defensive posture adopted toward the gentile world.[154]

The ethnic exclusivity of the "Portuguese" in Amsterdam had no basis in Jewish law. Some of its expressions actually contradicted Jewish law. For example, the ex-conversos were reluctant to accept into the community a convert to Judaism whose father was not "Portuguese."[155] Such a person was unequivocally Jewish; the problem was his or her ethnicity. Likewise, *negros e mulatos judeos*—converted servants or illegitimate children of servants—were denied the full privileges of communal membership, though there was no rabbinic justification for such a rule.[156] There are explicit decisions of the *Mahamad* of the Amsterdam community which also glaringly contradicted basic norms of Jewish communities. In 1657, for example, it prohibited "*tudescos*, Italian Jews and mulattos" from attending the communal school.[157] It decided in 1671 that "considering the difficulties that would arise," an Ashkenazi mate of a "Portuguese" woman could not be accepted as a member of the community or buried in Ouderkerk, and the same would hold for the offspring of such a marriage.[158] In 1697, it decided that even *Portuguese Jewish males* who married Jewish women who were not of "the Nation" would lose their rights as members.[159] And in 1709, in an effort to enforce these rulings, procedures were instituted for clarifying the origins of persons applying for membership in the community, if there was any reason for doubt.[160] These criteria for acceptance in a Jewish community are deviations of the first order from Jewish practice, and reflect the particular anxieties of the "Portuguese" about loss of their precarious sense of self.

Despite the considerable material which can be marshaled to show how the "Portuguese" leadership acted to protect the boundaries of "the Nation," it is difficult to convey in twentieth-century concepts how being "Portuguese" was perceived among the emigres in relation to being Jewish. The link was fluid and ambiguous and sometimes conflicted but, as we shall see in the next chapter, immensely powerful. Members of the communal elite drew both from deep-rooted converso patterns and from consciously developed ideas about Jewish history and theology to create an ethos that accommodated both loyalties.

6

❖

Maintaining "the Nation" in Exile

Ethnic Solidarity across National and Religious Boundaries

The ancestral élan vital that members of the rejudaized "Portuguese" elite believed they possessed implied an obligation to revive it where it lay dormant, that is, among those "Men of the Nation" who seemed content to live as Catholics in Catholic lands. Then, too, there was a need to encourage the ambivalent and the faint-hearted to make the leap, and to offer aid to those too impoverished to reach "lands of freedom." Given the fact that Portuguese Jews in Amsterdam and New Christians in Catholic lands belonged to a single, if scattered, population, bound together by commercial and kinship ties, common cultural traits, and a shared experience of stigma and persecution, some such role was quite natural. But the Amsterdam community's role vis-à-vis the New Christian diaspora was also prompted by more complex impulses. Alongside the immediate human concerns was an ideological one, a yearning to achieve not only partial, but full collective restoration. Only with the rejudaization of the entire "Nation" would the natural order, brutally upset by the Iberian "captivity," be set aright. This chapter will explore how Amsterdam's "Portuguese" leadership attempted to incorporate responsibility for the entire "Portuguese" diaspora into communal life, without compromising the rabbinic foundations of the community.

Theirs was not the only Jewish community to express concern for conversos in Catholic lands. In the early seventeenth century a number of Jewish communities possessed a Portuguese-Jewish emigre component, and major figures in these communities expressed concern for the "captives" of the New Christian diaspora. But no other community became as deeply engaged with the northward-spreading New Christian diaspora as Amsterdam's.

There were several reasons for this. The emigres who settled in Amsterdam were virtually the only Jews in the region when they arrived (aside from other Portuguese Jews who settled in a few smaller communities—in

Hamburg and its environs and elsewhere in Holland). They were thus not absorbed into a pre-existing Jewish communal structure as were ex-conversos who settled in the Mediterranean region. Their collective life remained overwhelmingly "Portuguese," and they did not experience a strong break with the New Christian diaspora.

When the Portuguese Jews in Amsterdam were eventually joined by Ashkenazi Jews from Germany and Poland, they had already established their own "Portuguese" cultural style, which they proceeded to protect jealously. The ethos they had cultivated, emphasizing their particular experience of suffering and heroism in the Peninsula and their Iberian social superiority, allowed them to feel secure even vis-à-vis Jews whose rabbinic roots were deeper and more natural than their own. If anything, as the most Europeanized Jews in early modern Europe, the arrival of Yiddish-speaking German Jews from the most uneducated and impoverished stratum of Ashkenazi society only intensified their sense of solidarity with the "Portuguese" diaspora.[1] They chose to stay aloof from the Ashkenazim, and their favorable legal status in Amsterdam gave them the freedom to do so. They did not need to unite with other Jews for self-protection and were not forced to live with other Jews in a ghetto, as in Venice. They thus felt free to construct their collective experience on their own terms, emphasizing their attachment to the "Portuguese" diaspora while distancing themselves from the Ashkenazim.

Finally, the relative geographical isolation of Amsterdam from other major Jewish populations (Poland-Lithuania, Moravia, Bohemia, Italy, the Balkans) had the effect of fostering closer ties between the "Portuguese" in Amsterdam and the population of New Christians in northwestern Europe. Even after Ashkenazim began to settle in large numbers, the combined crypto-Jewish and "rejudaized" converso population constituted the richest and most vital Jewish cultural presence in northwestern Europe. The Portuguese-Jewish community of Amsterdam quickly became a center for this far-flung "Nation" defined only by psychological and ethnic boundaries.

These circumstances—the emigres' experience of being pioneers of Jewish settlement (or resettlement), their ability to segregate themselves from local Ashkenazim, and their physical distance from other major Jewish populations—reinforced their continued identification with "the Nation." Their attachments to relatives and commercial correspondents in the Peninsula or in the New World were richer, more concrete, and more natural than their attachment to "the Jewish people." The term "the Nation" evoked an entire world of vivid memories and feelings; in contrast, "the Jewish people" remained a somewhat cerebral theological concept—one that had its place primarily in the synagogue and in theological discussion.

The communal elite thus instinctively sought to affirm and concretize the community's affiliation to the "Portuguese" diaspora as well as its affiliation to the wider Jewish world. But this meant deviating from established patterns of traditional Jewish communal life. Jewish societies in Christian Europe (that of late medieval Spain being a notable exception) were defined by theological, halakhic, social, biological, linguistic, and legal boundaries that had been virtually coextensive for centuries. These boundaries were quite difficult to cross.[2] To be sure, some Jews did convert to Christianity even outside Spain, willingly or under duress, and such persons were accepted back into the Jewish community when they returned or reverted to Judaism, on the principle that one could not sever oneself from the Jewish people even by conversion.[3] But an entire subsociety of conversos and ex-conversos—"the Nation," with its friars and nuns, its skeptics, its oblivious violators of the sabbath, and its technically non-Jewish members (those with gentiles in the female line)—was an utterly unfamiliar and bizarre entity. The affirmation by the leadership of Amsterdam's "Portuguese" that the community would take an active part in sustaining this entity represented a recognition that rejudaization, for them, did not necessarily mean imitating established precedents in Jewish life.

The most ambitious and original of the Amsterdam elite's efforts to involve itself with the entire "Portuguese Nation"—indeed, to serve as its center—was the establishment early in the community's existence, in 1615, of an institution which we have had occasion to mention. This was the *Santa Companhia de dotar orfans e donzelas pobres,* referred to commonly as the *Dotar.*[4] The apparent function of the society was to dispense dowries to poor girls. But the *Dotar* also served to give institutional expression to "the Nation." According to the provisional preamble to its statutes, the society was to be

> a society of Portuguese, established with divine favor, to marry poor orphans and poor maidens of this Portuguese Nation, and the Castilian, among residents [in the region stretching] from St. Jean de Luz to Danzig, including France and the Netherlands, England, and Germany; [a society] to which may be admitted all those who agree to aid in this pious work who belong to our Hebrew Nation, Portuguese or Castilian, or their descendants by the masculine or feminine line, residents in every part of the world.[5]

This passage is remarkable in several ways, not the least for its language of affiliation. It speaks of a) "a society of Portuguese," b) "the Portuguese Nation, and the Castilian," and c) "our Hebrew Nation, Portuguese or Castilian." Of the three terms of affiliation used, only the third betrays the fact that this was a *Jewish* society. As a whole, the preamble is a proclamation of the distinctiveness, unity, and solidarity of "the Nation" irrespective of religious or political boundaries.

The *Dotar* claimed to be established "in imitation of the *Hebra Kedossa de cazar orfas* of *K.K. Talmud Torah* [the so-called Ponentine community] of

Venice."[6] And indeed, a dowry society had been founded two years earlier in Venice by the "Ponentine" Jews (a Venetian congregation primarily of ex-conversos and their descendants). But the claim is highly misleading.

True, some of the unusual aspects of the *Dotar* had their precedent in the Venetian society. First, the Venetian society did not confine itself to the immediate, local community in which it was founded, unlike the countless confraternities which were part of seventeenth-century Catholic and Italian-Jewish life.[7] It was designed to serve a far-flung diaspora. At least on paper, the scope of its activity was unlimited by political or geographical boundaries. The statutes stipulate that a girl anywhere was eligible to apply for a dowry, whether "born here in Venice, or outside." Likewise, membership was open to persons in Venice "or outside," and members enjoyed equal privileges wherever they resided.[8] And these provisions by no means remained a dead letter. It is true that nearly all the members were recruited from within a fairly narrow Italian radius. But the philanthropic activity of the society was geographically quite far-ranging. Aside from the Venetian girls who applied, considerable numbers of candidates came from Salonica, Pisa, Monastir, Livorno, Corfu, Ferrara, Skoplje, Constantinople, and Tunis. Small numbers came from Amsterdam, Mantua, Ancona, Ismir, Jerusalem, Padua, Pazardzhik ("Patragic"), Lugo, Spoleto, Ragusa, Rovigo, Verona, Poland, and Safed. This series of place names is not merely a list. It offers an impressionistic map of the Sephardi diaspora in the early seventeenth century.

A second precedent set by the Venetian society was its adoption of Sephardi lineage as a criterion for eligibility. To be sure, this was not the first Jewish institution designed to serve a particular ethnic group within Jewish society. But to explicitly exclude other Jews on the basis of lineage was unheard of. The Venetian society did just that: it required applicants to be "poor Hebrew girls, Portuguese or Castilian on the father's or mother's side."[9] The society did not, however, draw an ethnic line where membership was concerned, and was glad to accept members of any "nation"—along with their entrance fees, of course. Moreover, non-Sephardi members could enter the names of their own poor female relatives as applicants for dowries. (They would have had little incentive to join otherwise.)

Where the Venetian institution differed from the *Dotar* essentially and fundamentally was in its indifference to conversos who were not practicing Jews living in Jewish communities. But its diaspora-wide activity apparently sparked the interest of Amsterdam's "Portuguese," suggesting to them an institutionalized means to reach out not just to Sephardi Jews, but to the entire scattered "Portuguese Nation," conversos and ex-conversos alike.

Thus inspired, in 1615 a group of fifteen Amsterdam "Portuguese" merchants, among them some of the most prominent figures in community life,[10] established their own society. They adopted both of the Venetian innovations: the principle of diaspora-wide activity, on the one hand, and the adoption of the criterion of Sephardi lineage, on the other. But the *Dotar*'s statutes reflect a radicalization of both principles. Concerning its diaspora activity, the *Dotar* founders extended the society's orbit beyond the Sephardi diaspora proper to include New Christians living in Catholic lands. And as for its ethnic requirements, the *Dotar* founders entirely excluded non-Sephardim from the ranks of its members and applicants.

These were not minor changes, but major, defining ones, reflecting a lingering ethnic bond that flourished on the soil of northern Europe in a way it could not in Venice. And the relevant by-laws were taken very seriously. In only two instances in the course of the seventeenth century did *Dotar* officers make an exception to the ethnic lines drawn in the statutes—and these were two exceptions that would have been difficult *not* to make. Both involved non-Sephardi rabbis on whom the community had depended in the early stages of its "restoration." One was already part of communal legend: the founding figure Uri Halevi, the Ashkenazi rabbi from Emden who had initiated the early settlers in Amsterdam to Jewish life. When a granddaughter of his asked to enter the lottery for a dowry in 1631, the officers of the *Dotar* were faced with a dilemma. They did allow the girl to enter, explaining that they made this exception because Uri Halevi was "a person who always demonstrated great virtue and good Judaism here, and virtually introduced Judaism to this land."[11] But this formulation is striking for what it does *not* say, namely that this Ashkenazi was *the first rabbinic figure in the community and a member of the Bet Jacob congregation.* By 1631, increasingly strained relations with Ashkenazi newcomers may have made such an admission unpalatable, however obvious.

That even being a major rabbi of the community did not make one a member of "the Nation" was shown again in 1640, when the *hakham* Saul Levi Mortera applied for membership in the *Dotar*. The officers of the *Dotar* voted to admit him although the statutes permitted only those of the "Portuguese or Spanish nation" to join because, they said, Mortera had been married to a "Portuguese" woman for twenty-four years and was such a "meritorious person." Even so, they made certain that his admission would not lead to further breaches of ethnic boundaries: they denied him the privilege, granted to other members, allowing their poor female relatives living outside the northwestern European orbit to apply for dowries.[12] Thus Mortera's non-Sephardi female relatives living in Venice were excluded.

This case reveals just how crucial biological lineage was in the "Portuguese" definition of their ethnicity. It now appears most likely that Mortera was of Italian-Jewish origin.[13] However, before the publication by a modern scholar in 1984 of the *Dotar* ruling, which reveals he was not of Sephardi origin, it had been argued by scholars, on good circumstantial evidence, that Mortera was of Portuguese converso origin.[14] He had come to Amsterdam as a young man bringing the body of the ex-converso physician Eliahu Montalto from Paris for Jewish burial. In Paris he had served as rabbi to Montalto and his entourage. He wrote in Portuguese and Spanish with ease. Moreover, soon after his arrival in Amsterdam he married a "Portuguese" orphan with a dowry from the *Dotar*. He was soon appointed *hakham* of the Bet Jacob congregation, and at the time he applied for *Dotar* membership he was a *hakham* of the recently united community *K.K. Talmud Torah*.[15] If ever there was a figure who, though not born "Portuguese," *became* "Portuguese," it was Mortera, and it is significant that admission to the *Dotar* even for this figure required discussion and a vote.

The ethnic inflexibility of the *Dotar* is especially noteworthy given its flexibility in the religious sphere. As a rabbinically approved institution in a Jewish community, it could not, to be sure, dispense dowries to *any* "Portuguese" girl who happened to have Jewish blood. But the religious criteria adopted reflect a kind of latitude lacking in ethnic matters. The *Dotar* statutes understandably excluded New Christians who were inclined to Catholicism, but welcomed those who, though outwardly Catholic in practice, were sympathetic to Judaism. Such sympathizers could become members even if they were not circumcised, and were required only to believe in two basic tenets of Judaism: "the unity of the Lord of the Universe" and "the truth of His Sacred Law."[16] These beliefs were also required for girls applying for dowries.[17] The *Dotar* officers thus affirmed the Jewish component of "Portuguese" identity, and encouraged New Christians living "outside Judaism" to affirm it as well, but their demands were minimal.

To receive reliable information about applicants and potential members living in Catholic lands, the *Dotar* maintained an elaborate communications network. This was perhaps the most important aspect of its activity—certainly more significant in its impact than the three to four dowries it dispensed annually. In its first year of operation, official representatives of the *Dotar* were appointed in St. Jean de Luz, Bordeaux, Paris, Rouen, and Antwerp to recruit new members and find suitable applicants for dowries.[18] By this and less formal means the society maintained contacts with converso and ex-converso families throughout Europe, the Ottoman Empire, and North Africa; later in the century it developed ties with families in the Americas as well.[19] The *Dotar* officers thus had a perhaps unequaled contemporary overview of the converso diaspora. Unfortunately, most of the material they collected and processed each year in order to evaluate applicants from a financial, moral, and religious point of view has not been preserved.

Penetrating forbidden territory as it did, the *Dotar* was a concrete expression of the freedom and power of the Amsterdam community. The society did not operate in the Peninsula but was active in Antwerp, where crypto-Jews were exposed to inquisitorial prosecution, as well as in France, where Jewish practice was illegal and could be dangerous. In Antwerp, members were recruited by means of a procedure that ensured the secrecy of the membership. It may be recalled that Isaac de Pinto's grandfather Manuel Alvares Pinto became a secret member of the *Dotar* in 1616 while living in Antwerp.[20] Such secret members (*secretos*) were represented by an acquaintance or family member in Amsterdam, who would sign in place of the *secreto* where required. The name of the *secreto* would be placed in a sealed envelope and would be revealed only if he (or his offspring) subsequently settled in a "land of Judaism."[21] The number of *secretos* was small, but their importance transcended their numbers.[22] They symbolized the solidarity of the diaspora and—no less important—the power of the Amsterdam community to outmaneuver its enemies.

The *Dotar* may have crossed boundaries in order to reach crypto-Jews, but it was not simply a vehicle of ethnic pride. It was an ambassador, so to speak, for a normative, halakhically anchored Portuguese-Jewish community. In fact its statutes provided that a rabbinically trained member be appointed whom the society's officers could call on to assist them with his rabbinic knowledge (*sua doctrina e sciencia*).[23] This *hakham* of the society had no formal authority, but his opinion would not have been ignored. The first to serve in this role was Rabbi Joseph Pardo, the most prominent rabbinic figure in Amsterdam in 1615.[24]

This gave clear rabbinic sanction to a body that perhaps needed it more than others. As we have seen, the society accepted as members and potential recipients of dowries persons who were outwardly practicing Catholics. This was not in itself inconsistent with Jewish law. Rather, it reflected a distinction contemporary rabbinic scholars made between conversos who lived in Catholic lands, on the one hand, and emigres to "lands of Judaism" or "lands of freedom" who resisted rejudaization (including circumcision), on the other. Conversos living in Catholic lands (other than Italy) were generally regarded as "infants taken captive among the gentiles," a status with specific rabbinic ramifications. These persons were not held responsible for their failure to observe Jewish law, since they had been raised from infancy "outside Judaism." In the words of Samuel Aboab, a Venetian rabbinic authority of the second half of the seventeenth century, the negative status of apostate was given only to "those particular persons who were forcibly converted and had previously been Jews, who understood the nature of the Jewish tradition." But "their children and later descendants who did not know and never saw the light of the Torah, what is the difference between them and an infant taken captive among the gentiles?"[25] Such persons were to be treated with kindness and with the hope that they would one day escape "captivity" and join a Jewish commu--

nity. In effect, then, different norms were applied to these conversos than to emigres who had reached free soil and had contact with a Jewish community—who had, that is, been exposed to the "light of the Torah" and moreover could undergo circumcision, if they were male, without putting themselves in danger.

This delicate legal distinction did not always temper angry feelings about those who lingered in "lands of idolatry." Extremely instructive, in this respect, is the correspondence of the ex-converso Eliahu Montalto in Venice with an in-law and paterfamilias who had fled to France with his family from the Peninsula. Montalto wrote several letters to this relative to persuade him to revert to Judaism; but in each successive letter, as he failed to get the desired response, Montalto became more impatient and intolerant.[26] In the third of his four letters he wrote that it pained him to see "a man of the seed of Israel" who was so learned (his relative was a physician) but so "blind in divine matters."[27] For those like Montalto who were deeply committed to the rejudaization of "the Nation," such lack of cooperation could only be explained as weakness of character, opportunism, or obtuseness in religious matters.

Revealing of the collective ambivalence of practicing Jews in Amsterdam toward converso relatives in the Peninsula are the terms of wills they left. Some testators disinherited relatives who remained in the Peninsula (or, in one case, a niece who became a nun in Italy). Others left bequests to such relatives, conditional on their leaving the Peninsula to live "in Judaism." Still others left bequests to such relatives with no conditions.[28]

Rabbinic and communal authorities confirmed the intuitive feeling of many ex-conversos that a distinction should be maintained between those who had "returned" and those who dallied "outside Judaism." Even the most unjudgmental rabbinic onlooker would not have put Jewishly identifying conversos living in "captivity" on a par with practicing Jews in a Jewish community. The need for such a distinction was made explicit in the decision of 1645, mentioned in chapter four, prohibiting the recitation in the synagogue of the *hashkavah* prayer for the deceased on behalf of a person who died "outside Judaism," for, as the entry explained, it was "a great public disgrace to treat those who died without the sign [of the Lord] [*sem o firmamento*] as equal to those who died with the sign [i.e., circumcision]." An exception was made only in the case of an uncircumcised person who died at sea directly en route to a "land of Judaism."[29]

More complex were cases involving the living. In 1640, the *Mahamad* received a request to help ransom "a Portuguese boy of our Nation" who was being held captive in Tunis. But the boy was not circumcised. Presumably the *hakhamim* were consulted as to whether money earmarked for the redemption of captives could be used to secure the release of someone living "outside Judaism." This was clearly an emotionally charged issue. It was resolved by offering to send a large sum toward the boy's redemption, on condition that he be circumcised immediately after his release.[30]

A similar policy of conditional eligibility for benefits was adopted in the many *Dotar* cases involving persons living "outside Judaism." There was the case of the eldest son of a deceased *Dotar* member whose father had lived in a Jewish community while he, the son, was living in a Catholic land. Such a person could not inherit his father's membership (as he otherwise would in most cases) until he emigrated and settled in a Jewish community. A rabbinic ruling was made, however, that he was not to be cut off from the inheritance. In keeping with the understanding that this son was a Jew and a potential emigre to a Jewish community, his father's membership was reserved for him to inherit as long as he was alive, even if he had younger brothers living in a Jewish community.[31] A similar approach was adopted in the matter of dowries. A girl might enter the annual lottery for a dowry even if she was living "outside Judaism." But she could not, if she was a winner, receive the sum set aside for her until she had married a circumcised Jew according to Jewish law.[32] This virtually required the recipient (and her groom, if he had not done so) to resettle in a place where Judaism was practiced. The conditions the rabbis and *Mahamad* posed made it clear that halakhic requirements, while sometimes flexible, ultimately outweighed ethnic loyalties in cases of conflict.

Halakhic demands did not, however, impede most areas of interaction between the rejudaized community and the New Christians. The most routine activity uniting members of the "Portuguese" diaspora was commercial. While these ties clearly contributed to maintaining such a diaspora, they were primarily instrumental, and did not give spiritual or emotional value to collective existence. It was in the realms of welfare and proselytizing activity that the value of the group was affirmed.

When we look at the diaspora-wide activity of the Amsterdam community in these realms, what stands out is the concentration of effort in the communities of southwest France. Again, the *Dotar* offers the best source of information. It was not all gratifying. Despite the confident stance of the statutes anticipating global membership, the *Dotar* had little success in attracting members outside the Amsterdam-Hamburg orbit.[33] But dowries were another matter. By far the largest number of outside applications were from France. Indeed, in the early years of the *Dotar*'s activity, the *majority* of applications were from France (though after that the great majority of applications came from families in the Amsterdam-Hamburg area). In the 1617 *pauta* (list of approved applicants), 37 out of a total of 66 applicants were from St. Jean de Luz (a French town on the Spanish border), while 23 were from Amsterdam and 5 were relatives of members[34] living in the Mediterranean area.[35] New Christians living in France, it would seem, had a special place in the life of the rejudaized "Portuguese."

There were both demographic and socioeconomic reasons for the conspicuous place of applicants from France. The poverty-stricken among those who fled the Peninsula tended to choose the least expensive route of exit and often ended their journey in settlements close to the Spanish border, particularly in St. Jean de Luz, Bayonne, Biarritz, Bidache, La Bastide, and Peyrehorade.[36] A French government report of 1636 concerning the New Christians in Bordeaux reported that 93 of the 260 "Portuguese" living in the city were poor.[37] And among those concentrated in small towns near the French-Spanish border, the degree of poverty was undoubtedly greater than that in Bordeaux. Lacking funds to continue elsewhere, and without a communal structure to which to appeal for relief, these emigres were quite isolated and helpless. The situation is described (no doubt with some exaggeration) in the memoirs of a local gentile resident (c. 1660):[38]

> Less than forty years ago there were not six families of this religion in Bourg St. Esprit [Bayonne]. Today there are more than four hundred, but of this number, there are scarcely ten who are reasonably prosperous. All the rest live only off charitable funds that they collect among themselves and that their brethren in Holland and England send.

Yet large numbers of poor emigres did manage to reach Amsterdam, which became an attractive destination as news spread of the support the Portuguese-Jewish community provided its poor. In some cases, wealthier emigres may have paid for passage to Amsterdam for the poor. In February, 1617, two "Portuguese" merchants in Amsterdam received instructions from three "Portuguese" merchants located elsewhere (apparently in southwest France) to hire a ship which was to sail from Amsterdam to St. Jean de Luz, where it was to take on as many passengers as possible with all of their belongings.[39] The organization of such a voyage—and there were other "mass" voyages like this one[40]—was in itself an act that reflected collective concern and responsibility.

But the arrival of such a ship would not have been greeted with unadulterated joy by the communal leaders in Amsterdam. While the community was relatively wealthy, the burden of caring for the poor—some chronically poor, some impoverished by inquisitorial confiscations or the death of the breadwinner—became increasingly difficult to bear. By 1618, toward the end of the Twelve Years Truce with Spain, with war about to be resumed, wealthy merchants were leaving Amsterdam—many for Hamburg, where they could carry on their trade with the Peninsula.[41] The community was faced with a growing population of poor along with a diminishing population of prosperous merchants to support them.

It was in this period that the practical problems of being the "mother" community for the entire northern "Portuguese" diaspora began to find expression. In 1617, the winners of all four of the *Dotar* dowries granted that year were, as luck would have it, from St. Jean de Luz.[42] Members of the society responded angrily and demanded a change in policy. An entry in the society's records conveys the mood: "Since this land [Holland] has been struck so hard by the poverty of needy widows and of female orphans without remedy [*faltas de remedio,* i.e., who could not marry because they had no dowry], and since last year all the dowries went to foreign girls so that those of this land have been left very disconsolate, and furthermore members are dissatisfied that the fruits of this *mizvah* [i.e., the profits from the fund] have not been distributed to girls of this land," it was unanimously decided that "the orphans and poor girls of this land shall be assured two dowries . . . , while one dowry shall be assured to outsiders [*os de fora*]."[43]

This was a recognition of the universal social principle that whatever one's larger loyalties, concern for those in one's midst comes first. The *Imposta* board, established in 1622 to deal with the increasingly burdensome welfare problems of the community, also set priorities that did not favor the "Portuguese" of southwest France. With its founding, its officers decided that the community would no longer extend aid to New Christians emigrating from France to Amsterdam, since funds for the poor "are reserved for those who have already settled here and for those coming directly from Spain, persecuted and seeking [an opportunity] to observe the laws of the Torah." Conversos in France were urged to emigrate to other "lands of Judaism" where the cost of living was lower than in Amsterdam.[44] To relieve the burden of the poor who had already arrived in Amsterdam, the *Imposta* board decided to grant a set sum of money to such persons on condition that they leave for lands at least as far away as Italy or Poland— that is, distant enough that their return to Amsterdam would be unlikely.[45] Communal leaders did not hesitate to enforce this policy; between the years 1622 and 1634 alone, they sent away 106 persons of "the Nation."[46] (Ashkenazi emigres were treated in the same fashion but, characteristically, were given smaller sums than members of "the Nation.")[47]

This did not reflect a developing callousness, but a new set of conditions. Amsterdam's communal leaders were unwilling to shoulder financial responsibility for the entire wave of "Portuguese" immigrating north from the Peninsula. But they did continue, in various ways, to offer aid to the emigres in France. These emigres, many of whom had strong Jewish inclinations, suffered not only from poverty but also from a lack of leadership, organization, and religious guidance. True, there were local figures who seem to have emerged as figures of influence. The persons appointed as representatives of the *Dotar* in St. Jean de Luz, Bordeaux, Rouen, Paris, and Nantes were undoubtedly informal authority figures in their settlements.[48] Indeed, the *Dotar* representative in Rouen, Antonio de Casseres (a relative and business partner of the Curiel brothers), was reported to have been called the "Jewish pope" by the French inhabitants of that town.[49] But such figures had no real authority and could not impose discipline or collect taxes.

In an effort to alleviate some of the problems of the French converso judaizers, various Jewish communities including Amsterdam sent emissaries to provide religious instruction and other services. Our best knowledge is from Rouen in the early 1630s, when the "Portuguese" colony there became the focus of an ecclesiastical—and then royal—investigation.[50] According to one report, two Jews from Amsterdam—Moses Montalto, son of the well-known physician Eliahu Montalto, and Rafael Buendia—visited Rouen in 1631 to conduct a Passover *seder* for local conversos.[51] Another document, a report by a French official from 1633, describes the activities of the person considered the key crypto-Jewish figure in Rouen, the poet João (Moses) Pinto Delgado. Delgado, the official claimed, "has with great effort learned Hebrew from two [visiting] rabbis here" and "has communicated with rabbis in Venice and other synagogues." He received money (presumably to aid the poor) from "Jews of Holland, Livorno, Venice, and other synagogues" who were passing through Rouen.[52] The reliability of such reports must naturally be questioned, but what lends them a certain credibility is the fact that the authorities dropped the case against the judaizers after the crown received a large bribe. The French authorities were clearly not obsessed with exposing judaizing among New Christians; indeed, they had encouraged their settlement knowing their judaizing inclinations.[53]

It should be stressed that not all "Portuguese" colonies in France chose the course of rejudaization. In Nantes, for example, the New Christian population was inclined to Catholicism, and cryptojudaizing died out rather quickly in the early seventeenth century.[54] But the majority of emigres in most French settlements did choose to practice Judaism, and by the late seventeenth century there was little reason for them to leave French territory. By then, they were practicing Judaism openly in organized communities. While no formal permission had been granted for them to do so, neither did officials interfere with Jewish life, and France gradually lost its status as a *terra de idolatria*.[55] Earlier in the century, the ex-conversos Eliahu Montalto and Immanuel Aboab had written impassioned letters urging conversos there to flee to *terras de judesmo* for the salvation of their souls.[56] But gradually France became a *terra de judesmo*. As late as 1663, the Amsterdam rabbi Moses Rafael d'Aguilar advised conversos in Bayonne, "Flee this Babylonia [*Fugi Fugi dessa Babilonia*] with all possible speed!" But he received back a letter explaining the great difference between France and the Peninsula in terms of the freedom to practice Judaism.[57]

As the French "Portuguese" colonies became Jewish communities, they faced some of the problems the Amsterdam "Portuguese" had experienced in the early years of the century. Indeed, Amsterdam assumed for them something of the role of authority that Venice had played earlier for Amsterdam. In 1684, for example, the rabbi of Bayonne, Haim de Mercado, wrote to Jacob Sasportas in Amsterdam to ask him to arbitrate in a dispute between him and the *parnasim* of the Bidache community.[58] This was one of many instances in which leaders of communities in southwest France appealed to Amsterdam to settle disputes or to answer halakhic questions.[59] By this time, clandestine visits and communications were unnecessary. The "Portuguese" of southwest France who lived as Jews had become, by a quiet process, an extension of the Sephardi diaspora.

It was not only New Christians in France to whom the Amsterdam community turned in the seventeenth century to aid, comfort, and rejudaize. But while it was fairly easy to proselytize and provide social assistance to New Christians in France (and, to an extent, in Antwerp), the difficulties of maintaining ties with "Portuguese" in the Peninsula were immense and involved danger for both sides. Even with its secret procedures, the *Dotar* did not attempt to establish contacts with conversos in the Peninsula. In fact crypto-Jews living in Spain and Portugal were explicitly excluded from participating in *Dotar* activities, undoubtedly to prevent exposing them to inquisitorial prosecution.[60] Despite the risks involved, however, Jews from outside the Peninsula did visit or otherwise contact conversos in Spain and Portugal.[61]

The impulse of Portuguese Jews in Amsterdam to persuade fellow "Portuguese" in the Peninsula to flee to "lands of freedom" is reflected in several urgent written messages that have been preserved, similar to those Eliahu Montalto and Immanuel Aboab addressed to New Christians in France. These messages may or may not have been delivered to the Peninsula; whatever the case, they reveal their authors' strong concern about the fate of those who lingered behind. We have already had occasion (in chapter two) to mention the poem composed in Amsterdam and addressed to Fernão Alvares Melo in Lisbon, urging him to flee before the Inquisition seized him.[62] The powerful conclusion of this poem—"Let pure self-interest move you, / Since God does not!"—reflects the author's opinion that those who stayed in the Peninsula, whatever their beliefs might be, were blind to the dangers the Inquisition posed to their lives and well-being. This theme was reiterated in two "open letters" to New Christians in Spain and Portugal composed in Amsterdam sometime before 1686 by the affluent ex-converso merchant Abraham Idaña (Gaspar Méndez del Arroyo). Both letters were intended to expose the self-delusion, as Idaña saw it, which held New Christians in the Peninsula.

Idaña's most scathing criticism and alarming prediction concerned the very wealthy conversos who, enthralled by their own *grandeza*, had no intention of giving up a privileged way of life. These persons were "abominable in the eyes of God," and divine punishment would come to them through the Inquisition, which would leave them languishing in its prisons, tortured to confess whatever the inquisitors needed to hear in order to confiscate their possessions, while their wives and children begged in the streets. (The Inquisition would seize the less privileged as well, to exact from them denunciations of the wealthy.) Like the author of the poem to Melo, Idaña saw both religious and practical reasons for fleeing: if not to serve God, then out of self-interest. Outside the Peninsula, the emigre could live in contentment, free of constant fear, and rewarded by God with worldly comforts.[63]

In his second letter, Idaña refuted certain theological arguments conversos used to absolve themselves of guilt for staying in the Peninsula. He attacked the notion which we examined in the last chapter, namely that it is enough to serve God in one's heart. This, Idaña wrote, was "a gross abuse, for the Law was given in order that it be observed." It was a particularly grave sin, Idaña continued (and in this he was echoing converso preoccupations and conflicts) to remain uncircumcised. One must flee to lands of freedom and be circumcised without delay. Nor should one delude oneself that good deeds could compensate for failure to observe the Law. Performing deeds of charity under such circumstances was (here Idaña used a rabbinic expression) like "immersing oneself [in waters of purification] with an impure creature in one's hand."[64]

Indirect evidence suggests that ex-conversos also made such efforts when they covertly visited the Peninsula. Since this evidence comes mainly from Inquisition files, it is spotty and less than wholly reliable. If we are to believe the records, Jews from outside the Peninsula engaged in several types of activity: disseminating literature on Judaism in the Peninsula, circumcising conversos, engaging in theological discussions, and attempting to persuade conversos to leave Spain. A 1673 report by an inquisitorial spy in Madrid described to the inquisitor-general how conversos living in Bayonne and Peyrehorade traveled to Spain under assumed names, either for commercial purposes or "in order to introduce Judaism to our New Christians who are ignorant of it, and to seduce them to leave for France or the northern countries."[65]

The carrying out of such activities was not a product of the inquisitorial imagination (which may, however, have exaggerated their extent). We have already discussed the evidence from communal registers recording the punishment and penance of merchants from Amsterdam who traveled to the Peninsula.[66] Surely while there they would have visited their business correspondents, relatives, and old friends—and, if they were so inclined, urged them to emigrate. While most such visitors were violating communal regulations by visiting the Peninsula, in some cases persons apparently acted with the approval of communal authorities. In the 1630s, *mohelim* (men trained to perform ritual circumcision) from Amsterdam were active in Castile, presumably with communal approval. Evidence given before the inquisitorial tribunal in Toledo in 1635 reveals that a *mohel* named Isaac Farhi from Amsterdam had circumcised conversos (probably of Portuguese origin) in Castile. At the time of the investigation, a witness reported that he had himself been circumcised by this *mohel* while in Amsterdam, and that he saw the same *mohel* in Madrid eight days before his testimony. "He comes here [to Madrid]," said the witness, "for no other purpose than to perform circumcisions in this city and elsewhere in Spain." He added that the *mohel* was paid handsomely for his work.[67] This story is corroborated by a witness for the Inquisition in Brazil who claimed that during his stay in Amsterdam in 1635 he had heard from the none-too-discreet Menasseh ben Israel that "every year certain Jews leave Holland for Madrid and for many other places in Spain in order to circumcise New Christians."[68] In such efforts as these, the "Portuguese" emigres in Amsterdam consistently demonstrated toward those who remained in the Peninsula a sense of collective responsibility and kinship. But their attachment to those who either did not wish to or could not share in the reconstruction of collective life was, as we have noted, conflicted. In principle, the ideologues of the "Portuguese" diaspora wished for the "return of the captives"—all of them. But faced with a flood of impoverished emigres from France, the hard-headed communal leaders drew a line. Their refusal to welcome the needy with open arms was partly a matter of financial self-interest (a key issue for any group) and partly a matter of self-image, a need to maintain a community that reflected their belief in "Portuguese" social superiority. (To be sure, they undertook to guide poor emigres to "lands of Judaism"—*other* lands.) Toward those who had no intention of "returning," the deeply committed among the rejudaized sometimes expressed anger and frustration. But the "Portuguese" elite in Amsterdam never hesitated to recognize either the destitute or the uncommitted of their "lineage" as anything but fellow "Members of the Nation."

By some combination of reflection and intuition, the communal leaders in Amsterdam were able to weave their attachment to "the Nation" into their construction of a normative Jewish community. To be sure, as the *Dotar* statutes and other measures demonstrate, communal expressions of ethnic solidarity with "the Nation" were hedged with halakhic restrictions. But the rabbinic leadership was sufficiently wise to accept the powerful, deep-rooted "Portuguese" allegiances of their congregants (which they sometimes shared), as long as they served ends consistent with Jewish life.

The Sephardi Diaspora and the Boundaries of "the Nation"

The ethnic insularity of Amsterdam's Portuguese Jews, expressed in their continuing identification with the "Portuguese Nation" and in their aloofness toward Ashkenazim, has often been noted by scholars. What has gone unobserved, however, is that in dealing with another group, the communal leadership quietly altered the meaning of "the Nation" and actually expanded its boundaries.

In the original sense of the term, being a member of "the Nation" meant being a judeoconverso or the descendant of judeoconversos in Portugal or Spain. What gave the group its identity was its particular history of forced conversion, assimilation, rejection, stigmatization, and inquisitorial persecution. Everyone who belonged to "the Nation" had shared in this experience to one degree or another. Occasionally members of Old Christian society referred to members of the group in more specific terms, such as "Men of the Hebrew Nation [*gente da nação hebrea*]" or "the Men of Commerce [*homens de negócios*]." But these did not capture the predicament conveyed by the elliptical term—the predicament of possessing an indeterminate identity. On rare occasions a somewhat more precise term was used, as when a Portuguese converso referred in inquisitorial testimony to "all the people of the Nation of *New Christians* [*todas as pessoas da Nação dos Christãos Novos*]."[69] But this, too, was not entirely accurate, since descendants of converted Moors were also known as "New Christians." Everyone knew, in any case, what "the Nation" meant.

On new soil in Amsterdam, however, conditions changed, and so, to some degree, did conceptions of affiliation to "the Nation." Most striking was the quiet inclusion of a group that had never shared the converso experience— the "old" Sephardim of the Mediterranean, descendants of the fifteenth-century exiles from Spain. This semantic (and to some degree sociological) change was never explicitly declared. But it did become an unwavering principle of policy. Communal and *Dotar* statutes that excluded persons who were not of "the Nation" from aspects of communal life did not exclude persons of "old" Sephardi origin. The latter were incorporated, at least statutorily, into the *nação*. It was taken for granted, for example, that Rabbi Joseph Pardo, of nonconverso Sephardi origins, was a member of the *nação* and as such was eligible to be a member (and indeed the *hakham*) of the *Dotar*, just as it was taken for granted that his granddaughter in Salonica belonged to the *nação*, and as such was eligible to apply for a dowry from the *Dotar*.[70] One "old" Sephardi figure—Jacob Sasportas from North Africa—served in an official or nonofficial rabbinic capacity not only in the Portuguese-Jewish community in Amsterdam, but in two other Portuguese-Jewish communities as well, those of Hamburg and London.[71]

Such cases were not concessions or exceptions. Given the "Portuguese" preoccupation with ethnic origins and the common origins (and languages) of the two groups, the inclusion of "old" Sephardim was a policy that required no explanation or justification. True, the descendants of the Spanish exiles and the recent refugees from the Peninsula were culturally very far apart. The contrast was especially conspicuous in Amsterdam, where members of the Portuguese-Jewish community, nearly all of them part of the wave of recent emigration from the Peninsula, came into contact with highly trained rabbinic figures from the Mediterranean Sephardi world. But however great the differences, there were good reasons for the "Portuguese" to affiliate themselves with the "old" Sephardim. Being members of the "Portuguese Nation" might mean a great deal for Portuguese Jews among themselves, but to other Jews of the diaspora it meant little. Being Sephardi, in contrast, had real weight in Jewish society. It was a rabbinically recognized and sanctioned status with significance in the realms of liturgy and Jewish law.[72] It conferred rabbinic respectability.

Affirming their identification with the "old" Sephardim also served another, perhaps more profound, function for the "Portuguese" of Amsterdam, who placed so high a value on lineage and tradition yet were unable to claim continuity with the medieval Spanish-Jewish tradition. By establishing ties with old Mediterranean Sephardi communities, the rejudaizing community was able to graft itself, so to speak, back to its "authentic" Spanish trunk and roots. It was this need to be rooted in continuous Sephardi traditions that led the community in its early years to turn to the Sephardi world (especially to Venice, but also to Livorno and Salonica) for institutional models, figures of authority to resolve conflicts, and trained rabbis. By the second half of the seventeenth century, the need to "import" from the Mediterranean was greatly diminished. The Portuguese-Jewish community of Amsterdam was producing its own rabbis and, as a result of economic and political circumstances, was thrust into a position of power within the Jewish world as a whole. Nevertheless, the Sephardi communities of the Mediterranean continued to represent for it an important link with unbroken ancestral traditions.

"Portuguese" identification with the Sephardi world was sometimes expressed with a subtly deceptive turn of phrase. An author would refer to the entire group of Jews who had suffered at the hands of Iberian regimes as "those of the Castilian and Portuguese exile" (in Portuguese, *judeus do desterro de Espanha e Portugal*). Thus, by a kind of semantic sleight-of-hand, the Expulsion of the Spanish Jews in 1492 was conflated with two centuries of converso flight from the Peninsula. Immanuel Aboab, for example, in his *Nomologia*, expanded on the theme of "the Hebrew exiles of Castile and Portugal [*los destierros de los Hebreos de Castilla y Portugal*]," joining together Spanish exiles and conversos in what would seem to be a single historical episode.[73] (The ambiguity of the terms *desterro* in Portuguese and *destierro* in Spanish, which can mean either "expulsion" or "exile," facilitated this rhetorical fusing of the two groups.) While there was indeed a link between the persecution of Jews and the persecution of conversos in the Peninsula, the wish to see the fate of the Spanish exiles and the Portuguese conversos as essentially the same was primarily a "Portuguese" wish.

There were reasons for such rhetoric, just as there were reasons to allow "old" Sephardi girls to apply to the *Dotar*. But these adaptations did not fundamentally change the sense of affiliation among the Amsterdam emigres and their descendants. In common parlance, the term *nação* continued to mean "Portuguese." The repeated use in ex-converso apologetic and polemical literature of the term *nossa nação portuguesa* attests to the continued centrality of this affiliation. Menasseh ben Israel wrote his *Thesouro dos dinim* "for the use of our Portuguese nation"[74]—not for the Sephardi "nation," most of whose members did not need such books. Likewise, in his Portuguese exposition of the 613 fundamental precepts of Jewish law, Abraham Farar identified himself on the title page as "Abraham Pharar, Judeu do desterro de Portugal"[75]—a member of the *Portuguese* exile he was addressing.

The wish to be identified with the Sephardi world, then, by no means displaced the more deep-rooted sense of being "Portuguese," but rather coexisted with it. Context determined what *nossa nação* meant. What it meant to a group of Portuguese-Jewish merchants discussing arrests in the Peninsula would not be what it meant to the same people when, as *Dotar* officials, they were drawing up a list of candidates for dowries. Such different boundaries suggested by a single term, depending on its context, are not alien to us. We mean one thing when we say, "They're a family of four," and quite another when we say, "They're having family for the holidays." There is no need to explain the difference, just as the "Portuguese" felt no need to define the different connotations of the term *nação*.

Demographic realities prevented any real fusion in Amsterdam of "old" Sephardim and "Portuguese." "Old" Sephardim were an exceptional presence. Their inclusion in the statutory definition of the *nação* in Amsterdam was, like other aspects of communal life, an inheritance from the Mediterranean Sephardi experience, in which different Sephardi types mixed freely and daily, and the boundaries between different Sephardi groups, though not entirely lost, tended to be blurred.

The obscuring of boundaries within the Sephardi world of the Mediterranean was a result of historical realities quite different from those in Amsterdam. In contrast to northern Europe, the Sephardi presence in the Mediterranean did not derive from a single wave of immigration. It was the result of complex migrations which occurred over several generations— migrations which brought together Spanish exiles (as well as pre-Expulsion conversos) and their descendants; early converso emigres from Portugal, many of whom had been among the Jewish exiles of 1492 and were

culturally indistinguishable from other exiles; and new waves of "Portuguese" emigres, each successive wave more deeply imprinted with the
converso experience than the previous one.

But any effort to distinguish discrete waves of Sephardi immigration in
the Mediterranean area is bound to be misleading. In fact, the Expulsion set
off a long period of wandering through the Mediterranean region for both
Jews and ex-conversos. Let us illustrate with the example of Venice. Emigres from the Peninsula might spend time in Venice and move on, or settle
in Venice after living for long periods in other Jewish communities in the
Mediterranean. Especially conspicuous was the movement of Sephardi
merchants from the Ottoman Empire to Venice, where they gained a
foothold as "Levantine" transients. In 1541, the Venetian authorities allowed the permanent settlement of these merchants, allotting to them an
extension of the ghetto known as the *ghetto vecchio*.[76] Their ranks undoubtedly included some "Portuguese" ex-conversos (and descendants of ex-
conversos) who had first settled in the Levant and then gravitated to Italy.
But the experience of these "Portuguese" in the Ottoman Empire would
have given them cultural traits (in dress, for example,[77] and in Jewish
practice) that made them indistinguishable from other Levantine Jews.
They would have been quite different from the ex-conversos who settled in
Venice in the 1580s after the Ferrara community broke up.[78]

The "Portuguese" never really became, then, a distinct ethnic component in the Venetian ghetto. From 1541 to 1589, conversos who arrived
directly from the Peninsula continued to claim status as "Levantines" and
joined the Levantine congregation, seeking to avoid identification as baptized persons reverting to Judaism (who were, strictly speaking, regarded
as heretics in Catholic Italy). It was only in 1589 that the Venetian government openly recognized the "Ponentine" ("western") Jews (in effect, a
euphemism for "New Christians") as distinct from the "Levantine" Jews,
thus permitting the establishment of a separate "Ponentine" congregation.[79] But by this time there was no way to differentiate clearly between
"Portuguese" and "old" Sephardim. The blurring is reflected in the terminology used to distinguish the two congregations. The "Ponentine" Jews
referred to their synagogue as "Spanish" (not "Portuguese") (*scuola Spag-
nola*); the "Levantines" referred to theirs as the *scuola Levantina*. Members of
both Sephardi congregations lived together in the crowded *ghetto vecchio*,
often cooperating at a social and organizational level.[80] The wide range of
Sephardi types in the *ghetto vecchio*—from the transient Turkish merchant
to the Italianized Levantine, from the thoroughly conditioned Jew with
converso parents or grandparents to the newly arrived refugee from the
Iberian Peninsula—encouraged mediation rather than segregation. For
many or perhaps most of the emigres from the Peninsula who settled in
Venice in the seventeenth century, being "Portuguese" did not long remain
a primary aspect of self-definition.

Did the formal communal alliance with the "old" Sephardi world have a significant impact on the ethos and character of the Amsterdam community? Probably not. However powerful the impact of Mediterranean Sephardi realities on the development of Amsterdam's Portuguese-Jewish institutions, ultimately the exclusivist impulses of the "Portuguese" in northern Europe proved more powerful than the formal institutional habits they adopted from the south. The most intense experience of belonging continued to be that of belonging to the *Portuguese* "Nation." The presence of the occasional "old" Sephardi did not upset this fundamental sociological and emotional reality. Northern Europe remained the sphere of "Portuguese" Sephardim, while the "old" Sephardim remained concentrated in the Mediterranean region. There was no danger that Amsterdam's Portuguese Jews would be dominated culturally by their mostly distant "old" Sephardi cousins. Everyday life in Amsterdam continued to unfold in a "Portuguese" orbit, with its distinctive converso ethos.

Conclusion

To build a community that would survive, Amsterdam's "Portuguese" elite wrestled with a number of problems, from the glaring challenges of heresy to the more delicate issue of relations with Dutch Reformed clergy. No problem, however, was more critical in the making of this community than that of balancing the two clusters of ideas about collective self, one associated with Jewish religion and peoplehood, the other with "the Nation." The problem was not clearly defined even by communal leaders who dealt with it, but nonetheless dominated the dynamics of community building. Other issues, important as they might have been, tended to be corollary to this one: the ambivalence about Ashkenazi Jews; the policies adopted toward New Christians who lived "outside Judaism"; the enforcement of halakhic norms within the community; and so on. In dealing with the entire array of issues that arose around this core problem, communal leaders revealed two somewhat conflicting (though not contradictory) aims: first, building a community belonging fully to the rabbinic-Jewish world, and second, preserving a distinct identity based on quasi-ethnic foundations alien to rabbinic Judaism. The first aim was pursued primarily through institution building and intercommunal relations. The second, though given institutional expression in the *Dotar*, was mainly sustained at an informal level—in the language and lore of the community, in ties to friends and relatives throughout the "Portuguese" diaspora, and in shared responses to news of arrests or convictions in the Peninsula.

In general, communal leaders seemed unaware of any conflict between these aims. The sense of triumph that accompanied their collective rejudaization tended to overshadow the issues that remained unresolved. When necessary (as in the case of Saul Levi Mortera's admission to the *Dotar*), a measure was taken to resolve quietly an obvious conflict. As in any society, practical solutions were found when theoretical quandaries arose. But the need to leave unacknowledged the very fact of conflict was particularly acute among the Portuguese Jews, who wished to represent their "return" to Judaism as an unproblematic, natural event.

It was thus only on rare occasions that communal leaders addressed the issue of the complex relationship between "Portuguese" and Jewish identity. When they did make an attempt to distinguish the two aspects of identity, they seem to have taken the path of detaching ethnicity from religion. Menasseh ben Israel made such a distinction when he introduced the visionary converso António de Montesinos (Aharon Levi) in his work *The Hope of Israel* (1650): Menasseh described Montesinos as "Portuguese in nation, and a Jew in religion."[1]

It is striking to find such a distinction between religious and ethnic affiliation among seventeenth-century Jews. Indeed, more than a century would pass before European Jews, pressured by demands to demonstrate national allegiance, would begin actively to confine their Jewish affiliation to the sphere of religion. But Menasseh's formulation was not a response to that dilemma. It was an effort to identify coherently a person (and, by extension, an entire group) who had undergone an extreme cultural transition.

Other sources, too, attest to such a dualistic course of explanation. One of these is the first of two letters we have mentioned, written in 1683 by the Amsterdam merchant Abraham Idaña to an inquisitorial official in Madrid. Wrote Idaña:

> In this city there are . . . two synagogues in which the Jews of the German Empire, known as *tudescos,* gather to worship along with Polish Jews. They observe the same holy Law of Moses with its rituals as the Portuguese, but in matters of governance [*en la política*] they are very different, because they are of an alien native character [*estraña naturaleza*], and for this reason, even if today many of them are wealthy, they are held in low esteem, for in fact they are debased in spirit.[2]

Particularly striking in this passage is Idaña's conviction that the "Portuguese" are different from Ashkenazim because Ashkenazim are of an alien *naturaleza* (literally, "nature")—a seventeenth-century term (in Portuguese, *natureza*) that eludes easy translation when used in this particular sense. The term thus used reflects an idea about the origin of differences in collective character that was discussed in contemporary Iberian writings, an idea more often associated with Montesquieu and the eighteenth century—namely, that the distinctive customs and manners observed in different peoples are a consequence of their milieux. The term *naturaleza*, then, could be used to refer to the collective characteristics produced by a certain milieu. Thus, for example, the statesman Cristobal Suarez de Figueroa wrote that "Mores go hand in hand with the nature of the place, with various countries producing various natures [*naturalezas*] in man."[3] Similarly, the statement of Luis Alfonso de Carballo, "I could give you a thousand examples showing that the place where we are born produces in us a certain nature [*naturaleza*] which constantly inclines us toward that which has produced us."[4]

This notion of an acquired Iberian identity appears to have been accepted implicitly by Portuguese Jews, and it is striking to find them expressing it explicitly. Interestingly, a formulation very similar to Idaña's is found in an entry scrawled in a record book of the "Portuguese" community of Hamburg. It is precisely the casual nature of these remarks that makes them such convincing evidence. They refer to an embarrassing incident that occurred in 1670. The "Portuguese" leadership of Hamburg had investigated a report that a member of the community had taken it upon himself to visit a new pastor in Hamburg. The latter apparently arrived at the pastor's house without prior notice, for he came at an hour when the pastor was not accustomed to receiving visitors, and was therefore turned away. The following was the interesting conclusion of the *Mahamad*, which had failed to uncover the identity of the culprit:

> It may very well be that the elders of the Ashkenazim were the ones who did this [that is, sent the man]; for although they belong to our nation, and the Torah is one, this [unity] does not extend to matters of conduct [*governo*].[5]

The appeal to the Portuguese Jews of the idea of possessing a Portuguese "essence" must have been great, given their pride in their Iberian linguistic and cultural traits. Presumably it appealed to conversos in the Peninsula as well as outside. A wealthy New Christian in Lisbon, Duarte Gomes Solís— one of the many *arbitristas* urging the Spanish monarch to introduce mercantilist reforms—had adopted this idea, and indeed used it to challenge indirectly the ideological basis of Iberian racialism. The Portuguese conversos, he argued, gained from their Iberian experience the tools which rendered them particularly valuable to the state, yet fled the Peninsula and obtained high office elsewhere. He concluded:[6]

> These are the reasons why the Men of the Portuguese Nation may pride themselves on the character [*natureza*] which Portugal bestows on them, [giving them] the most highly esteemed glory—so highly [esteemed], that is, in the countries of [other] Christian rulers, and so little in their own country [*propria patria*].

Something of this idea seems to have entered the thinking of the Amsterdam "Portuguese" when they contemplated what, indeed, it meant to be "Portuguese" after reverting to Judaism. It was precisely in the area of mores, customs, and manners—*natureza*—that they felt themselves to be Iberian, even if they observed the Law of Moses.

The key to sustaining a "Portuguese" legacy within a rabbinic community, then, was the idea that the traits and ideas encoded in the term "Portuguese" were different—or at least not always congruent—with the traits and ideas encoded in the term "Jew." Jewish ancestry dictated one's religious loyalties; Portuguese experience determined one's behavioral traits. Yet both clusters of traits, while at times they could be distinguished and separated, were capable of coexisting and even merging.

Harmony, or at least the expectation of it, was provided in the realm of theology and myth. Themes of exile and redemption which were a key element of crypto-Jewish theology in the Peninsula[7] were also themes that had assumed unusual potency throughout the Jewish world in the seventeenth century.[8] It was through these themes, elaborated about a uniquely converso core, that members of the Portuguese Jewish intellectual elite of northwestern Europe were able to anticipate the resolution of the tensions inherent in their condition. It was for them an unfortunate fact that many of their fellow conversos tarried in the Peninsula, practicing Catholicism out of prudence, conviction, or inertia. The divine scenario ensured, however, that they too would one day "return," bringing to an end their condition of spiritual exile.[9]

Such expectations had the potential for resolving other tensions as well. The conditions of exile and dispersion had given rise to different Jewish "nations" with limited natural affinity between them. But viewed on a wider stage, these different Jewish "nations" were playing out a single drama. The specific experience of the "Portuguese Nation" was an integral part of the unfolding story of exile and redemption that touched all groups of Jews in all ages.[10] Full reconciliation would come in the days of messianic redemption.

But at a concrete everyday level, the tensions were far from resolved. A superficial look at "Portuguese" patterns of behavior might lead to the convenient formula, echoing Menasseh's, that members of this group were sociologically "Portuguese" and religiously Jewish. This, however, would be a distorted representation of the fluid, situationally determined way in which the ex-conversos of northwestern Europe actually behaved and thought.

True, they stubbornly maintained the system of social ties they had established in the Peninsula, and indeed reinforced it. But the need to be part of the wider Jewish world, even if at a distance, was a real and urgent one; gaining a recognized, legitimate role in that world was a goal pursued persistently by the merchant-banker communal leadership. Moreover, the themes of exile and redemption, while rarely determining behavior in everyday life (except during the brief sabbatian enthusiasm), did hover in the mind and were part of the constantly reconfigured bundle of notions of self and group among the "Portuguese."

Just as "Jewish" patterns and impulses permeated social life, so too did "Portuguese" experience invade religious life and thinking. "Converso" assumptions, formulations, and experiences informed even the most orthodox ex-converso interpretations of Jewish life.[11] Jewish life itself—not just its interpretation—adapted to the realities of "Portuguese" society. In ex-converso communities, for example, adult circumcision became a Jewish life-cycle event with no equivalent in traditional communities. Feeling at ease with the synagogue service required a process of both conditioning and deconditioning for ex-conversos that no doubt entailed frustration and, at times, resistance. Imagine, for example, the university-trained physician, fluent in Spanish, Portuguese, French, and Latin, struggling to make sense of the Hebrew characters in a prayer book, or the conscientious young woman in the gallery trying to accustom herself to a form of worship in which one did not kneel or place one's hands together in prayer. There was no escape from the legacy of the past, from conscious comparison. What is clear (and remarkable) is that for most emigres, the sense that this was, despite everything, one's natural place developed quickly.

The task of collective self-definition undertaken by the "Portuguese" elite in Amsterdam was, of course, an ongoing one—at any rate, until the *Mahamad*'s authority was sharply curtailed in the late eighteenth century. To be sure, the most fateful decisions about communal boundaries were made by 1640. But the story did not end there. Nor did it end with the rather sudden decline in the community's fortunes (and vitality) toward the end of the seventeenth century. While it is beyond the scope of this book to carefully chart the course of "Portuguese" self-perception into the eighteenth and nineteenth centuries, it would be unfortunate to conclude without suggesting in broad strokes the subsequent history of "Portuguese" ethnicity in Amsterdam.

In the early period of the community's existence examined in this book, the forces favoring the cultivation of "the Nation" as the primary reference group were quite powerful. This sense of affiliation was the only pre-existing, surviving one among the emigres in their new environment. It was reinforced by habits of language and culture with roots in the Peninsula, as well as the common experience of stigma and persecution. During the period when the community underwent rejudaization, being "Portuguese" was a source of esteem and psychological security. The communal leadership was shrewd and purposeful enough to harness this residual sense of collective self to promote the "return" of emigres to rabbinic Judaism both in Amsterdam and throughout the "Portuguese" diaspora. Indeed, Jewish communal life became the only organized structure for preserving "Portuguese" identity.

Yet by the time De Barrios published his tribute to the community, unabashedly entitled *Triumpho del govierno popular* (1683), the mental and institutional structures which had been created with so much effort were already facing severe challenges, with others to come. This was not immediately evident. The community—now numbering about 2,800 persons— was still affluent, largely self-sufficient and autonomous. Its imposing synagogue, dedicated in 1675, was a concrete symbol of its wealth and self-confidence. But in retrospect, one can see in the French invasion which interrupted the synagogue's construction in 1672 an important watershed. From this point onward, Dutch trade entered a process of permanent decline which was to have devastating consequences for the community.[12]

In the eighteenth century there were still fabulously wealthy Portuguese Jews in Amsterdam like the De Pintos and Suassos. But as the crisis of the

Dutch economy deepened, the community as a whole became increasingly impoverished. In fact, within Dutch society the "Portuguese" community was hit especially hard because of the concentration of its members in occupations connected with overseas commerce, and because of its members' continued exclusion (until 1809) from guild occupations. Communal revenues declined and then were further hit when some well-to-do merchants left for London or elsewhere. In a tract of 1748, the eighteenth-century economist Isaac de Pinto (a descendant of the Isaac de Pinto who left us an autobiography) saw no way out of the crisis except to step up the decades-old policy of financing the emigration of poor members of the community to the Dutch colonies, especially to Surinam.[13] But the situation continued to degenerate. Astonishingly, by 1799 it is estimated that more than half the members of the Portuguese-Jewish community were on poor relief.[14]

Not only diminished opportunities in overseas trade, but also the changing financial behavior of the wealthy merchant families contributed to a weakening of pan-diaspora "Portuguese" ties. Like their Dutch counterparts, the great "Portuguese" merchant families tended toward the end of the seventeenth century to withdraw from commerce and pursue what they perceived to be a more genteel rentier existence, living off the profits of their investments. If they remained financially involved with Dutch colonial trade, it was passively, through their shares in the East India Company.

The community's engagement with the "Portuguese" diaspora also waned as it ceased to absorb large numbers of immigrants from the Peninsula. Conversos continued to arrive from the Peninsula well into the eighteenth century, but their numbers dwindled sharply.[15] By the end of the seventeenth century, most conversos who wished to leave the Peninsula had done so.[16] Under these circumstances, the Amsterdam community could no longer view itself as the nerve center of the "Portuguese" diaspora.

The weakening of ties with the diaspora is reflected in the shrinking of the horizons of the *Dotar* society. The grand global aims of the founders eroded as other ties to the "Portuguese" diaspora, familial and commercial, contracted. Indeed, as early as 1658, the first signs of a narrowing geographical focus appeared. A decision was made (compatible with the prosperity of the community at the time) to double the sums of the dowries given to Amsterdam recipients, while raising up to fifty percent those given to recipients elsewhere in the region (i.e., the Netherlands and the environs of Hamburg), but freezing altogether the sums granted to recipients outside this region.[17] In the early eighteenth century, new regulations restricted the scope of the society's activity still more: the Mediterranean region was entirely excluded.[18]

And the inexorable process of constriction continued. It can be seen in the *Dotar* society as it exists today. (Astonishingly, it has survived the ravages of both nineteenth-century assimilation and twentieth-century castastrophe.) Today, it reflects nothing of its original outward-reaching aims. In the postwar period it has granted "dowries" only to Amsterdam Jews with Dutch citizenship—though also, it should be added (*mirabile dictu*), to men as well as women, Ashkenazim as well as "Portuguese."[19] The history of the *Dotar* illustrates nicely how short-lived, relatively speaking, were the impulses to preserve a "Portuguese" diaspora in the wake of the scattering of the emigres from the Peninsula.

Equally important for the collective self-image of the "Portuguese" in Amsterdam was the fact that by the late seventeenth century they were losing their demographic strength in relation to the overall Jewish population of Amsterdam. That population was becoming increasingly—indeed overwhelmingly—Ashkenazi. The "Portuguese" population peaked around the mid-eighteenth century at about 3,000. In contrast, the Ashkenazi population grew at an ever accelerating rate. It was estimated at 5,000 in 1674, at 10,000 in 1748, and at almost double that in 1780.[20] And this trend continued into the twentieth century.[21]

With the community's economic impoverishment and demographic stagnation, the influence of the Amsterdam "Portuguese" in the Jewish world at large suffered decline. So did their self-image. An anonymous "Portuguese" author wrote in 1770:[22]

> Our nation becomes poorer from year to year. Our principal commercial houses are hurt in many ways, some through bankruptcy and others through ever increasing luxury and extravagance. The middle classes have to be very cautious in their expenditure. There are no special ways to make a living and business becomes worse and worse and more insecure, especially the share transactions in which our most important men are solely concerned. Taken all in all, the Portuguese Jewish nation has had her summer and approaches her winter, while the Ashkenazi Jews, who for the most part came here in poverty, despised by us at that time (but in truth more industrious and economical than we are), are over their winter and see a prosperous time drawing near. We fall and they rise.

This passage draws a distorted picture of the Ashkenazi community (it was still shockingly poor), but reflects new perceptions and the impact of "modern" values on the author. He clearly identified with the Portuguese-Jewish nation. But he viewed it with a critical, utilitarian eye, questioning its aristocratic (or pseudo-aristocratic) values. He had evidently absorbed Enlightenment attitudes which favored efficiency and diligence and what were to be known as bourgeois ideals.

Events of the late eighteenth century, which saw the emergence of new political as well as philosophical principles, threatened the entire structure on which Portuguese-Jewish life in Amsterdam was founded. With the events of 1787 to 1813—the Patriot rebellion of 1787, the invasion of the Netherlands by the French in 1794, the reign of Louis Napoleon, and the annexation of the Netherlands to France from 1810 to 1813—the political organization of the Netherlands was radically (and in many ways permanently) transformed. The installation of a centralized government influenced by French revolutionary notions brought an end to autonomous self-government as the "Portuguese" (and Ashkenazim) of Amsterdam had known it. Among both Ashkenazim and, to a lesser extent, "Portuguese," there were persons who found the new ethos persuasive and liberating and were eager to see a greater integration of Jews into Dutch life. It was natural for such "enlightened" Jews, Portuguese and Ashkenazi, to act together (merely one more benighted taboo to break) in order to undermine the desperate efforts of the established communal leadership to resist incursions on its authority.

It was a matter of self-interest, perhaps, but also an instinctive response to the possible loss of a cherished way of life that led the leadership of both communities in Amsterdam to oppose changes in the traditional, established patterns of communal governance and education. Given the constellation of forces, it is not surprising that the Ashkenazi *parnasim* made overtures to the "Portuguese" *Mahamad* to act together with them to defend autonomy and orthodoxy. But the "Portuguese" *parnasim* just as naturally resisted such efforts.[23] Their own form of communal traditionalism was too deeply enmeshed with "Portuguese" particularism to allow them to defend the former at the cost of the latter.

In any case, the battle to retain communal autonomy was a lost cause. Powerful political forces were pressuring Jewish communities throughout Europe to relinquish their judicial and civil powers and become religious institutions with limited functions. Napoleon struck the first decisive blow in the Netherlands when the republic fell under his rule. In September 1808, six months after he had imposed a government-supervised consistorial system on the French Jews, his brother King Louis Napoleon introduced a similar system in the Netherlands. The *parnasim* were stripped of all coercive and punitive powers, and government officials were charged with negotiating reforms in Jewish life to suit the needs of the state.

In the complex negotiations that ensued after Dutch sovereignty was restored (as a constitutional monarchy) in 1813, some concessions to Jewish particularistic aspirations—both "Portuguese" and Ashkenazi—were made. In 1814, for example, the "Portuguese" were permitted to revert to independent management of their own synagogue affairs.[24] However, they did not succeed in their effort to remove their community from consistorial supervision. The *parnasim*, now subordinated to a government-backed "enlightened" Jewish elite, were reduced to mere communal functionaries. Gone were the days when they could view themselves as protectors of a great, scattered "Nation."

Internally, too, the bonds that held the "Portuguese" together as an ethnic group lost their strength. They were under severe ideological assault. The political principles of modern European states (which among other things required emancipation of the Jews, officially declared in the Netherlands on September 2, 1796) were deeply antithetical to the ideological and sociological underpinnings of "Portuguese" religio-ethnic solidarity. The paternalistic (and autocratic) leadership of the *Mahamad* had been widely accepted in a seventeenth-century community whose members revered ancestral traditions. But in the nineteenth century that leadership, stripped of its powers and contending with a system of values in which individual choice and freedom of conscience prevailed, could not continue to play such a role.

Under these conditions, communal institutions became less central to the lives of Amsterdam's "Portuguese." They continued to affirm the value of being "Portuguese," but this was achieved more and more by evoking a glorious past. While Daniel de Barrios wrote to a large extent about a community he lived in, David Franco Mendes, whose chronicle of the community was completed in 1772, wrote about a community he looked back on, often with the help of archival documents.[25]

A parallel change can be detected in the realm of language. In the seventeenth century, Portuguese was the tongue of everyday speech among members of "the Nation." By the first half of the nineteenth century, it was Dutch. To be sure, Portuguese was still spoken, but it was becoming the language of Talmud instruction and sermons.[26] In general, the task of perpetuating the "Portuguese" legacy of the community was increasingly relegated to rabbis, talmud students, communal librarians, and archivists. It was part of the job of these functionaries to preserve the memory of a collective "golden age" that was highly valued—but gone.

The Law of Moses did not fare much better than the Portuguese language in eighteenth- and nineteenth-century Amsterdam. The enthusiasm and momentum of the rejudaization effort of the seventeenth century could not be maintained indefinitely, especially when the stream of emigres ceased. To be sure, many in the community remained committed to Jewish observance. By now such persons were fully conditioned to rabbinic life. They also remained proud of the particular aspects of "Portuguese" synagogue practice. (The conservation of "Portuguese" ritual still prevails in what is left of the community, as can be witnessed on sabbaths at the recently renovated landmark synagogue—a structure still known by the Portuguese term *esnoga*.) But the religious aspect of "Portuguese" identity, fragile from the start, was challenged in the nineteenth century by trends that were a far cry from those to which Saul Levi Mortera and Orobio de Castro had responded. The secular spirit that pervaded European society, together with a diminished wish or need among later generations of Portuguese Jews to live within the orbit of "Portuguese" communal life, led to increasing apathy toward Jewish practice. Indeed, in the nineteenth century many members of the Portuguese-Jewish elite converted to Christianity. By this time they were no doubt indifferent to the horror this would have evoked in some of their forebears.

Despite the trends that have tended to erode "Portuguese" identity—the loss of economic status, the prevalence of Enlightenment ideals, the dissolution of the autonomous community, and growing indifference to religious practice—a certain sense of (admittedly attenuated) pride and solidarity has persisted quite stubbornly among the "Portuguese" in modern times. Iberian names and coats of arms are treasured even among those who have converted to Christianity.[27]

Thus a rich and complex climate of ideas which, in the conditions of seventeenth-century Amsterdam, led to the foundation of a community and the flowering of its particular "ethnic" culture, became, in the very different conditions of modern European society, a somewhat sorrowful refuge of shared memory for some and, for others, a token of inherited individual status. But that is another story.

PERSONALIA

ABOAB DA FONSECA, ISAAC, 1605–1693. Aboab was born Simão da Fonseca in Castro Daire, Portugal. As a child he and his family emigrated to St. Jean de Luz and then to Amsterdam. Aboab eventually became an outstanding student of Isaac Uziel, a Sephardi rabbi from Fez who had settled in Amsterdam. In 1626, at the age of only twenty-one, he was appointed *hakham* of the Bet Israel congregation—an achievement for both Aboab and the community, which had shown that it could now produce its own rabbis. Financial incentives may have encouraged Aboab to leave Amsterdam for Brazil after the Dutch conquest of the northeastern part of that territory. He served as *hakham* of the rapidly growing Portuguese-Jewish community in Recife from 1641 until the Portuguese reconquest of the territory in 1654. He returned to Amsterdam where he became a senior figure in the rabbinic leadership and authored a number of religious works reflecting his kabbalistic leanings.

BARRIOS, DANIEL LEVI DE (Miguel de Barrios), 1635–1701, poet and playwright. De Barrios was born in Spain of Portuguese converso parents. After a family member was condemned to death by the Inquisition, De Barrios settled in Italy, where he reverted to Judaism. After the death of his first wife he moved to Amsterdam, joined the Portuguese-Jewish community, and in 1662 remarried. But he soon took a commission as a captain in the Spanish Netherlands, and spent the next twelve years as an outwardly practicing Catholic in Brussels, though he maintained contact with the Portuguese-Jewish community in Amsterdam. After 1674, he returned to Amsterdam and lived a somewhat tortured life as a Jew. He was a prolific, if uneven, writer. Among his better-known works are *Contra la verdad no hay fuerza* (before 1672), memorializing victims of the Inquisition, and *Triumpho del govierno popular* (1683), a flattering portrayal of the Portuguese-Jewish community in Amsterdam.

BELMONTE, JACOB ISRAEL (Diogo Nunes Belmonte), 1572/73–1629. Belmonte emigrated from Madeira to Amsterdam in the late 1590s. An ex-converso eager to adopt Jewish life, he became one of the key figures in the institutional life of the early community. Like many other "Portuguese," he traded in colonial commodities, and by 1614 he was the wealthiest member of the community. He apparently produced some poetry, which has been lost, but also kept a diary in which he recorded major family events (mainly births) after his marriage to Guiomar Nunes in 1608. The diary offers insight into Belmonte's simple piety and increasing familiarity over the years with rabbinic Judaism.

COSTA, URIEL DA (Gabriel da Costa), c. 1583–1640. Born in Porto, Portugal, into a converso merchant family, Da Costa was early on driven by a searching religious impulse. He studied theology at Coimbra and became a minor church official. He and other members of his family emigrated to Amsterdam in 1615, where they adopted Judaism. Uriel and his brother Jácome soon resettled in Hamburg, where Uriel engaged in commerce (mainly the sugar trade) under the name Adam Romez. In 1616 Uriel sent a tract challenging rabbinic (as distinct from biblical) law to rabbinic authorities in Venice. For this he was excommunicated in 1618. By 1623 Da Costa was in Amsterdam, where he published an attack on rabbinic tradition. His social isolation, however, led him to seek a reconciliation with the community in 1633, but his doubts led him to even more radical ideas, including rejection of the divinity of the Torah. He was again excommunicated, and again, after seven years, attempted reconciliation with the Amsterdam community. By his own account (the authenticity of which is problematic), the humiliating ceremony of penitence to which he was subjected in the synagogue led to his suicide in 1640.

CURIEL, DAVID (Lopo da Fonseca Ramires), 1594–1666. Curiel was born into a crypto-Jewish family in Portugal, a son of the eminent Lisbon physician Jeronimo Nunes Ramires and Maria da Fonseca, a sister-in-law of Eliahu Montalto. Curiel settled in Amsterdam in the 1610s and remained associated with the Bet Jacob congregation, supporting the faction of David Farar at the time of the 1618 split. Along with his brother Jacob Curiel (Duarte Nunes da Costa) and other relatives, he contributed to creating a far-flung Portuguese-Jewish family commercial empire. Interestingly, several members of the family served the Portuguese and Spanish crowns in diplomatic and mercantile roles. Especially prominent in the service of the Portuguese crown was Jacob Curiel's son Moses (Jeronimo Nunes da Costa). But the Curiel family, while pursuing its own commercial, diplomatic, and social interests, devoted considerable energy to supporting Jewish communal institutions in Amsterdam.

FARAR, DAVID (Francisco Lopes Henriques), 1573–1624. Farar was one of the earliest university-trained physicians in the Amsterdam "Portuguese" community, as well as a merchant. He had settled in Amsterdam by 1608, as we know from an account of his religious disputation with the English Protestant theologian Hugh Broughton that year, and became a leader of the Bet Jacob congregation. A rationalist in religious beliefs, Farar was attacked in 1618 by a more traditionalist faction led by Joseph Pardo, whose members broke off from Bet Jacob to form a new congregation (Bet Israel).

HALEVI, URI (Philips Joosten), c. 1544- ?. An Ashkenazi rabbi from Emden, Halevi settled in Amsterdam with his son Moses in 1602 at the age of about sixty, and there attended to the ritual needs of the early Portuguese-Jewish community. In 1622, the elderly Halevi was still in Amsterdam, but apparently returned to Emden shortly thereafter.

MELO, DAVID ABENATAR (Fernão Alvares Melo), 1569–1632. Born and baptized in Fronteira in 1569, Melo was active as a merchant in Lisbon. He was arrested and imprisoned there in April 1609, on charges of judaizing, which he denied. After incarceration and torture he was released in August 1611, but was forbidden to leave the country without permission from the Inquisition. By

June 1612, he was in Amsterdam with his wife, where he joined the Bet Jacob congregation and engaged in the shipping trade. His brother António (Eliahu) had already settled in Amsterdam, as did a number of other members of the family. Melo set up a press in Amsterdam which published a prayer book for the High Holidays in Spanish translation (1617) and a Spanish translation of the Haggadah (1622). In 1626 he published his own translation and deeply personal adaptation of Psalms. He died in Hamburg in 1632, and was buried with his wife in the Portuguese Jewish cemetery there.

MONTALTO, ELIAHU (Felipe Rodrigues), d. 1616. Born to converso parents in Castelo Branco, Portugal, Montalto was active in crypto-Jewish circles in the Peninsula. He studied medicine at Salamanca, but fled the Peninsula and practiced medicine first in Florence, then in Venice where he reverted openly to Judaism. In 1611 he became the personal physician to Queen Marie de Médicis in Paris, having obtained permission to live openly as a Jew. He took the young Saul Levi Mortera to France with him. When Montalto died suddenly in 1616, Mortera accompanied Montalto's body to Amsterdam for burial in the Ouderkerk cemetery.

MORTERA, SAUL LEVI, c. 1596–1660. Mortera, apparently an Italian Jew (i.e., neither Sephardi nor Ashkenazi), was born in Venice and studied under the great Italian rabbi Leon de Modena. In 1611 he accompanied the ex-converso physician Eliahu Montalto to Paris, where he served as rabbi of a small Jewish colony. When Montalto died in 1616, Mortera brought his body for Jewish burial to Amsterdam, where he was asked to stay and serve in a rabbinic position. He married a Portuguese-Jewish woman and settled in Amsterdam permanently. With his rigorous rabbinic training and his familiarity with Portuguese-Jewish life, he became a leading rabbinic figure in the community. His polemical and apologetic writings, directed to an ex-converso audience, circulated widely.

OROBIO DE CASTRO, ISAAC, c. 1617–1687. Orobio was born Balthazar Alvares de Orobio into a merchant family in Braganza, Portugal. Sometime after his birth his family resettled in Málaga, Spain. Balthazar pursued a medical career in Andalusia and was appointed to a chair in medicine in Seville in 1641. In the 1640s various members of his family came under inquisitorial suspicion, though without dire consequences. But in 1654 Balthazar was arrested by the Seville Inquisition along with other members of his immediate family. He was reconciled at an auto-da-fé in 1656 and released in 1658. By 1660 he had left the Peninsula and soon obtained a medical appointment at the University of Toulouse. In 1662 he arrived with his wife and children in Amsterdam, where for the rest of his life he practiced medicine and was known as an outstanding apologete for Judaism.

PARDO, JOSEPH, d. 1619. Pardo, a Sephardi rabbi and merchant, was born in Salonica but settled in Venice by 1589, where he served as rabbi of the Levantine Jewish community. He fell into bankruptcy and by 1608 had resettled in Amsterdam, where he served as rabbi of the Bet Jacob congregation.

He was an avid organizer rather than a prominent rabbinic scholar, and played a key role in the institutional development of the community.

PINTO, ISAAC DE (Manuel Álvares Pinto), 1629–1681. Pinto was born in Antwerp into a Portuguese converso family some of whose members were part of the Madrid-centered *asentista* network which financed the Spanish crown. Pinto and other members of his family fled Antwerp for Rotterdam in 1646 when war and other conditions rendered their commercial activity highly vulnerable. In Rotterdam they reverted to Judaism, and in 1648 Pinto married his cousin Rachel (she died in childbirth, and he was remarried to another cousin). Most of the Pintos moved to Amsterdam in the years after their arrival in the Netherlands. They became patrons of Jewish life and settled into a comfortable rentier existence. Isaac de Pinto has left a highly valuable family history which he wrote in 1671.

ABBREVIATIONS

EH	Ets Haim Collection
DJH	*Dutch Jewish History*
GAA	Gemeentelijke Archief, Amsterdam
GJN	H. Brugmans and A. Frank, eds., *Geschiedenis der Joden in Nederland* (Amsterdam 1940)
HUCA	*Hebrew Union College Annual*
JQR	*Jewish Quarterly Review*
JSS	*Jewish Social Studies*
PA	Particuliere Archieven
REJ	*Revue des Études Juives*
SDH	*Mehkarim al toledot yehadut holand*
SR	*Studia Rosenthaliana*
TGP	*Triumpho del govierno popular*
VA	*De Vrijdagavond*

NOTES

Preface

1. There is unfortunately no adequate ungendered translation for the terms *homens da nação* and *gente da nação*.

2. Cecil Roth, *A History of the Marranos* (Philadelphia 1932), 170, 181.

3. The most influential statement of this view, though largely implicit, is Yitzhak Baer, *A History of the Jews in Christian Spain*, 2 vols. (Philadelphia 1978), 2: 334–423. It is given explicit expression by his students. See, for example, Haim Beinart, "The Records of the Inquisition: A Source of Jewish and Converso History," *Proceedings of the Israel Academy of Science and Humanities* 2 (1967), 211–27.

4. This basic position is argued in E. Rivkin, "The Utilization of Non-Jewish Sources for the Reconstruction of Jewish History," *JQR* 48 (1957–58), 191–203; and B. Netanyahu, *The Marranos of Spain from the Late XIVth to the Early XVth Century* (New York 1966). (It is also argued, from a Marxist point of view, by the Portuguese scholar A. J. Saraiva, *A Inquisição portuguesa* [Lisbon 1956].) Recently this position has been reiterated for fifteenth-century Spain in B. Netanyahu, *The Origins of the Inquisition in Fifteenth Century Spain* (New York 1995), and Norman Roth, *Conversos, Inquisition, and the Expulsion of the Jews from Spain* (Madison 1995).

5. A classic statement of this view is the final paragraph of Yitzhak Baer's *History of the Jews in Christian Spain*, in which Baer wrote that "in Spain we see recapitulated, as it were, what took place . . . on two other occasions in the history of the Jews: once in the course of the drawn-out struggle with the united powers of Graeco-Roman civilization and early Christianity, and again in our own times, that began with the call to assimilate among the nations of Europe and whose continuation may be seen in all that has happened to the Jewish people ever since, down to our own generation." (This was written in the original Hebrew text of Baer's work in 1945.)

6. Américo Castro, *España en su historia. Cristianos, moros, judíos* (Buenos Aires 1948); idem, *La realidad histórica de España* (Mexico 1954); Claudio Sánchez-Albornoz, *España, un enigma histórico* (Buenos Aires 1956), 2 vols.

7. Carl Gebhardt, *Die Schriften des Uriel da Costa* (Amsterdam 1922), xix. In the same vein is J. A. van Praag's discussion of the "split souls" among the rejudaized conversos. See J. A. van Praag, "Almas en litigio," *Clavileño* 1 (1950), 14–26.

8. "Les Marranes," *REJ* 118 (1959–60), 53.

9. Ibid., 55.

10. Of a large and expanding literature, a few particularly suggestive studies are Fredrik Barth, ed., *Ethnic Groups and Boundaries: The Social Organization of Culture Difference* (Boston 1969); John Armstrong, "Mobilized and Proletarian Diasporas," *American Political Science Review* 70 (1976), 393–408; idem, *Nations before Nationalism* (Chapel Hill 1982); Eric Hobsbawm and Terence Ranger, eds., *The Invention of Tradition* (Cambridge 1983); Anthony Smith, "Ethnic Myths and Ethnic Revivals," *European Journal of Sociology* 25 (1984), 283–305; Anthony Cohen, *The Symbolic Construction of Community* (London 1985); Anthony Smith, *The Ethnic Origins of Nations* (Oxford 1986).

1. Introduction

1. J. Z. Kennegieter, "De Bloemstraat en haar zijstraten, 1613–1625," *Jaarboek van het Genootschap Amstelodamum* 54 (1962), 92, and see also 98–102 for data on birthplaces of Bloemstraat residents.

2. Philipp von Zesen, *Beschreibung der Stadt Amsterdam* (Amsterdam 1664), 232–33.

3. See Jonathan Israel, "The Changing Role of the Dutch Sephardim in International Trade, 1595–1715," in *DJH* 1 (Jerusalem 1984), 31–51.

4. It is telling that when the first eminent, unattached rabbi arrived in Amsterdam (this was Saul Levi Mortera), he was not immediately besieged by wealthy potential fathers-in-law. In fact, he married an orphan who received her dowry from a charitable fund. It should be mentioned that he was also probably undesirable because he was an Italianate, not a Sephardi, Jew. But it is significant that there were quite a few marriages between rabbis and poor girls who obtained dowries through public assistance.

5. For a detailed account of the occupations of the "Portuguese," see Herbert I. Bloom, *The Economic Activities of the Jews of Amsterdam in the Seventeenth and Eighteenth Centuries* (Williamsport 1937).

6. See I. S. Révah, "Une famille de 'nouveaux-chrétiens': les Bocarro Francês," *REJ* 116 (1957), 73–86.

7. Guido Zernatto, "Nation: The History of a Word," *Review of Politics* 6 (1944), 352–55.

8. It may well have been the term preferred by conversos in the Peninsula. See Yerushalmi, *Spanish Court*, 19 n. 28.

9. On the riots of 1391, see Baer, *Jews in Christian Spain*, 2: 95–135; and Philippe Wolff, "The 1391 Pogrom in Spain. Social Crisis or Not?" *Past and Present* 50 (1971), 4–18.

10. A discussion of the pattern of violent outbreaks can be found in Angus MacKay, "Popular Movements and Pogroms in Fifteenth-Century Castile," *Past and Present* 55 (1972), 33–44. For a more detailed and descriptive account, see Baer, *Jews in Christian Spain*, 2: 170–232, 244–51.

11. On the term *marrano*, see Révah, "Les Marranes," 30.

12. On this legislation, see José María Monsalvo Antón, *Teoría y evolución de un conflicto social: El antisemitismo en la Corona de Castilla en la Baja Edad Media* (Madrid 1985), 150, 251. Such legislation did little to halt this form of harassment. In the late fifteenth century, soon after the Expulsion, conversos petitioned the Catholic Monarchs, complaining of being called *judíos* and *tornadizos*. See Luis Suarez Fernandez, ed., *Documentos acerca de la Expulsión de los Judíos* (Valladolid 1964), No. 260, 528–29.

13. This obvious conclusion has led to speculation as to whether there was any cryptojudaizing in the Peninsula at all. The scholarly evidence on inquisitorial activity that has been brought to light has by now rendered this hypothesis utterly untenable. For the literature of the scholarly polemic on this issue (discussed briefly in the preface to this book), see Yerushalmi, *Spanish Court*, 21–22, nn. 31–34. For more detailed bibliographical information, see ch. 2, n. 4, below.

14. How unclear the boundary was, in the minds of Spaniards, between "judaizing" and nonconformist speech has been demonstrated by John Edwards, "Religious Faith and Doubt in Late Medieval Spain: Soria circa 1450–1500," *Past and Present* 120 (1988), 3–25. The lack of clear differentiation between skepticism and "judaizing" is evident in the material discussed by José María Monsalvo Antón, "Herejía conversa y contestación religiosa a fines de la Edad Media: las denuncias

a la Inquisición en el obispado de Osana," *Studia Historica* 2 (1984), 109–38. See also Alisa Meyuhas Ginio, "Self-Perception and Images of the Judeoconversos in Fifteenth-Century Spain and Portugal," *Tel Aviver Jahrbuch für deutsche Geschichte* 22 (1993), 143–47.

15. See Carlos Carrete Parrondo, "Nostalgia for the Past (and for the Future?) among Castilian Judeoconversos," *Mediterranean Historical Review* 6 (1991), 32.

16. See, for example, the evidence from Aragon in the series of articles by Encarnación Marín Padilla, "Relación judeoconversa durante la segunda mitad del siglo XV en Aragón," *Sefarad* 41 (1981), 273–300; 42 (1982), 59–77, 243–98; 43 (1983), 251–344.

17. Haim Beinart, *Conversos on Trial: The Inquisition in Ciudad Real* (Jerusalem 1981), 237–85.

18. The riots and their aftermath have been studied in detail by Eloy Benito Ruano, *Toledo en el siglo XV* (Madrid 1961), 33–81; and idem, "La 'Sentencia-Estatuto' de Pero Sarmiento contra los conversos toledanos," *Revista de la Universidad de Madrid* 6 (1957), 277–306. See also Nicholas Round, "La rebelión toledana de 1449," *Archivum* 16 (1966), 385–446; Baer, *History of the Jews,* 2: 277–83; and Nicholas Round, *The Greatest Man Uncrowned: A Study of the Fall of don Alvares de Luna* (London 1986). For details on Alfonso Cota and his family consult F. Cantera Burgos, *El poeta Ruy Sanchez Cota (Rodrigo Cota) y su familia de judíos conversos* (Madrid 1970).

19. Benito Ruano, *Toledo en el siglo XV,* 194.

20. Manuel Nieto Cumplido, "La revuelta contra los conversos de Córdoba en 1473," in *Homenaje a Antón de Montoro en el V centenario de su muerte* (Montoro 1977), 31–49.

21. Baer's view of the anticonverso violence reflects his general conviction that religious factors were paramount (*Jews in Christian Spain,* 2: 277–83, 300–12). More recent research, however, has tended to emphasize the role of powerful socioeconomic conflicts. See especially the analysis of Francisco Márquez Villanueva, "Conversos y cargos consejiles en el siglo XV," *Revista de Archivos, Bibliotecas y Museos* 63 (1957), 503–40; and more recently, idem, "El problema de los conversos: cuatro puntos cardinales," in *Hispania Judaica* 1 (Barcelona 1980), 52–56.

22. The issue of approximate numbers is a thorny one. Before the 1391 riots there were perhaps 250,000 Jews in the Spanish kingdoms. (See Isidore Loeb, "Le nombre des juifs de Castille et d'Espagne," *REJ* 14 [1887], 161–83. For a recent discussion of the difficulties in estimating figures, see Henry Kamen, "The Mediterranean and the Expulsion of Spanish Jews in 1492," *Past and Present* 119 [1988], 30–55.) Estimates of the number of Jews who were converted during the 1391 riots and in their aftermath vary greatly, from Baer's tens of thousands (*Jews in Christian Spain,* 2: 246) to B. Netanyahu's exaggerated 200,000 (*Marranos of Spain,* 235–40). By the time of the Expulsion, the number of conversos had grown significantly, the standard estimate being 300,000. To this number were later added the Jews in Portugal who were baptized in 1497; the latter perhaps numbered some tens of thousands.

23. On Jewish visitors to post-Expulsion Spain, see Yosef Hayim Yerushalmi, "Jews in Post-Expulsion Spain and Portugal," *Salo Wittmayer Baron Jubilee Volume* (Jerusalem 1974), 2: 1023–58; Haim Beinart, "A Jew of Salonica in Spain in the Seventeenth Century" (Hebrew), *Sefunot* 12 (1971–78), 189–97; idem, "Jews and Conversos between Italy and Spain" (Hebrew) in H. Beinart, ed., *Yehudim be-Italyah* (Jerusalem 1988), 275–88; Salo Wittmayer Baron, *A Social and Religious History of the Jews,* 18 vols. (New York 1952–83), 15: 162, 481 n. 71; Julio Caro Baroja, *Los judíos en la España moderna y contemporánea,* 3 vols. (Madrid 1978), 3: 361 (Appendix 29).

24. Esther 4: 16. For the special place given to Purim, see Cecil Roth, "Religion of the Marranos," 26–27; Yerushalmi, *Spanish Court*, 38n.

25. For this testimony and its background, see I. S. Révah, "La religion d'Uriel da Costa, Marrane de Porto," *Revue de l'Histoire des Religions* 161 (1962), 45–76; the passage quoted is on p. 68.

26. For two quite different discussions of racial views about the conversos, see Yosef Hayim Yerushalmi, "Assimilation and Racial Anti-Semitism: The Iberian and the German Models," *The Leo Baeck Memorial Lecture* 26 (New York 1982); and D. Gracia Guillén, "Judaísmo, medicina y mentalidad inquisitorial en la España del siglo XVI," in A. Alcalá et al., *Inquisición española y mentalidad inquisitorial* (Barcelona 1984), 330–39. Yerushalmi analyzes these views in the context of the history of antisemitism; Gracia Guillén, in the context of sixteenth-century anthropological thinking.

27. See Linda Martz, "Pure Blood Statutes in Sixteenth-Century Toledo," *Sefarad* 54 (1994), 83–108; John Edwards, "Race and Religion in Fifteenth- and Sixteenth-Century Spain: The 'Purity of Blood' Laws Revisited," *Proceedings of the Tenth World Congress of Jewish Studies*, B, 2 (Jerusalem 1990), 159–66.

28. On the history of the "purity of blood" statutes, see Albert A. Sicroff, *Les controverses des statuts de pureté de sang en Espagne du XVe au XVIIe siècle* (Paris 1960). See also Antonio Domínguez Ortiz, *La clase social de los conversos en Castilla en la edad moderna* (Madrid 1955). For a more recent evaluation, arguing the persistence of opposition to the statutes in Spanish society, see Henry Kamen, "Una crisis de conciencia en la edad de oro en España: Inquisición contra 'limpieza de sangre,'" *Bulletin Hispanique* 88 (1986), 321–56.

29. See Yerushalmi, *Spanish Court*, 4–5; Révah, "Les Marranes," 36–39.

30. For the migration of the Portuguese conversos to Castile and their subsequent activity there, see Julio Caro Baroja, *La sociedad criptojudía en la corte de Felipe IV* (Madrid 1963), 35–128; Antonio Domínguez Ortiz, *Política y hacienda de Felipe IV* (Madrid 1983), 121–33; James C. Boyajian, *Portuguese Bankers at the Court of Spain, 1626–1650* (New Brunswick 1983).

31. For discussion of this development, see Henry Kamen, *Inquisition and Society in the Sixteenth and Seventeenth Centuries* (Bloomington 1985), 225–31; Boyajian, *Portuguese Bankers*, 117–20.

32. On this term, see Castro, *La realidad histórica*, 23–57.

33. For example, see Caro Baroja, *Los judíos en la España*, 1: 221.

34. António Vieira, *Obras escolhidas* (Lisbon 1951–54), 4: 182. And see Caro Baroja, *Los judíos en la España*, 1: 361.

35. The *moriscos* were deported between 1609 and 1614. See, inter alia, J. H. Elliott, *Imperial Spain, 1469–1716* (London 1990), 305–308.

36. There are numerous discussions of this phenomenon. For an important study of its socioeconomic aspects, see Márquez Villanueva, "Conversos y cargos consejiles." For a more vivid and encompassing (albeit brief) description, see Caro Baroja, *La sociedad criptojudía*, 22–29.

37. Juan de Lucena, *Tratado de Vita Beata* (Burgos 1502), fol. 11. Quoted in Domínguez Ortiz, *Clase social*, 159.

38. On the phenomenon of such reversal or inversion from the point of view of social anthropology, see Cohen, *Symbolic Construction of Community*, 58–63.

39. For a characterization of the ethos of medieval Spanish Jewry, see H. H. Ben-Sasson, "The Generation of Spanish Exiles on Itself" (Hebrew), *Zion* 26 (1961), 23–64.

40. See H. P. Salomon, "The 'De Pinto' Manuscript: A Seventeenth-Century Marrano Family History," *SR* 9 (1975), 13; Yosef Kaplan, *From Christianity to Judaism: The Story of Isaac Orobio de Castro* (Oxford 1989), 312.

41. E. Cunha de Azevedo Mea, "Orações judaicas na Inquisição Portuguesa—século XVI," in Y. Kaplan, ed., *Jews and Conversos, Studies in Society and the Inquisition* (Jerusalem 1985), 168.

42. For sources, see Louis Ginzberg, *Legends of the Jews*, 6 vols. (Philadelphia 1946–47), 3: 22; 6: 6–7 n. 36.

43. See Alisa Meyuhas Ginio, "Las aspiraciones mesianicas de los conversos en la Castilla de mediados del siglo XV," *El Olivo* 13 (1989), 217–33; Yitzhak Baer, "The Messianic Movement in Spain at the Time of the Expulsion" (Hebrew), *Me'asef Zion* 5 (1933), 61–74; Isaiah Tishby, *Messianism in the Time of the Expulsion from Spain and Portugal* (Hebrew) (Jerusalem 1985); Carrete Parrondo, "Nostalgia for the Past," 36; Carlos Carrete Parrondo and Yolanda Moreno Koch, "Movimiento mesiánico hispano-portugués: Badajoz 1525," *Sefarad* 52 (1992), 65–68 (the document presented clearly describes hopes stirred by the visit of David Reuveni, although the authors do not refer to this); Haim Beinart, "A Prophetic Movement in Cordova in the Years 1499–1502" (Hebrew), *Zion* 44 (1979), 190–200; Haim Beinart, "The Prophetess Inés and her Messianic Movement in Herrera del Duque" (Hebrew), in *Studies in Kabbalah, Jewish Philosophy and Ethical Literature in Honor of Isaiah Tishby on his Seventy-fifth Birthday* (Jerusalem 1986), 459–506.

44. David Ruderman, "Hope against Hope: Jewish and Christian Messianic Expectations in the Late Middle Ages," *Exile and Diaspora* (Jerusalem 1991), 185–202, and see literature cited there, 187 n. 8.

45. Carrete Parondo, "Nostalgia for the Past," 36.

46. Révah, "Les Marranes," 53–54.

47. Andres Bernáldez, *Memorias del reinado de los Reyes Católicos*, ed. Gomez-Moreno and Carriazo (Madrid 1962), 102.

48. Salomon, "'De Pinto' Manuscript," 46.

49. See Miriam Bodian, "Some Ideological Implications of Marrano Involvement in the International Arena," *Society and Community: Proceedings of the Second International Congress for Research of the Sephardi and Oriental Jewish Heritage 1984* (Jerusalem 1991), 207–217.

50. S. Seeligmann, *Bibliographie en Historie, Bijdrage tot de Geschiedenis der eerste Sephardim in Amsterdam* (Amsterdam 1927), 42–44. At some point—perhaps at the time of the unification of the three congregations—the pelican became the symbol for the community. It was this bird which was depicted on the title page of the revised regulations for the Talmud Torah and Ets Haim educational institutions in 1728. (See B. M. Teensma, "Van Marraan tot Jood: 17e en 18e-eeuwse Amsterdamse Sephardim en hun iberische achtergrond," *Jaarboek Amstelodamum* 50 [1988], 119, 123.) I have heard it suggested that the phoenix was readopted only in the wake of World War II.

51 . See, for example, *Elogios que zelosos dedicaron a la felice memoria de Abraham Nuñez Bernal* (Amsterdam 1655), 41, 49, 55–56, 112, 115, 154.

52. It is difficult to capture this phrase in translation, with its Spanish *señores* and its Hebrew *parnasim* (officers), *gabay* (treasurer), and *Kahal Kados* (the common title preceding the name of a Jewish community, a term of respect for the community).

53 . It is known that De Barrios received financial aid from the communal leaders. See W. Chr. Pieterse, *Daniel Levi de Barrios als geschiedschrijver van de Portugees-Israelitische Gemeente te Amsterdam in zijn "Triumpho del Govierno popular"* (Amsterdam 1968), 22–23 and Appendix 3, 144–45. For further evidence of his financial difficulties during the period in question, see his "Al Muy Inclito Govierno del Kahal Kados de Londres" in *TGP*, (Amsterdam 1683–84), 719–22. (All citations of *TGP* are from the Ets Haim Collection exemplar 9E43, according to its pagination by hand.)

54. An elaborate tale of how Uri Halevi and his congregants got to Amsterdam

was told by Halevi's grandson in a narrative published in the early eighteenth century: Uri ben Aron Halevy, *Narração da Vinda dos Judeos espanhões a Amsterdam* (Amsterdam 1711), reprinted in facsimile edition by J. S. da Silva Rosa (Amsterdam 1933). For a detailed bibliographical description of this work, see S. Seeligmann, "Über die erste jüdische Ansiedlung in Amsterdam," *Mitteilungen zur jüdischen Volkskunde* 17 (1906), 1–13. An English translation has been published by H. P. Salomon, "Myth or Anti-Myth? The Oldest Account Concerning the Origin of Portuguese Judaism at Amsterdam," *Lias* 16 (1989), 280–82.

55. De Barrios, *TGP*, "Casa de Jacob," 404–408. (A somewhat different, rhymed version of the story appears later in De Barrios's essay in the same work, in the opuscule "Maskil el Dal." In that version Uri Halevi's arrest is included as part of the story.)

56. E. M. Koen, "Notarial Records in Amsterdam Relating to the Portuguese Jews up to 1639," *SR* 1 (1967), 111, No. 1.

57. This was also how the story was told by Uri Halevi's grandson in his *Narração da vinda*.

58. See Jacob Zwarts, "De eerste rabbijnen en synagogen van Amsterdam naar archivalische bronnen," *Bijdragen en Mededelingen van het Genootschap voor de Joodsche Wetenschap in Nederland* 4 (1928), 168ff.; Uri Halevi, *Narração da vinda*, 4–5.

59. For the records of the marriages of Maria Nunes, her sister Justa Pereyra, and her brother Manuel Lopes Pereyra, see Pieterse, *Daniel Levi de Barrios*, 45 n. 3. Incidentally, all married first cousins, the children of one uncle.

60. H. P. Salomon, *Os primeiros portugueses de Amesterdão* (Braga 1983), 21–24.

61. S. Seeligmann, *Bibliographie en Historie*, 17–19.

62. Jonathan Israel, *Empires and Entrepôts: The Dutch, the Spanish Monarchy and the Jews, 1585–1713* (London 1990), 252–53. The deed revealing this fact is published in Koen, "Notarial Records," *SR* 6 (1972), 123, No. 599.

63. See Pieterse, *Daniel Levi de Barrios*, 46–47.

64. Israel, *Empires and Entrepôts*, 247–64.

65. De Barrios, *TGP* ("Casa de Jacob"), 400; and see Israel, *Empires and Entrepôts*, 249.

66. In particular, Francisco Nunes Homem (David Abendana), among the founders of the *Dotar*; his uncle Michael Lopes Homem, who signed the 1610 contract for the provision of ritually slaughtered meat, and was thus probably a *parnas* of the Bet Jacob community; and Antonio Lopes Pereyra (Joseph Abendana), who was among the founders of the *Dotar* and also served as administrator of the Ouderkerk cemetery.

2. The Forging of a Community

1. Salomon, *Os primeiros portugueses*, 21–24; Pieterse, *Daniel Levi de Barrios*, 45 n. 3; *SR* 3 (1969), 245 n. 38.

2. See J. M. Millás Villacrosa, "Emigración masiva de conversos por la frontera catalano-francesa en el año 1608," *Sefarad* 19 (1959), 142–44.

3. For a discussion of this episode, see Haim Beinart, "The Exodus of Conversos from the Iberian Peninsula in the Fifteenth to Seventeenth Centuries" (Hebrew), *Scritti in Memoria di Umberto Nahon* (Jerusalem 1978), 63–106.

4. Cecil Roth, in his pioneering *History of the Marranos*, set the stage for the debate with his heroic view of the *marranos* (a term almost synonymous for him with crypto-Jews), a view that was shared in some ways by more careful scholars, particularly Yitzhak Baer and Haim Beinart. This view was challenged from various quarters. Ellis Rivkin, in his article "The Utilization of Non-Jewish Sour-

ces," esp. 191–203, argued with more passion than evidence that the "judaizing" reported by the Inquisition was fabricated. Benzion Netanyahu, in his book *The Marranos of Spain*, made a similar argument using problematic evidence. António José Saraiva, in his *Inquisição e Cristãos-Novos* (Porto 1969) and elsewhere, argued that the Portuguese New Christians were exclusively a socioeconomic entity, with no religious or ethnic significance of their own. Rivkin and Saraiva were criticized by Révah in "Marranes," 45–52; in addition, Saraiva and Révah conducted a vitriolic debate in the *Diário de Lisboa* from May to September 1971 (republished in the fifth edition of Saraiva, *Inquisição e Cristãos-Novos* [Lisbon 1985], 213–91). Netanyahu's book has been criticized by Albert Sicroff, *Midstream* 12 (October 1966), 71–75; Gershon Cohen, *JSS* 29 (1967), 178–84; and Yerushalmi, *Spanish Court*, 22 n. 34. No serious scholar today would argue that cryptojudaizing was entirely a fabrication of the Inquisition.

5. For this view, see, for example, Beinart, "Records of the Inquisition."

6. See Boyajian, *Portuguese Bankers*, 133–53.

7. For analyses of this phenonomen, see Jonathan Israel, *European Jewry in the Age of Mercantilism, 1550–1750* (Oxford 1991), 35–52; Baron, *Social and Religious History*, 15: 3–160; Arthur Hertzberg, *The French Enlightenment and the Jews* (New York 1968), 12–28.

8. On the stimulus for immigration, see Jonathan Israel, "Sephardic Immigration into the Dutch Republic, 1595–1672," *SR*, special issue published with vol. 23 (1989), 45–46. On the colony's religious character, see Hans Pohl, *Die Portugiesen in Antwerpen (1567–1648): zur Geschichte einer Minderheit* (Wiesbaden 1977), 331–48.

9. I. S. Révah, "Pour l'histoire des Marranes à Anvers; recensements de la 'Nation Portugaise' de 1571 à 1666," *REJ* 122 (1963), 130, 132–35 (Document A).

10. J. Denucé, "Een geheime Synagoge te Antwerpen in de XVI^{de} eeuw," *Antwerpsch Archievenblad*, 3rd ser. 4 (1929), 151–54; Kopel Liberman, "La découverte d'une synagogue secrète à Anvers à la fin du dix-septième siècle," *REJ* 100 (1935), 36–48; Lucien Wolf, "Jews in Elizabethan England," *Transactions of the Jewish Historical Society of England* 11 (1954), 19–20.

11. Israel, "Sephardic Immigration," 47.

12. According to Hermann Kellenbenz, by 1595 Hamburg had a "Portuguese" community of about twelve families. Hermann Kellenbenz, *Sephardim an der unteren Elbe* (Wiesbaden 1958), 27–28.

13. *SR* 1 (1967), 111–12. On Rodrigues Vega, see R. G. Fuks-Mansfeld, *De Sefardim in Amsterdam tot 1795* (Hilversum 1989), 39 n. 10. Of course Rodrigues Vega was not necessarily the first "Portuguese" merchant to settle in Amsterdam in the 1590s. The 1607 marriage registration of Rafael Cardoso Nahemias from Lisbon states that the latter had been living in Amsterdam for fifteen years, indicating his arrival was in 1593; there is however no documentation of his presence then. (E. M. Koen, "The Earliest Sources Relating to the Portuguese Jews in the Municipal Archives of Amsterdam up to 1620," *SR* 4 [1970], 39. And see A. M. Vaz Dias, "De Stichters van Beth Jaäcob," *VA* December 25, 1931, 195.)

14. Evidence for Fernandes's crypto-Jewish involvement derives from a letter of February, 1594, published in Wolf, "Jews in Elizabethan England," 20. The letter indicates that crypto-Jews in London sent sums for the secret synagogue in Antwerp via Luis Fernandes. For further information on Fernandes consult Pohl, *Die Portugiesen in Antwerpen*, index.

15. Israel, "Sephardic Immigration," 49. A detailed account of Rodrigues Vega can be found in Daniel Swetschinski, "The Portuguese Jewish Merchants of Seventeenth-Century Amsterdam: A Social Profile" (2 vols., Brandeis University diss. 1980), 152–60.

16. For example, the twenty-one Jewish congregations listed in a Salonica tax list

drawn up between 1520 and 1535 include a "Lisbon" and an "Evora" congregation. (Bernard Lewis, *Notes and Documents from the Turkish Archives: A Contribution to the History of the Jews of the Ottoman Empire* [Jerusalem 1952], 25.) "Portuguese" congregations were also established in Constantinople, Adrianople, Valona, Arta, and Smyrna (Morris Goodblatt, *Jewish Life in Turkey in the Sixteenth Century as Reflected in the Legal Writings of Samuel de Medina* [New York 1952], 111).

17. E. H. Kossman and A. F. Mellink, *Texts Concerning the Revolt of the Netherlands* (Cambridge 1974), 169–70.

18. Israel, *European Jewry in the Age of Mercantilism*, 50–51.

19. *Copia do Livro das gerasoins prinsipiado p[or] o señor Jahacob Belmonte desde o anno 1599*, Ms. EH 47B 4.

20. The date of the prayer seems to contradict the date of 1597 for his arrival in Holland given by David Henriques de Castro, *Keur van Grafstenen op de Nederl.-Portug.-Israël. Begraafplaats te Ouderkerk aan den Amstel* (Leiden 1883), 54.

21. See the discussion of De Barrios's ambiguous statement in David Henriques de Castro, *Keur van Grafstenen*, 54.

22. Pieterse, *Livro de Bet Haim*, 183–84.

23. As an official of the Bet Jacob congregation, as an officer of the *Imposta* Board, and as a key figure in the administration of the *Dotar* from its establishment in 1615 to 1627. See Pieterse, *Livro de Bet Haim*, 183–84, and *Dotar* records.

24. M. H. Gans, *Memorbook: History of Dutch Jewry from the Renaissance to 1940* (Baarn 1977), 31.

25. Israel, "Sephardic Immigration," 49.

26. Pieterse, *Daniel Levi de Barrios*, 57. This is somewhat puzzling, however, since Carvalho was one of seven Portuguese Jews who signed a contract for the supply of ritually slaughtered meat in 1610 (*SR* 5 [1971], 222, No. 436). It should also be noted that Hector Mendes Bravo, in 1617, listed among those living in conformity with Jewish law in Amsterdam "Manoel Carvalho, of Porto. He has lived many years in Brazil, he is of an advanced age and unmarried." (Cecil Roth, "The Strange Case of Hector Mendes Bravo," *HUCA* 18 [1944], 235). This, of course, is consistent with Carvalho's own statement.

27. *SR* 2 (1968), 113, No. 44, and see n. 46.

28. Ibid., 26.

29. Pieterse, *Livro de Bet Haim*, 93. And see Salomon, *Os primeiros portugueses*, 49 n. 68.

30. Salomon, *Os primeiros portugueses*, 46–48.

31. Jonathan Israel, "The Jews of Venice and Their Links with Holland and with Dutch Jewry (1600–1710)," in *Gli Ebrei e Venezia, secoli XIV-XVIII* (Venice 1987), 97.

32. For a more thorough discussion of this issue, see M. Bodian, "The 'Portuguese' Dowry Societies in Venice and Amsterdam: A Case Study in Communal Differentiation within the Marrano Diaspora," *Italia* 6 (1987), 30–61, esp. 46–55.

33. Unlike Salomon, who believed Melo was "judaized" by his experience with the Inquisition, Révah believed Melo to have been a committed judaizer at the time of his arrest: "He was arrested by the Inquisition but refused to confess, even under torture, his ardent marranism" (*Annuaire de l'Ecole Pratique des Hautes Etudes* 4 [1971], 482–83).

34. H. P. Salomon, *Portrait of a New Christian: Fernão Alvares Melo (1569–1632)*, 285–86 (Paris 1982).

35. There is nothing curious about the fact that Abenatar chose psalms as biblical material to rework. Psalms were central prayers among crypto-Jews in the Peninsula, where they were available from Latin Bibles, the Books of Hours, and other Catholic devotional writings. The direct emotionalism of the many psalms dealing

with suffering at the hands of an enemy and eventual redemption must have seized converso attention. In Portugal in the second half of the sixteenth century psalms were frequently recited by crypto-Jews, who however omitted the Catholic doxology (the *Gloria patri*) appended to each psalm.

36. David Abenatar Melo, *Los CL Psalmos de David en lengua española, en varias rimas* (Frankfurt 1626), dedication "del Autor al D. B." (n.p.). I have relied to some extent on the English translation in Salomon, *Portrait of a New Christian*, 160–61.

37. Melo, *CL Psalmos*, unpaginated "Advertencias al letor."

38. Salomon, *Portrait of a New Christian*, 167.

39. A similar about-face was made by Isaac Cardoso, at one time a physician in fashionable Madrid circles. See Yerushalmi, *Spanish Court*, 375–76.

40. The Curiel are among the best-documented families in the "Portuguese" diaspora of northern Europe. See, inter alia, Edgar Samuel, "The Curiel Family in 16th-Century Portugal," *Transactions of the Jewish Historical Society of England* 31 (1990), 111–36; Daniel Swetschinski, "An Amsterdam Jewish Merchant-Diplomat: Jeronimo Nunes da Costa (1620–1697), Agent of the King of Portugal," in Dasberg and Cohen, eds., *Neveh Ja'akov: Jubilee Volume Presented to Dr. Jaap Meijer on the Occasion of his Seventieth Birthday* (Assen 1982), 3–30; Jonathan Israel, "An Amsterdam Jewish Merchant of the Golden Age: Jeronimo Nunes da Costa (1620–1697), Agent of Portugal in the Dutch Republic," *SR* 18 (1984), 21–40; Jonathan Israel, "Duarte Nunes da Costa (Jacob Curiel) of Hamburg, Sephardi Nobleman and Communal Leader, 1585–1664," in *Empires and Entrepôts*, 333–53; Jonathan Israel, "The Diplomatic Career of Jeronimo Nunes da Costa," *Bijdragen en Mededelingen betreffende de Geschiedenis der Nederlanden* 98 (1983), 167–90.

41. On Eliahu Montalto, see Harry Friedenwald, "Montalto, A Jewish Physician at the Court of Marie de Medicis and Louis XIII," *Bulletin of the Institute of the History of Medicine* 3 (1935), 129–58; J. M. Pelorson, "Le Docteur Carlos García et la Colonie Hispano-Portugaise de Paris (1613–1619)," *Bulletin Hispanique* 71 (1969), 520–40; Cecil Roth, "Quatre Lettres d'Elie de Montalte," *REJ* 87 (1929), 137–65.

42. Pieterse, *Livro de Bet Haim*, 73.

43. Israel, "Diplomatic Career," 168.

44. Israel, "Duarte Nunes da Costa," 335.

45. Ibid., 337–39, 351–53; Swetschinski, "An Amsterdam Jewish Merchant-Diplomat," 5–6.

46. Israel, "An Amsterdam Jewish Merchant," 22.

47. Swetschinski, "Portuguese Jewish Merchants," 1: 228, and see there 242–43.

48. Salomon, "'De Pinto' Manuscript," 21 n. 75; 29 n. 96.

49. James Boyajian, "The New Christians Reconsidered: Evidence from Lisbon's Portuguese Bankers, 1497–1647," *SR* 13 (1979), 153.

50. Jonathan Israel, "Spain and the Dutch Sephardim," in idem, *Empires and Entrepôts*, 399.

51. Boyajian, *Portuguese Bankers*, Appendix A–10.

52. See Ibid., Appendices A–10 and A–1, second page, and Salomon, "'De Pinto' Manuscript," 48.

53. The discussion of the Pinto family's financial situation and behavior relies on Boyajian, *Portuguese Bankers*, 48, 66, 74–84, 150–51.

54. Israel, *Empires and Entrepôts*, 403.

55. It was published in 1975 by H. P. Salomon, "'De Pinto' Manuscript,'" *SR* 9 (1975), 1–62. Its importance was recognized earlier by I. S. Révah, "Généalogie de l'économiste Isaac de Pinto (1717–1787)," in *Mélanges à la Mémoire de Jean Sarrailh* (Paris 1966), 2: 267.

56. See Salomon, "'De Pinto' Manuscript," 7–8.

57. Ibid., 49.

58. Ibid., 13.

59. Ibid., 46.

60. Ibid., 51.

61. Ibid.

62. Ibid., 61.

63. Ibid., 24.

64. Ibid., 27.

65. The grandfather, Manuel Alvares Pinto, was accepted as a member on July 7, 1616. He died in Antwerp, and his son, Gil Lopez Pinto (Abraham de Pinto), father of the author, inherited the membership on his arrival in Holland in 1647 (GAA, PA 334, No. 1143, 64v).

66. See the provision in the 1615 statutes published by I. S. Révah, "Le premier règlement imprimé de la 'Santa Companhia de dotar orfans e donzelas pobres,'" *Boletim internacional de bibliografia luso-brasileira* 4 (1963), 674.

67. Salomon, "'De Pinto' Manuscript," 47.

68. See Jonathan Israel, "Spain, the Spanish Embargoes, and the Struggle for the Mastery of World Trade, 1585–1660," in *Empires and Entrepôts*, 195 (and cf. notarial deeds dealing with "Portuguese" trade via Emden cited by Israel).

69. Zwarts has published the notarial deed with this information in "De eerste rabbijnen," Appendix IV. The deed has been published in English in *SR* 2 (1968), 271, No. 116.

70. Jan Lokers, *Die Juden in Emden 1530–1806* (Aurich 1990), 40–45.

71. Zwarts, "De eerste rabbijnen," 197.

72. GAA, PA 334, No. 1142, 137 (entry for 16 Adar 5401). See also the *Yizkor* prayer said for Uri Halevi in Emden, Zwarts, "De eerste rabbijnen," 186. Skepticism about the chronicle accounts has led one scholar to question whether Uri Halevi served as anything but a ritual slaughterer. In view of the evidence, this is an untenable position. See Odette Vlessing, "New Light on the Earliest History of the Amsterdam Portuguese Jews," *DJH* 3 (1993), 44–53.

73. A. M. Vaz Dias, "Een verzoek om de Joden in Amsterdam een bepaalde woonplats aan te wijzen," *Jaarboek van het genootschap Amstelodamum* 35 (1938), 187. Vaz Dias does not state his source. It was Vaz Dias who identified Jacob Tirado with James Lopes da Costa, in the above article.

74. Zwarts, "De eerste rabbijnen," 148 cites *VA* of 7 August 1925 as stating that the breastplate was donated in 1607. The author of a study of the community's ceremonial objects states that the breastplate was made in Amsterdam between 1603 and 1609 by Leendert Claes van Emden. (Julie-Marthe Cohen, "From Rimmonim to Persian Rugs," in Judith Belinfante et al., *The Esnoga: A Monument to Portuguese-Jewish Culture* [Amsterdam 1991], 74.)

75. Seeligmann, *Bibliographie en Historie*, 44.

76. The poem appears in Francisco de Caceres's *Los siete dias de la semana*. On its printing, see Pieterse, *Daniel Levi de Barrios*, 51 n. 6, and document of November 8, 1612, summarized in *SR* 6 (1972), 119, No. 583.

77. The date of Pardo's arrival in Amsterdam was established by Seeligmann, *Bibliographie en Historie*, 23–30.

78. Meir Benayahu, *Relations between Greek and Italian Jewry* (Hebrew) (Tel Aviv 1980), 177.

79. On Pardo, see Seeligmann, *Bibliographie en Historie*, 23–30, and bibliography, 30 n. 2; D. Tamar, "Two New Letters from Rabbi Judah Aryeh of Modena Concern-

ing Safed" (Hebrew), in *Yitzhak F. Baer Jubilee Volume* (Jerusalem 1960), 300–301; Benayahu, *Relations*, 173–85; idem, in *SDH* 4, 1–6.

80. Benayahu, *Relations*, 181.

81. See Vlessing, "New Light," 46–47.

82. Joseph Shalom ben Gallego, *Sefer imrei no'am* (Amsterdam 1628), fol. 141r. On Gallego's role in the community, see Edwin Seroussi, "Rabbi Joseph Shalom Gallego, Salonican Hazzan in Amsterdam in the Early Seventeenth Century" (Hebrew), *Asufoth* 6 (1992), 89–91.

83. Zwarts, "De eerste rabbijnen," 199–202.

84. This estimate is based on payments made in 1614 for the purchase of the cemetery in Ouderkerk. See J. d'Ancona, "Komst der Marranen in Noord-Neder-land: De Portugese gemeenten te Amsterdam tot de vereniging (1639)," in *GJN*, 219. But there is no agreement on this. According to another estimate, about 340 families had come to Amsterdam by 1615, and most of them stayed. See Koen, "Earliest Sources," 38–40.

85. A. M. Vaz Dias, "Het Amsterdamsche Jodenkwartier," in *Gedenkschrift der stichting "Bouwfonds Handwerkers Vriedenkring"* (Amsterdam 1937), 17–22.

86. *SR* 5 (1971), 240–42, No. 524.

87. One *pez* is close to 28 centimeters, a little less than an English foot.

88. These records have been published by W. Chr. Pieterse, *Livro de Bet Haim do Kahal Kados de Bet Yahacob* (Assen 1970).

89. *SR* 4, 120 (No. 249); 108; 114 (No. 571). On Coronel's commercial activity, see Kellenbenz, *Sephardim an der unteren Elbe*, 124; Koen, "Notarial Records," *SR* 6 (1972), 108 n. 31.

90. H. Z. Hirschberg, *A History of the Jews in North Africa* (Hebrew), 2 vols. (Jerusalem 1965), 2: 103.

91. Payment of his salary is first mentioned in that year. GAA, PA 334, No. 9, 4. Cf. Pieterse, *Daniel Levi de Barrios*, 63.

92. M. Bodian, "Amsterdam, Venice, and the Marrano Diaspora," *DJH* 2 (1989), 49.

93. For a detailed discussion of the episode, see Bodian, "Amsterdam, Venice and the Marrano Diaspora," 54–57.

94. The *Imposta* board's revenues derived from an impost (*imposta*) levied on all commercial transactions involving imported and exported goods, precious stones, silver and gold, money, insurance policies, and brokerage fees. GAA, PA 334, No. 13, 3–4.

95. Israel, "Sephardic Immigration," 51.

96. Yosef Kaplan, "Jewish Refugees from Germany and Poland in Amsterdam during the Thirty Years War and at the Time of the Chmielnitsky Massacres" (Hebrew), in *Culture and Society in Medieval Jewish History: A Collection in Memory of Haim Hillel Ben Sasson* (Hebrew) (Jerusalem 1989), 593.

97. David Franco Mendes, "Memorias do estabelecimento e progresso dos judeos portuguezes e espanhoes nesta famosa cidade de Amsterdam," *SR* 9 (1975), 46.

98. The merger agreement has been published in Pieterse, *Daniel Levi de Barrios*, 156–67. The clauses providing for the election of the first and future *Mahamad* boards are #4 and #6.

99. For parallel cases, see Salo Baron, *The Jewish Community*, 3 vols. (Philadelphia 1942), 2: 46–49.

100. GAA, PA 334, No. 19, 21.

3. The Dutch Context

1. A notable exception is Daniel Swetschinski, "The Portuguese Jews of Seventeenth-Century Amsterdam: Cultural Continuity and Adaptation," in Malino and Albert, eds., *Essays in Modern Jewish History, A Tribute to Ben Halpern* (Rutherford, N.J. 1982), 56–80.

2. Most importantly, Zwarts, "De eerste rabbijnen"; Ancona, "Komst," 201–69; Baron, *Social and Religious History,* 15: 3–73; Swetschinski, "Portuguese Jewish Merchants."

3. For a detailed analysis of the role these liberties played in the revolt, see J. J. Woltjer, "Dutch Privileges, Real and Imaginary," *Britain and the Netherlands* 5 (The Hague 1975), 19–35.

4. A note on the structure of Amsterdam's government may be helpful. There was a rather powerless city council (*vroedschap*) which chose the city's *schepenen* or aldermen, responsible for judicial matters. The figures who truly governed Amsterdam were the burgomasters, chosen by the city's merchant elite from among themselves. The *schout* was responsible for police matters. The term "magistrates" refers to the city's governing officials together.

5. Pieter de la Court, *Interest van Holland ofte Gronden van Hollands-Welvaren* (Amsterdam 1662), 38–40.

6. On Dutch attitudes to foreigners, see A. Th. van Deursen, *Plain Lives in a Golden Age: Popular Culture, Religion and Society in Seventeenth-Century Holland* (Eng. trans. Cambridge 1991), 32–43.

7. Van Deursen, *Plain Lives,* 32–43. See also Geoffrey Parker, *The Dutch Revolt* (Ithaca 1977), 281–82 n. 8.

8. On population figures for Amsterdam, see Jan de Vries, *The Dutch Rural Economy in the Golden Age, 1500–1700* (New Haven 1974), 90.

9. Van Deursen, *Plain Lives,* 33.

10. Gans, *Memorbook,* 88.

11. The motto is inscribed on Beggar half-moon medals on permanent display in the Rijksmuseum, Amsterdam.

12. On the prolonged restriction of public Catholic worship, see J. van den Berg, "Church and State Relations in the Netherlands," in J. A. Hebly, ed., *Lowland Highlights: Church and Oecumene in the Netherlands* (Kampen 1972), 38.

13. There was one exception to this, in 1629, but mercenaries may have been responsible (Van Deursen, *Plain Lives,* 33).

14. For a convenient collection of seventeenth-century Dutch images of Jews, see the exhibition catalogue *The Jews in the Age of Rembrandt* (Rockville, Md., 1981–82).

15. Joseph Lecler, *Toleration and the Reformation,* 2 vols., English translation from the French (London 1960), 2: 212.

16. On Hooft's views, see Lecler, *Toleration,* 2: 292–97; Zwarts, "De eerste rabbijnen," 221.

17. For a thorough discussion of the debate, see Lecler, *Toleration,* 2: 189–323; Martin van Gelderen, *The Political Thought of the Dutch Revolt, 1555–1590* (Cambridge 1992), 213–59.

18. Lecler, *Toleration,* 2: 268.

19. See J. H. Prins, "Prince William of Orange and the Jews" (Hebrew), *Zion* 15 (1950), 93–105. And see Baron, *Social and Religious History,* 15: 17–19.

20. Zwarts, "De eerste rabbijnen," 249, Appendix 3. And see Bloom, *Economic Activities,* 22–24.

21. In 1598, the same year the resolution was passed, the great jurist Hugo

Grotius expressed no doubt about the religious identity of the "Portuguese": he referred to them as "refugees from Portugal, part of the Jews remaining in that kingdom," who had come to Amsterdam "for fear of an [inquisitorial] investigation into their ancestral religion, and others with a view to greater gain." Hugo Grotius, *Nederlandtsche Jaerboeken en Historien* (Amsterdam 1681), 330.

22. Hermanus Noordkerk, *Handvesten ofte Privilegien ende Octroyen . . . der Stad Amstelredam* (Amsterdam 1748), 1: 138 (9 March 1632).

23. Koen, "Earliest Sources," 30; Bloom, *Economic Activities,* 22–23.

24. Perhaps it was no coincidence that only four months later Manuel Rodrigues Vega's petition to the Amsterdam authorities to establish silk mills there received a favorable response. Bloom, *Economic Activities,* 34; Zwarts, "De eerste rabbijnen," 186–88.

25. M. Wolff, *De Geschiedenis der Joden te Haarlem 1600–1815* (Haarlem 1917), Appendix I, 57–63.

26. *SR* 5 (1971), 240–42, No. 524.

27. This decision has been published by Vaz Dias, "Een verzoek," 185 n. 1.

28. Abraham Coster, *Historie der Joden . . . uyt verscheyde autheuren vergadert* (Rotterdam 1608), unpaginated preface.

29. Zwarts, "De eerste rabbijnen," 209–16 and Appendices 260–64; E. M. Koen, "War en voor vie werd de synagoge van 1612 gebouwd?" *Maandblad Amstelodamum* 57 (1970), 209–12; idem, "Nicolaes van Campen als huiseigenaar van de Portugees-Israelitische synagoge," *Maandblad Amstelodamum* 58 (1971).

30. Paul Zumthor, *Daily Life in Rembrandt's Holland* (London 1962), 90.

31. H. Brugmans, "De houding van Staat en Kerk ten opzichte van de Joden; hun betrekkingen tot de overige bevolking," in *GJN*, 617–42.

32. Bloom, *Economic Activities,* 27–28 n. 120.

33. Brugmans, "De houding," 633.

34. They could also be physicians, surgeons, apothecaries, brokers, printers, or tobacco workers, and engage in a few other guild-related occupations. Bloom, *Economic Activities,* 23–24.

35. Wolff, "De eerste vestiging," 383–84.

36 A. W. Wijbrands, "Overgang tot het Jodendom," *Studiën en bijdragen op 't gebied der historische theologie* 3 (1876), 455–75.

37. Pieterse, *Livro de Bet Haim,* xiii.

38. On Grotius's *Remonstrantie,* see Jacob Meijer, "Hugo Grotius' *Remonstrantie,*" *JSS* 17 (1955), 91–104; A. K. Kuhn, "Hugo Grotius and the Emancipation of the Jews in Holland," *Publications of the American Jewish Historical Society* 31 (1928), 173–80; Baron, *Social and Religious History,* 15: 25–30.

39. *Resolutiën van de Heeren Staten van Hollandt ende West-Vrieslandt . . . January . . . 1619* (printed, n.d., n.p., GAA, Arch. 5038, No. 52), 283 (Dec. 12, 1619), 287 (Dec. 13, 1619), 172 (July 6, 1619).

40. *Resolutiën van Hollandt,* 283, 287.

41. Daniel Swetschinski, "Portuguese Jewish Merchants," 1: 12.

42. Noordkerk, *Handvesten,* 2: 472.

43. It is not surprising that the only two prosecutions I have run across occurred in 1616. One case concerned Abraham Israel, a Portuguese Jew from Lisbon and an apothecary, who cohabited with a certain Maria Granjean first in Bordeaux and then in Amsterdam. On August 23, 1616, a court found him guilty of adultery with his Christian servant and banned him from the States of Holland and Westfriesland with a fine of 100 guilders. Yet from 1623 to 1626, he was again in Amsterdam, where he appears in the records of the Neve Salom community. (See *SR* 10, 213–14

[No. 948], and see 214 n. 27.) In the same year, David Bravo was hoisted up with a weight of two hundred pounds on his feet to make him confess that he had had sexual relations with Lysbeth Egmontsdochter (Koen, "Earliest Sources," 34).

44. Later in the century, England would follow a course similar to that of the Dutch, reflecting important early modern shifts in notions about the governance of Jews.

45. Zwarts, "De eerste rabbijnen," 224 and Appendices 22a and 22b.

46. Ibid. 224–25, 229, and Appendices 22c, 22d, 23a, 23b.

47. GAA, PA 334, No. 19, 25 (*Haskamah* No. 39).

48. Zwarts, "De eerste rabbijnen," 157–58 and Appendix 3.

49. GAA, PA 334, No. 19, 26 (*Haskamah* No. 51) and see ibid., p. 56, decision of 15 Shevat 5400 to limit the number of persons accompanying a bride or groom to twelve.

50. GAA, PA 334, No. 20, f. 200ᵛ (5456).

51. GAA, PA 334, No. 20, p. 279 (6 Shevat 5460).

52. Abraham ben Yosef Halevi, *Sefer ein mishpat* (Salonica 1896/97), No. 45.

53. For an analysis of the emergence of the regent class, see H. F. K. Nierop, *The Nobility of Holland: From Knights to Regents, 1500–1650* (Cambridge 1993).

54. Brugmans, "De houding," 631.

55. For a thorough study of this topic, see Jacob Katz, *Exclusiveness and Tolerance* (London 1961).

56. For a discussion of the economic activities and social rise of the Trip family, see P. W. Klein, "The Trip Family in the Seventeenth Century: A Study of the Behaviour of the Entrepreneur on the Dutch Staple Market," *Acta Historiae Neerlandica* 1 (1966), 187–211.

57. *SR* 2, 124, No. 78; *SR* 3, 114, No. 124; *SR* 3, 248, No. 197 (see also *SR* 6, 242–43, Nos. 660, 661, and *SR* 7, 120, Nos. 693 and 696); *SR* 4, 255, No. 315; *SR* 7, 268, No. 743; *SR* 8, 301, No. 844 (and see *SR* 8, 304, Nos. 855, 860, and 861, also *SR* 10, 97, No. 883); *SR* 10, 213–14, No. 948; *SR* 11, 91, No. 1157; *SR* 13, 227, No. 1522; *SR* 13, 234 n. 45; *SR* 15, 146, No. 1779 (charge of rape); *SR* 24, 76, No. 2896. See also Salomon, *Portrait of a New Christian*, 135–39. On the liaisons of the extremely wealthy Antonio and Francisco Lopes Suasso, see *The Lopes Suasso Family, Bankers to William III* (Amsterdam 1988), 59.

58. Swetschinski, "Portuguese Jewish Merchants," 1: 16–17.

59. Van Deursen, *Plain Lives,* 161. For similar comments by surprised visitors, see Peter Burke, "Patrician Culture: Venice and Amsterdam in the Seventeenth Century," *Transactions of the Royal Historical Society,* fifth series, 23 (1973), 137.

60. See a description of the auction catalogue of Aboab's library in A. Marx, *Studies in Jewish History and Booklore* (New York 1944), 210–11; Shlomo Berger, "Codices Gentium: Rabbi Isaac Aboab's Collection of Classical Literature," *SR* 29 (1995), 5–13; Aaron L. Katchen, *Christian Hebraists and Dutch Rabbis* (Harvard 1984), 114–15.

61. *Sermões que pregaraõ os doctos ingenios do K. K. de Talmud Torah, desta cidade de Amsterdam no alegre estreamento publica celebridade da Esnoga* (Amsterdam 1675). The explanation of L. and R. G. Fuks in "The Inauguration of the Portuguese Synagogue of Amsterdam, Netherlands in 1675," *Arquivos do Centro Cultural Portugues* 14 (1974), 504–505, that delivering the sermons in Spanish might have seemed politically provocative to the Dutch, does not seem compelling to me.

62. Benjamin Teensma, "De taal der Amsterdamse Sefardim in de 17e en 18e eeuw," in R. Kistemaker and T. Levie, eds., *Êxodo: Portugezen in Amsterdam, 1600–1680* (Amsterdam 1987), 70.

63. Benjamin Teensma, "The Suffocation of Spanish and Portuguese among Amsterdam Sephardi Jews," *DJH* 3 (Jerusalem 1993), 137–77.

64. See Van Praag, "Almas en litigio," 14–26; L. Fuks and R. G. Fuks-Mansfeld, "Joodse geschiedschrijving in de Republiek in de 17e en 18e eeuw," *SR* 6 (1972), 138.

65. Van Praag, "Almas en litigio," 21.

66. Swetschinski, "Portuguese Jews," 65–68.

67. Menasseh ben Israel, *Gratulação de Menasseh ben Israel em nome de sua nação ao celsissimo Principe de Orange . . .* (Amsterdam 1642), 7. Elsewhere, likewise—in his *Conciliador,* published for both a Jewish and gentile audience—Menasseh described himself as "Portuguese by birth but Dutch in spirit [*Lusitano con anima Batavea*]." See Menasseh ben Israel, *Conciliador o de la conveniencia de los lugares de la S. Escriptura que repugnantes entre si parecen,* pt. 2 (Amsterdam 1641), unpaginated dedication.

68. On the relative indifference of Ashkenazi Jews to the Christian world in this period, see Katz, *Exclusiveness and Tolerance,* 134–38. To be sure, in the 1520s, there had been at least a few such Jews who viewed Martin Luther's break with the Church as a momentous event—indeed, the dawn of the messianic era, a sign of the approaching defeat of the fourth empire as prophesied in the Book of Daniel (i.e., Rome, according to Jewish interpretation). Rumors even circulated that Luther was a "crypto-Jew": that he rejected the divinity of Jesus and intended to win the gentiles over to Judaism. But such illusions had soon been dispelled. By the 1540s, Luther was writing virulently hostile tracts on Jews and Judaism; and as the years passed it became evident that neither Luther's message nor the best-trained Protestant armies would bring about a decisive defeat of the Catholic Church. See H. H. Ben-Sasson, "The Reformation in Contemporary Jewish Eyes," in *Proceedings of the Israel Academy of Sciences and Humanities* 4 (Jerusalem 1970), 239–327.

69. This had been Luther's approach in the 1520s when he wrote the treatise *Dass Jhesus Christus eyn geborner Jude sey* (1523), but he soon abandoned it.

70. Meijer, "Hugo Grotius' *Remonstrantie,*" 95. On Jewish converts to the Reformed church, and efforts of the latter to bring this about, see Brugmans, "De houding," 634–37.

71. See L. Fuks and R. G. Fuks-Mansfeld, *Hebrew Typography in the Northern Netherlands, 1585–1815,* 2 vols. (Leiden 1984–87), 1: 98–99.

72. Broughton, who appears to have been contentious by nature and not well-disposed to the Jews, published an account of the debate "for Amsteldam and the Portugalles and our Iscariots [i.e., his theological opponents]," in Latin in 1605, and in English in 1608. See Hugh Broughton, *Our Lordes Familie and many other poinctes depending upon it: opened against a Iew, Rabbi David Farar who disputed many houres, with hope to overthrow the Gospel* (Amsterdam 1608). If Farar published his version of the debate in Latin, as Broughton's account claims he intended to do, it has not been found. .

73. Noordkerk, *Handvesten,* 2: 472.

74. GAA, PA 334, No. 19, 25 (*Haskamah* No. 38).

75. GAA, PA 334, No. 19, 769.

76. On this figure, see *SR* 11 (1977), 221 n. 56.

77. S. B. J. Zilverberg, "Jan Pieterszoon Beelthouwer (c. 1603–c. 1669) en de Joden," *SR* 3 (1969), 158–60; L. Hirschel, "Jan Pieterszoon Beeldthouwer en de rabbijnen," *VA* 7 (1930), 210–11, 227–28.

78. Their correspondence (in Hebrew) was printed at the end of Alting's *Fundamenta punctationis Linguae Sanctae* (Groningen 1673), paginated separately 1–8; see discussion in Jacob Silva Rosa, *Over de verhouding tusschen Joden en niet-joden in de*

Republiek der vereenigde Nederlanden gedurende de 17e en 18e eeuw (Amsterdam 1922), 24.

79. Hulsius published his correspondence with Abendana in Latin in 1669: *Disputatio epistolaris . . . super loco Haggaei cp. 2 v. 9 . . .* (Leiden 1669). See J. van den Berg, *Joden en Christenen in Nederland gedurende de zeventiende eeuw* (Kampen 1969), 12–13; Fuks-Mansfeld, *De Sephardim in Amsterdam*, 102–103.

80. See P. T. van Rooden and J. W. Wesselius, "J. S. Rittangel in Amsterdam," *Nederlands Archief voor Kerkgeschiedenis* 65 (1985), 131–52.

81. It began as an oral discussion in 1683 but developed into a lengthy debate by correspondence. Limborch published a record of the written discussion in 1687: *De veritate religionis christianae amica collatio cum erudito judaeo* (Gouda 1687).

82. P. T. van Rooden and J. W. Wesselius, "The Early Enlightenment and Judaism: The 'Civil Dispute' between Philippus van Limborch and Isaac Orobio de Castro (1687)," *SR* 21 (1987), 140–53. On the debate, see also Yosef Kaplan, *From Christianity to Judaism: The Story of Isaac Orobio de Castro* (Oxford 1989), 270–85.

83. Van den Berg, *Joden en christenen in Nederland*, 24.

84. Silva Rosa, *Over de verhouding*, 19–22; Van den Berg, *Joden en christenen*, 36–37.

85. For example, concerning the doctine of transubstantiation. Inquisition files reveal that a New Christian cleric in the sixteenth century was accused of complaining, before saying mass, that "they want me to believe that the Host which the priest is kneading at night with his mistress becomes the next day the true and complete God!" (Antonio Baião, *A Inquisição em Portugal e no Brasil* [Lisbon 1921], 151). Compare this with a jingle by a Dutch Protestant in the seventeenth century: "I have visited countries, hear my tale, / Where the people present a piece of bread as their God. / Afterwards they eat him. Are these not strange customs? / But the greatest wonder above all wonders deep, / Every day a new God is kneaded there again" (van Deursen, *Plain Lives*, 242).

86. It is true that Menasseh ben Israel published ideas contrary to Calvin's doctrine of predestination, but he did not directly attack Calvin, and a view similar to his was openly supported by the Arminians or Remonstrants in the Netherlands. See his *De termino vitae* (Amsterdam 1639), 226–28; *De la fragilidad humana y inclinación del hombre al pecado* (Amsterdam 1642).

87. Mortera's manuscript work has recently been published by H. P. Salomon, ed., *Tratado da verdade da lei de Moisés* (Coimbra 1988). Mortera was not a Portuguese Jew of converso origin—he was apparently an Italian Jew—but he had become a part of the ex-converso diaspora quite early in his life, and devoted himself to serving its needs until his death. On Mortera, see Bodian, "Amsterdam, Venice, and the Marrano Diaspora," 49–50.

88. Mortera, *Tratado da verdade*, 1–3.

89. Zechariah 14: 9.

90. Mortera, *Tratado da verdade*, 174–203.

91. Ibid., 192.

92. Ibid., 52.

93. Ibid., 388–90.

94. *Prevenciones divinas contra la vana Idolatría de las Gentes.* There are a number of manuscript copies of this work. I have used Ms. EH 48 D 6. On Orobio de Castro, see Kaplan, *From Christianity*.

95. *Prevenciones divinas*, 121^v–122^r.

96. *TGP*, 1–58 and passim.

97. *Pseudo-Philo's Liber Antiquitatum Biblicarum*, ed. G. Kisch (Notre Dame, Indiana 1949), 123–30.

98. His proof text was Genesis 10: 30, describing the dwelling place of the descendants of Yoqtan: "And their dwelling was from Mesha, as thou goest to

Sefar, a mountain of *kedem.*" De Barrios cited sources showing that *kedem* refers to Spain or some part of it, and that "Mesha" refers to the river Maas in the Netherlands—Mosa in Latin. From this he concluded that the Netherlanders were originally a Celtiberian tribe (*Arevacas*) which relocated in the Low Countries. See *TGP,* 8–9, 42–43, 46–47.

99. On the classical humanist roots of the Batavian myth, see I. Schöffer, "The Batavian Myth during the Sixteenth and Seventeenth Centuries," *Britain and the Netherlands* 5 (1975), 78–101.

100. In fact, Alexander Polyhistor relates only that a woman named Moso gave the Law to the Jews (M. Stern, *Greek and Latin Authors on Jews and Judaism,* 3 vols. [Jerusalem 1974–1984], 1: 163). Suidas, also cited by De Barrios, gives the same information (*Suidae Lexicon,* Ada Adler, ed., I, 104 line 34). De Barrios also cites Tomás de Pinedo's commentary on Stephen of Byzantium as a source, but I have not seen this.

101. *TGP,* 18, 22, 47–48.

102. Ibid., 421.

103. On the self-defining iconography of the Dutch in the seventeenth century, see Simon Schama, *The Embarrassment of Riches: An Interpretation of Dutch Culture in the Golden Age* (New York 1987). On the many chronicles written by the Dutch in the seventeenth century in an effort to construct a Dutch national past, see J. L. Price, *Culture and Society in the Dutch Republic during the Seventeenth Century* (London 1974), 13, 188–94.

4. Iberian Memory and Its Perpetuation

1. António Borges Coelho, *Inquisição de Évora,* 2 vols. (Lisbon 1987), 1: 211–12.

2. Cecil Roth, "Les Marranes à Rouen: Un chapitre ignoré de l'histoire des Juifs de France," *REJ* 88 (1929), 113–55; I. S. Révah, "Le premier établissement des Marranes portugais à Rouen (1603–1607)," *Mélanges Isidore Levy* (*Annuaire de l'Institut de Philologie et d'Histoires Orientales et Slaves* 13, 1953) (Brussels 1955), 539–52.

3. For a study of domestic problems among conversos fueled by differences of conviction, see David Gitlitz, "Divided Families in 'Converso' Spain," *Shofar* 11 (1993), 1–19.

4. See, for example, Rafael de Lera García, "Venta de oficios en la Inquisición de Granada (1629–1644)," *Hispania: Revista Española de Historia* 48 (1988), 909–62.

5. Salomon, "'De Pinto' Manuscript," 47.

6. On the nostalgia of two converso poets for the Peninsula, see Yosef Kaplan, "The Travels of Portuguese Jews from Amsterdam to the 'Lands of Idolatry' (1644–1724)," in Kaplan, ed., *Jews and Conversos,* 198; Antonio Enríquez Gómez, "Cuando contemplo mi pasada gloria," in Timothy Oelman, trans. and ed., *Marrano Poets of the Seventeenth Century: An Anthology of the Poetry of João Pinto Delgado, Antonio Enríquez Gómez, and Miguel de Barrios* (Associated University Presses, 1982), 140–50, and idem, *Las Academias morales de las Musas* (Rouen 1642).

7. C. Roth, "Immanuel Aboab's Proselytization of the Marranos," *JQR* 23 (1932), 143.

8. I. S. Révah, "Les écrivains Manuel de Pina et Miguel de Barrios et la censure de la communauté judéo-portugaise d'Amsterdam," *Tesoro de los Judíos Españoles* 8 (1965), lxxxi-lxxxii.

9. See Kaplan, "Travels of Portuguese Jews."

10. Cecil Roth, "Strange Case of Hector Mendes Bravo," 221–45.

11. Roth, *History of the Marranos,* 142.

12. "p[or] nao saber consertar mentiras, que forao as palauras que dizen" (Salomon, "'De Pinto' Manuscript," 51).

13. B. N. Teensma, "Fragmenten uit het amsterdamse convoluut van Abraham Idaña, alias Gaspar Méndez Arroyo (1623–1690)," *SR* 11 (1977), 146, 153, 155.

14. This is a free rhymed translation. In the original Portuguese: "Aqui se faz o justo criminozo, / Jurando o que não viu, nem foy soñado, / Aquy se fazem trassas e ardis seus, / Que os Cristãos se convertem em Judeos" (Salomon, *Portrait of a New Christian*, xiii).

15. Its mobilization was no doubt facilitated by the fact that Dutch rhetoric also condemned anything that smacked of "the Inquisition."

16. See Cecil Roth, "Religion of the Marranos," 6; António José Texeira, *António Homem e a Inquisição* (Coimbra 1895), 161–62; João Lúcio d'Azevedo, *História dos Christãos-Novos portugueses* (Lisbon 1921), 177.

17. Révah, "La religion d'Uriel da Costa," 59.

18. Cecil Roth maintains this prayer could be found in "the prayer books of the time" (Roth, *History of the Marranos*, 141), but I have found it in only one.

19. *Seder Brachot, Orden de Bendiciones y las ocaziones en que se deven dezir, con muchas adiciones a las precedentes impreciones, y por mejor methodo dispuestas* (Amsterdam 1687) (Hebrew and Spanish on facing pages), 300–303. In the Hebrew version the prayer is entitled *Hashkavat ha-serufim al kiddush ha-shem.*

20. In the Spanish version, the expression is *su siervo el santo (hulano)* for a male and *su sierva la Santa (Señora hulana)* for a female.

21. GAA, PA 334, No. 19, f. 195 (21 Av 5405).

22. Isaac Orobio de Castro, "Respuesta a un escrito que presentó un Predicante Francés a el Author contra la observancia de la Divina Ley de Mosseh," Ms. EH 48D 6, f. 294 (pp. 20–21 in the text published by M. B. Amzalak [Coimbra 1925]).

23. On Abendana, see Meyer Kayserling, *Biblioteca Española-Portugueza-Judaica,* ed. Y. H. Yerushalmi (New York 1971), 23–24.

24. *Elogios que zelosos dedicaron a la felice memoria de Abraham Nuñez Bernal, que fue quemado vivo santificando el Nombre de su criador en Cordova a 3 de Mayo 5415* [Amsterdam 1655], 169.

25. From a poem by Antonio Enríquez Gómez published in Oelman, *Marrano Poets,* 148–49. I have used Oelman's translation.

26. Anita Novinsky, *Cristãos novos na Bahía* (São Paulo 1972), 149.

27. See Arnold Wiznitzer, "Isaac de Castro, Brazilian Jewish Martyr," in Martin Cohen, ed., *The Jewish Experience in Latin America* (New York 1971), 2: 205–17; Elias Lipiner, *Izaque de Castro: o mancebo que veio preso do Brasil* (Recife 1992).

28. For bibliographical details on the literature on Isaac de Castro, see George Alexander Kohut, "Jewish Martyrs of the Inquisition in South America," *Publications of the American Jewish Historical Society* 4 (1896), 166–71; Cecil Roth, "An Elegy of João Pinto Delgado on Isaac de Castro Tartas," *REJ* 21 (1962), 355–66; and see Lipiner, *Izaque de Castro,* 253–55.

29. The entire text of the poem, in the original Hebrew and with a rough English translation, is published in Kohut, "Jewish Martyrs," 167–70. And compare it with the verse in Castro Tartas's memory by João Pinto Delgado, an important "Portuguese" poet who eventually settled in Amsterdam (Roth, "Elegy of João Pinto Delgado," 365–66).

30. *Elogios que zelosos dedicaron a la felice memoria de Abraham Nuñez Bernal.* The title of the collection does not indicate the material in honor of Isaac d'Almeida Bernal. Isaac was only seventeen years old when seized by the Inquisition and twenty-two when burned at the stake. The story of his martyrdom was recounted in passionate detail, perhaps embellished, by Daniel de Ribera (*Elogios,* 125–28).

31. De Barrios wrote an allegorical *comedia* in honor of Athias and two other judaizers burned alive at this auto. See Daniel Levi de Barrios, *Contra la verdad no ay fuerça, Panegirico a los tres bienaventurados martires Abraham Athias, Yahacob Rodriguez Càceres, y Raquel Nuñes Fernandez, que fueron quemados vivos en Córdova, por santificar la unidad divina. En 16 de Tamuz, Año de 5425* (Amsterdam n.d.).

32. Fuks and Fuks-Mansfeld, *Hebrew Typography*, 2: 291–92.

33. GAA, PA 334, No. 1141, 47, 64. Another candidate in St. Jean de Luz was listed that year as "a daughter of Beatris de Mercado, widow of Alvaro de Fonseca Peres who suffered in this auto-da-fé in Coimbra" (GAA, PA 334, No. 1141, 64).

34. See, for example, João Pinto, "A la salida de Lisboa," "Poema de la Reina Ester," "Lamentación 1: 13," "Canción, aplicando misericordias divinas y defetos proprios a la salida de Egipto hasta la Tierra Santa"; Antonio Enríquez Gómez, "Romance al divín mártir, Judá Creyente, martirizado en Valladolid por la Inquisición"—all published in Oelman, *Marrano Poets*, in the original and in English translation.

35. Salomon, *Portrait of a New Christian*, 190–94.

36. See, inter alia, José Antonio Maravall, *Poder, honor y élites en el siglo XVII* (Madrid 1979); J. A. Jackson, ed., *Estratificación social* (Barcelona 1971); J. G. Peristiany, ed., *El concepto del honor en la sociedad mediterránea* (Barcelona 1968).

37. H. H. Ben-Sasson, "Generation of Spanish Exiles," 23–64.

38. Hermann Kellenbenz, "Tradiciones nobiliarias de los grupos sefardíes," *Actas del Primer Simposio de Estudios Sefardíes* (Madrid 1970), 50.

39. Biblioteca Nacional, Madrid, Ms. 13043, 117v.

40. Carlos Carrete Parrondo, "Nostalgia for the Past," 35. And see Yolanda Koch, "La comunidad judaizante de Catillo de Garcimuñoz: 1489–1492," *Sefarad* 37 (1977), 370, for a similar statement reportedly overheard in 1485.

41. Angela Selke, *Los Chuetas y la Inquisición* (Madrid 1972), 115.

42. Dedication to *Additiones ad postillam Magistri Lyra* (1429).

43. The claims to levitic descent of a distinguished seventeenth-century converso, Manuel Fernandes Villareal, were apparently part of the testimony used to convict him of judaizing (Roth, *History of the Marranos*, 160).

44. Diego de Valera, *Espejo de verdadera nobleza* in Balenchana, ed., *Epístolas, Sociedad de Bibliófilos Españoles*, vol. 16 (Madrid 1878), 204–205, and in M. Penna, ed., *Prosistas castellanos del siglo XV*, vol. 116 of *Biblioteca de Autores Españoles* (Madrid 1959), 102–105.

45. *TGP*, "Casa de Jacob," 404.

46. Salomon, "'De Pinto' Manuscript," 46.

47. Ibid., 47.

48. Ibid., 48.

49. Ibid., 49.

50. Ibid.

51. Racial ideas, while marginal, can be found in rabbinic literature, particularly in the thinking of the medieval Spanish poet and thinker Judah Halevi, whose *Kuzari* was known in the "Portuguese" diaspora. But racial ideas were not common in rabbinic literature, and in any case Jewish law recognizes no racial principle.

52. Cardoso, *Excelencias*, 32–33. Cf. Yerushalmi, *Spanish Court*, 385.

53. Salomon, *Portrait of a New Christian*, 167. Incidentally, the claim of Jewish purity of blood was put to apologetic use in Menasseh ben Israel's *Humble Addresses* to Oliver Cromwell—as if this claim was one that could impress gentiles as well. One of the three reasons Jews should be readmitted to England, Menasseh argued, was the "nobleness and purity of their blood." He did not, however, elaborate on the point, explaining that it was "enough known amongst all Chris-

tians." See Lucien Wolf, ed., *Menasseh ben Israel's Mission to Oliver Cromwell* (London 1901), 81, 103.

54. The rejudaized Pereiras and Pimentels made similar modifications to eliminate a cross or crosses on their coats of arms. See Isaac da Costa, *Noble Families among the Sephardic Jews* (London 1936), 126, 129 n. 1.

55. Hermann Kellenbenz, "Das Testament von Manuel Texeira," *SR* 3 (1969), 53; idem, *Sephardim an der unteren Elbe*, 164–65.

56. Arnold Wiznitzer, *The Jews in Colonial Brazil* (New York 1960), 16.

57. See H. Reinhold, "Joseph Salvador: His Life and Ideas" (Hebrew), *Zion* 9 (1944), 115.

58. Da Costa, *Noble Families*, 134.

59. Ibid.

60. Salomon, "'De Pinto' Manuscript," 11 n. 29.

61. Gans, *Memorbook*, 110. I would like to express my appreciation to Ms. Judith Belinfante at the Jewish Historical Museum in Amsterdam for allowing me to view a color slide of the marriage contract.

62. Da Costa, *Noble Families*, 112.

63. Of course titles were not eagerly granted to Jews elsewhere in Europe. In 1673, Emperor Leopold II made Manuel de Belmonte a Count Palatine in recognition of his efforts in the defense of the Spanish Netherlands. However, when the Emperor learned that Belmonte was a Jew, he ordered that the certificate be withheld. Manuel de Belmonte nevertheless proudly called himself a Count Palatine whenever the occasion presented itself—for example, in every notarial deed drawn up in his name. He must have been immensely gratified when in 1693 Carlos II of Spain elevated him to baron, making him lord of a territory situated in the Spanish Netherlands (Swetschinski, "Portuguese Jewish Merchants," 1: 269–70).

64. Swetschinski, "Portuguese Jewish Merchants," 1: 263.

65. A color reproduction of the portrait can be found in *The Lopes Suasso Family: Bankers to William III* (catalogue of the Jewish Historical Museum of Amsterdam) (Amsterdam 1988), 10.

66. *Sermões que pregaraõ*, 57–58.

67. On the different roles of the Spanish and Portuguese languages, see Cecil Roth, "The Role of Spanish in the Marrano Diaspora," in Frank Pierce, ed., *Hispanic Studies in Honour of I. González Llubera* (Oxford 1959), 299–308. On the relatively pure character of the Spanish and Portuguese used by the Amsterdam Sephardim in the seventeenth century, see Teensma, "De taal der Amsterdamse Sefardim," 70.

68. Teensma, "Van Marraan tot Jood," 122.

69. On the Spanish literary academies, see José Sánchez, *Academias literarias del siglo de oro español* (Madrid 1961); W. F. King, *Prosa novelística y academias literarias en el siglo XVII* (Madrid 1963).

70. See Kaplan, *From Christianity*, 286–302; Swetschinski, "Portuguese Jews," 71–73.

71. See Daniel Levi de Barrios's opuscules "Metros Nobles," and "Academia de los Floridos, Memoria plausible de sus juezes y Academicos."

72. Kaplan, *From Christianity*, 289–90.

73. See the discussion of Swetschinski, "Portuguese Jewish Merchants," 2: 536–42.

74. See Kaplan, *From Christianity*, 294–95.

75. See Swetschinski, "Portuguese Jews," 71–73, and 80 nn. 71–73; Kaplan, *From Christianity*, 297–302. To Swetschinski's list of published works resulting from the academies' activities may be added De Barrios's *Repuesta panegírica a la Carta que escrivio el muy ilustre R. Joseph Penso Vega al muy sapiente Doctor Ishac Orobio,*

presented at the *Academia de los Sitibundos* (Amsterdam 1677; see Kayserling, *Biblioteca*, 41).

76. Salomon, "'De Pinto' Manuscript," 41.

77. See Daniel Heiple, "Life as Dream and the Philosophy of Disillusionment," in Frederick A. de Armas, ed., *The Prince in the Tower: Perceptions of "La vida es sueño"* (Associated University Presses 1993), 123.

78. GAA, NA 3580, 100, 131. Cited in Daniel Swetschinski, "Portuguese Jews," 63.

79. Swetschinski, "Portuguese Jews," 63.

80. Ibid.; J. S. da Silva Rosa, "De joden in den Schouwburg en in de Opera te Amsterdam gedurende de 17de en 18de eeuw," *VA*, 1925.

81. GAA, PA 334, No. 13, 86. The text of the decision has been published in Pieterse, *Daniel Levi de Barrios*, 155.

82. GAA, PA 334, No. 19, 107.

83. Swetschinski, "Portuguese Jews," 63–64.

84. From the prologue to his *Rumbos peligrosos* (Antwerp 1683). See Julia Rebollo Lieberman, "El teatro alegorico religioso de Miguel (Daniel Levi) de Barrios y la colonia de sefarditas de Amsterdam en el siglo XVII" (Yale University diss. 1989), 50–51.

85. Dan Pagis, *Hebrew Poetry of the Middle Ages and the Renaissance* (Berkeley 1991), 36–37; idem, "Ziburei dimuyim," *Jerusalem Studies in Hebrew Literature* (Hebrew) (Jerusalem 1981), 1: 207.

5. The Rejudaization of "the Nation"

1. Salomon, "'De Pinto' Manuscript," 59.

2. Ibid.

3. Ibid.

4. Ibid., 60.

5. Cardoso, *Las excelencias*, 90–91. Cf. Yerushalmi, *Spanish Court*, 380.

6. The popular converso conception of circumcision as a kind of sacramental act must have had implications for women. Given the social and economic dependence of women on men and the strongly patriarchal character of Iberian society, it is not surprising that the issue was not raised. One would like to know how women responded to the absence for them of such a differentiating act.

7. Caro Baroja, *Los judíos en la España*, 3: 361.

8. While the entire testimony is fascinating, some of it is of doubtful reliability, and there is no evidence that the witness, Esteban de Ares de Fonseca, was pressured into being circumcised in Amsterdam by being put in *herem*, as he told the Inquisition. The entire account is published in Caro Baroja, *Los judíos en la España*, 3: 359–64.

9. Samuel Aboab, *Sefer ha-zikhronot* (n.p., n.d.), fol. 75. Cf. Yerushalmi, *Spanish Court*, 200. A similar position was adopted not long afterward by the "Portuguese" rabbi Moses Rafael d'Aguilar of Amsterdam, when a forged rabbinic opinion was sent to conversos in Bayonne advising them that without circumcision their observance of other precepts was useless for their salvation. "Reposta e discurso sobre certas perguntas de Bayona e foy em nome dos Hahamim," Ms. EH 48A11, 213v–225v. And see Yosef Kaplan, "Rabbi Moshe Rafael d'Aguilar's Role with Spanish and Portuguese Emigres in the Seventeenth Century" [Hebrew], *Proceedings of the Sixth World Congress of Jewish Studies* [1976], Part B, 99–100.)

10. Yosef Hayim Yerushalmi, "The Re-education of the Marranos in the Seventeenth Century," *The Third Annual Rabbi Louis Feinberg Memorial Lecture in Judaic Studies* (March 26, 1980), 4–5.

11. Stephen Gilman, *The Spain of Fernando de Rojas* (Princeton 1972), 197.

12. Elvira Cunha de Azevedo Mea, *Sentenças da Inquisicão de Coimbra em metropolitanos de D. Frei Bartolomeu dos Mártires* (Porto 1982), 450.

13. Antonio Baião, *A Inquisição em Portugal e no Brasil* (Lisbon 1921), 137–38.

14. Ibid., 178.

15. Ibid., 157.

16. Feliciano Sierro Malmierca, *Judíos, moriscos e Inquisición en Ciudad Rodrigo* (Salamanca 1990), 178.

17. Baião, *A Inquisição em Portugal*, 129.

18. Ibid., 141.

19. María Antonia Bel Bravo, *El auto de fe de 1593: los conversos granadinos de origen judío* (Granada 1988), 151.

20. Révah, "Les Marranes," 53–54.

21. See Tishby, *Messianism in the Time of the Expulsion*, 44, n. 111.

22. Jaime Contreras, *El Santo Oficio de la Inquisición de Galicia, 1560–1700: poder, sociedad y cultura* (Madrid 1982), 607.

23. Roth, "Religion of the Marranos," 5.

24. Cunha de Azevedo Mea, *Sentenças*, 344.

25. Ibid., 375.

26. Coelho, *Inquisição de Évora*, 1: 223–24.

27. Ibid., 211.

28. For a discussion of some of the Christian works frequently cited by Portuguese Jews, see Swetschinski, "Portuguese Jews," 68.

29. Cunha de Azevedo Mea, "Orações," 159–63.

30. "Bento tu, Adonay, nosso Deos, que com teu mandamento anoitecem as noites e com sabedoria abre as portes e com entendimento mudas as horas e ordenas as estrellas no ceo como he tua vontade e crias dia e crias noite e envolves a luz entre as escuridades. . . ." (Cunha de Azevedo Mea, "Orações," 162).

31. Cunha de Azevedo Mea, "Orações," 166–67.

32. Cunha de Azevedo Mea, Sentenças, 378.

33. See Yerushalmi, *Spanish Court*, 276–99; idem, "Professing Jews," 1023–58; idem, "Conversos Returning to Judaism in the Seventeenth Century: Their Jewish Knowledge and Psychological Readiness" (Hebrew), *Proceedings of the Fifth World Congress of Jewish Studies* (1969), vol. 2 (Jerusalem 1972), Hebrew section, 201–209.

34. See I. S. Révah, *Spinoza et le Dr. Juan de Prado* (Paris/The Hague 1959), 24; idem, "Aux origines de la rupture spinozienne: nouvel examen des origines, du déroulement et des conséquences de l'affaire Spinoza-Prado-Ribera" (part 3), *Annuaire de Collège de France* 70 (1970), 650; Kaplan, *From Christianity*, 125–27.

35. Joseph Shalom ben Gallego, *Sefer imrei no'am* (Amsterdam 1628–1630), fol. 141r.

36. Yerushalmi, "The Re-education of Marranos," 7.

37. See the discussion of this literature in Yerushalmi, "The Re-education of Marranos," 7–12.

38. This has been suggested by Roth, "The Role of Spanish," 302–303.

39. See A. K. Offenberg, "The *Primera Parte del sedur* (Amsterdam 1612)," *SR* 15 (1981), 234–37.

40. See Kayserling, *Biblioteca*, 59–64.

41. Harm den Boer and Herman Prins Salomon, "Another 'Lost' Book Found: The Melo Haggadah, Amsterdam 1622," *SR* 29 (1995), 119–34.

42. See Kayserling, *Biblioteca*, 50–52.

43. The most important published works of this kind are Immanuel Aboab's *Nomologia* (Amsterdam 1629) and Isaac Cardoso's *Las Excelencias de los Hebreos* (Amsterdam 1679). Worthy of note is the early translation of the polemical Karaite work *Hizzuk emunah* by Isaac Athias, *Fortificacion de la Ley de Mosse* (Hamburg 1621). Many of the important polemical works attacking Christianity, however—among them those of Isaac Orobio de Castro—circulated in manuscript, for obvious reasons.

44. *Libro intitulado Obligacion de los coraçones, compuesto por el excelentissimo senor el grande Rabenu Moseh de Aegypco* (!) translated by David Pardo, son of Joseph Pardo (Amsterdam 1610); *Hobat Alebabot, Obrigaçam dos coraçoes*, translated into Portuguese by the Amsterdam rabbi Samuel Abas (Amsterdam 1670).

45. The work was translated by the Amsterdam-trained rabbi Jacob Abendana, using ibn Tibbon's translation into Hebrew of the original Judeo-Arabic work. The *Kuzari*, which pits Judaism successfully against Greek philosophy, Islam, and Christianity, had obvious appeal for the "Portuguese," an appeal which may have been enhanced by Halevi's notions about the superiority of Jewish "lineage."

46. *Tratado de la Thesuvah o Contricion* (Amsterdam 1613); *Tratado de los Articulos de la Ley Divina* (Amsterdam 1652).

47. On the hesitations that delayed such translations, see Yerushalmi, "The Re-education of the Marranos," 8–10.

48. Menasseh ben Israel, *Thesouro dos dinim, que o povo de Israel he obrigado saber, e observar* (Amsterdam 1645–47), dedication, n.p.

49. *TGP*, 61–76 (Keter Torah); 77–112 (Torah Or); 113–16 (Pinto Yeshiva); 117–31 (Meirat Yenaim). Cf. Pieterse, *Daniel Levi de Barrios*, 106–17.

50. See Pieterse, *Daniel Levi de Barrios*, 110.

51. Shabbetai Sheftel Horowitz, *Sefer vav ha-amudim* (Amsterdam 1653), fol. 9v (published at the end of his father's work *Shenei luhot ha-brit*; appropriate excerpts published in Simha Assaf, *Documents on the History of Jewish Education*, 4 vols. [Hebrew] [Tel Aviv 1925–1930], 1: 70–71).

52. Jacob Katz, *Tradition and Crisis* (New York 1993), 162.

53. Clause 22 of the merger agreement, published in Pieterse, *Daniel Levi de Barrios*, 160.

54. Shabbetai Bass, *Sefer siftei yeshenim* (Amsterdam 1680), fol. 8r-v. The passage has been published in Assaf, *Documents*, 1: 155–56.

55. Swetschinski, "Portuguese Jewish Merchants," 2: 388–89.

56. See Katz, *Tradition and Crisis*, 158–62.

57. There they "did not have to flatter and ingratiate themselves to anyone." And see Katz, *Tradition and Crisis*, 161–62, 163.

58. Pieterse, *Daniel Levi de Barrios*, 97.

59. GAA, PA 334, No. 19, fol. 459.

60. See Katz, *Tradition and Crisis*, 65–68.

61. The second clause of the merger agreement states that the means of enforcing the *Mahamad's* authority would be like those exercised in Venice (*segindo ho estilo de Veneza*). See the merger agreement published in Pieterse, *Daniel Levi de Barrios*, 156. Unfortunately, no copy of the statutes of the Venetian community has survived, so no detailed comparison is possible. For other ways in which the Venetian community served as the model for the Amsterdam community, see Bodian, "Amsterdam, Venice, and the Converso Diaspora."

62. See Abraham Neuman, *The Jews in Spain: Their Social, Political and Cultural Life during the Middle Ages*, 2 vols. (Philadelphia 1948), 1: 53.

63. "Que o Mahamad terá autoridade e superioridade sobre tudo" (GAA, PA 334, No. 19, 21).

64. Most importantly, it accepted the right of the *Mahamad* to impose the ban or

herem. See Yosef Kaplan, "The Social Functions of the Herem in the Portuguese Jewish Community of Amsterdam in the Seventeenth Century," *DJH* 1 (1984), 113 n. 4. But this acceptance was not absolute. In at least two cases city authorities intervened on behalf of persons who had been placed under the ban (ibid., 144, 145).

65. See Kaplan, "Social Functions of the Herem," 118–19.

66. GAA, PA 334, No. 19, 204. Cf. Kaplan, "Social Functions of the Herem," 136.

67. GAA, PA 334, No. 13, fol. 6v. Cf. Kaplan, "Social Functions of the Herem," 118. The patterns of behavior of generally uncommitted conversos living outside the Peninsula have been explored in two studies based on Venetian inquisitorial documents: Brian Pullan, "'A Ship with Two Rudders': 'Righetto Marrano' and the Inquisition in Venice," *The Historical Journal* 20 (1977), 25–58; idem, "The Inquisition and the Jews of Venice: The Case of Gaspare Ribeiro, 1580–1581," *Bulletin of the John Rylands University Library* 62 (1979), 207–31. On uncommitted or minimally attached "Portuguese" in London, see Matt Goldish, "Jews, Christians and Conversos: Rabbi Solomon Aailion's Struggles in the Portuguese Community of London," *Journal of Jewish Studies* 45 (1994), 227–57; Isaiah Tishby, "New Information on the 'Converso' Community in London According to the Letters of Sasportas from 1664/1665" in *Exile and Diaspora: Studies in the History of the Jewish People Presented to Professor Haim Beinart on the Occasion of His Seventieth Birthday* (Hebrew volume) (Jerusalem 1988), 470–96; Yosef Kaplan, "Wayward New Christians and Stubborn New Jews: The Shaping of a Jewish Identity," in Gartner and Stow, eds., *The Robert Cohen Memorial Volume* (Haifa 1994), 27–41; and Yosef Kaplan, "The Jewish Profile of the Spanish and Portuguese Community of London in the Seventeenth Century," in Katz and Kaplan, eds., *Exile and Return: Anglo-Jewry through the Ages* (Jerusalem 1993), 133–45.

68. Rafael Meldola, *Mayim rabbim* (Amsterdam 1737), part 2, Nos. 51 and 52. See also No. 53, Meldola's later prohibition, on more legalistic grounds.

69. GAA, PA 344, No. 10 (Bet Israel records), 60.

70. Lionel Barnett, *El libro de los Acuerdos, Being the Records and Accompts of the Spanish and Portuguese Synagogue of London from 1663 to 1681* (Oxford 1931), 23. A year earlier, in 1665, the rabbi Jacob Sasportas had expelled from the synagogue those who refused to be circumcised (Tishby, "New Information," 478–80).

71. Two such cases are recorded in the cemetery records in the years 1617 and 1618. See Pieterse, *Livro de Bet Haim*, 91 (a twelve-year-old boy "uncircumcised in life"), 93 (Baruch Senior, "who was circumcised after his death").

72. Pieterse, *Livro de Bet Haim*, 45.

73. Ibid., 102, 106, 107.

74. It is misleading both in its implication that it entailed complete expulsion and in its implication that the *herem* was imposed by ecclesiastical authorities. In fact it was imposed by the lay authorities in consultation, at most, with the rabbis. The issue has been discussed, inter alia, by Henri Méchoulan, "Le herem à Amsterdam et 'l'excommunication' de Spinoza," *Cahiers Spinoza* 3 (1979/80), 117–34.

75. For a discussion of the many infractions for which a *herem* was threatened, see Kaplan, "Social Functions of the Herem."

76. The rather pathetic story is related in Roth, *Menasseh ben Israel*, 52–57.

77. GAA, PA 334, No. 19, 413. Cf. Kaplan, "Social Functions of the Herem," 118–19.

78. See Kaplan, "Travels of Portuguese Jews."

79. Punishments imposed by the *Mahamad* have been studied in detail by Yosef Kaplan, "Social Functions of the Herem."

80. *SR* 2, 124, No. 78; *SR* 3, 114, No. 124; *SR* 3, 248, No. 197 (see also *SR* 6, 242–43,

Nos. 660, 661, and *SR* 7, 120, Nos. 693 and 696); *SR* 4, 255, No. 315; *SR* 7, 268, No. 743; *SR* 8, 301, No. 844 (and see *SR* 8, 304, Nos. 855, 860, and 861, also *SR* 10, 97, No. 883); *SR* 10, 213–14, No. 948; *SR* 11, 91, No. 1157; *SR* 13, 227, No. 1522; *SR* 13, 234 n. 45; *SR* 15, 146, No. 1779 (charge of rape); *SR* 24, 76, No. 2896.

81. *SR* 2, 124, No. 78.

82. *SR* 20, 110–11, No. 2508; *SR* 24, 70, No. 2863.

83. *Lopes Suasso Family,* 59.

84. Kaplan, "Social Functions of the Herem," 129.

85. Révah, "Premier règlement," 677.

86. See Swetschinski, "Portuguese Merchants," 67–68.

87. GAA, PA 334, No. 19, 25.

88. See Révah, "Les écrivains," lxxiv-xci.

89. See Harm den Boer, "Ediciones falsificadas de Holanda en el siglo XVII: escritores sefarditas y censura judaica," *Varia Bibliographica: Homenaje a José Simón Díaz* (Kassel 1987), 99–103.

90. Révah, "Les écrivains," lxxxv-lxxxvii.

91. Seven years earlier the *Mahamad* had prohibited the printing in Amsterdam of De Barrios's poetic work *Flor de Apolo,* partly due to criticism that in this work De Barrios attributed divinity to gentile gods—even though the critic acknowledged the purely rhetorical purposes of De Barrios in doing so. Révah, "Les écrivains," lxxxii-lxxxiii.

92. On the censorship of De Pina's work *Chanças del ingenio,* deemed indecent by the *Mahamad,* see Révah, "Les écrivains," lxxiv-lxxvii.

93. Shlomo Simonsohn, ed., *Responsa of R. Yehuda Aryeh of Modena* (Hebrew) (Jerusalem 1956).

94. While Modena was not a Sephardi Jew, his stature and his close ties to the Sephardi congregations of Venice made him a logical figure to turn to. Ample evidence of his ties with Sephardim can be found in his autobiography *Chayye Yehuda* (Hebrew), ed. Daniel Carpi (Tel Aviv 1985) or in the English translation with extensive notes prepared by Mark Cohen, *The Autobiography of a Seventeenth-Century Venetian Rabbi* (Princeton 1988).

95. Modena's summary of Da Costa's arguments has been published by Gebhardt, *Schriften,* 3–10.

96. As Révah has shown, despite his claims to the contrary Da Costa must have been familiar with some aspects of postbiblical Judaism while still a "judaizer" in the Peninsula. See Révah, "La religion d'Urieol da Costa," 45–76.

97. See Modena's opening statement, *Magen ve-zinnah,* ed. A. Geiger (Breslau 1856), fol. 1r.

98. Modena's 1616/17 letter to the Hamburg community excommunicating Da Costa was published by L. Blau, *Leo Modenas Briefe und Schriftstücke* (Budapest 1905), No. 156, 146, and again by Gebhardt, *Schriften,* 150. That this letter refers to Da Costa was established by N. Porges, "Leon Modena über Uriel da Costa," *Zeitschrift für Hebräische Bibliographie* 15 (1911), 80–82. The ban placed on Da Costa by the Venetian community on 23 Ab 5378 (August 14, 1618) was published in Blau, *Briefe und Schriftstücke,* 95ff., and Gebhardt, *Schriften,* 181–82. Again, it was Porges who established that the ban refers to Da Costa, in his above-cited article.

99. The Amsterdam ban was published by Gebhardt, *Schriften,* 181–82.

100. A copy of this book, *Exame das tradições phariseas* (Examination of Pharisaic Traditions), has only recently been found (and republished): Uriel da Costa, *Examination of Pharisaic Traditions,* with facsimile of the original, translation, notes, and introduction by H. P. Salomon and I. S. D. Sassoon (Leiden/New York/Cologne 1993).

101. Da Costa, *Examination,* 234.

102. Ibid., 246–48.

103. Ibid., 195.

104. Meijer, "Hugo Grotius' *Remonstrantie,*" 97–98.

105. Da Costa, *Examination,* 429.

106. The Remonstrant theologian Philip van Limborch published the autobiography in 1687 as an appendix to his *De Veritate Religionis Christianae Amica Collatio cum Erudito Judaeo,* titling it *Exemplar humanae vitae.* It has been published by Gebhardt, *Schriften,* 105–23.

107. See especially Révah, "La religion d'Uriel da Costa," 45–56.

108. See the sources cited by Salomon in Da Costa, *Examination,* 23. Johan Müller's report of Da Costa's death has been published by Gebhardt, *Schriften,* 202–204.

109. Alexander Altmann, "Eternality of Punishment: A Theological Controversy within the Amsterdam Rabbinate in the Thirties of the Seventeenth Century," *Proceedings of the American Academy of Jewish Research* 40 (1972), 17–20.

110. The debate has been thoroughly examined, and the relevant documents published, by Altmann, "Eternality of Punishment," 1–88.

111. Altmann, "Eternality of Punishment," 53.

112. Gerschom Scholem, *Sabbatai Sevi: The Mystical Messiah* (Princeton 1973).

113. On the movement in Amsterdam, see Scholem, *Sabbatai Sevi,* 518–45, 749–64; also Yosef Kaplan, "The Attitude of the Leadership of the 'Portuguese,' Community in Amsterdam to the Sabbatian Movement" (Hebrew), *Zion* 39 (1974), 198–216.

114. See Yerushalmi, *Spanish Court,* 303–13.

115. See Scholem, *Sabbatai Sevi,* 893–95.

116. This circle and its evolution have been studied with great skill by Révah, *Spinoza et Juan de Prado;* idem, "Aux origines de la rupture spinozienne: nouveaux documents sur l'incroyance dans la communauté judéo-portugaise d'Amsterdam à l'époque de l'excommunication de Spinoza," *REJ* 123 (1964), 359–83; idem, "Aux origines de la rupture spinozienne: nouvel examen des origines du déroulement et des consequences de l'affaire Spinoza-Prado-Ribera," *Annuaire de Collège de France* 70 (1970), 562–68; 71 (1971), 574–89; 72 (1972), 641–53.

117. On Prado's flirtation with deism in the Peninsula, see Révah, "Aux origines," (1972), 650–51.

118. The *herem* is published in Révah, *Spinoza et Juan de Prado,* 57–58.

119. The entire deposition of the monk is published in Révah, *Spinoza et Juan de Prado,* 61–65; for the statement concerning Spinoza, see p. 64.

120. Révah, "Aux origines" (1964), 371–83.

121. On the measures (not always consistent) taken by the Dutch authorities from the 1640s to the 1670s concerning heterodox religious ideas, see Jonathan Israel, *The Dutch Republic: Its Rise, Greatness, and Fall, 1477–1806* (Oxford 1995), 889–933.

122. See Jacob Teicher, "Why Was Spinoza Banned?" *The Menorah Journal* 45 (1957), 57; Révah, *Spinoza et Juan de Prado,* 29–30; Méchoulan, "Le herem à Amsterdam," 123–24.

123. See Kaplan, *From Christianity,* 122–26, 146–47.

124. For a detailed analysis of Orobio's correspondence and the *Mahamad,* see Kaplan, *From Christianity,* 146–56.

125. On Orobio's functions as a communal leader, see Kaplan, *From Christianity,* 189–99.

126. Bringing an analogue from the discipline he shared with Prado, namely medicine, he asked what Prado would think of someone who held a medical opinion that contradicted the opinion of Galen, Avicenna, Vallés, Garcia, Fernelio,

"and others of this class." This was indeed clinging to tradition, in the second half of the seventeenth century!

127. Isaac Orobio de Castro, *Epístola invectiva contra Prado, un Philósopho Médico que dudava o no creía la verdad de la divina escriptura y pretendió encubrir su malicia con la afectada confessión de Dios y Ley de Naturaleza,* published in abridged form in Révah, *Spinoza et Juan de Prado,* 86–129.

128. Révah, *Spinoza et Juan de Prado,* 97.

129. Ibid., 109–10.

130. See the discussion of this in Kaplan, *From Christianity,* 167–69. On "fideistic skeptics," see Richard Popkin, "Scepticism, Theology and the Scientific Revolution in the Seventeenth Century," in I. Lakatos and A. Musgrave, eds., *Problems in the Philosophy of Science* (Amsterdam 1968), 12–17.

131. Kaplan, *From Christianity,* 169.

132. Pieterse, *Livro de Bet Haim,* 4, No. 2.

133. Presumably due to the paucity of material from Venice, the first instance I have encountered of the use of the term *tudesco* among the Ponentine Jews dates from 1660, in a letter in Portuguese concerning the redemption of a captive: "chegou aqui Davi [sic] tudesco polaco" ("Copie di lettere, Resc. de Schiavi de T.T.," Archivio della Communità Israelitica, Venezia, file 7, fol. 30v; Central Archives for the History of the Jewish People, Jerusalem, HM 5221).

134. Pieterse, *Livro de Bet Haim,* 92.

135. See Yosef Kaplan, "The Portuguese Community in Seventeenth-Century Amsterdam and the Ashkenazi World," *DJH* 2 (Jerusalem 1989), 29.

136. The *Mahamad* lent the *tudescos* 300 guilders of the 410 guilders needed to buy the land for the cemetery. GAA, PA 334, No. 19, 131.

137. Gans, *Memorbook,* 29.

138. He was taxed only two guilders for the purchase of the cemetery in 1614 (Pieterse, *Livro de Bet Haim,* 150, 176).

139. GAA, PA 334, No. 1142, p. 143 (17 Adar Sheni, 1631).

140. GAA, PA 334, No. 1142, p. 88 (12 Ab, 1627).

141. On the different attitude of the *Mahamad* to "Portuguese" and Ashkenazi poor, see the revealing description of the changing roles of the *Avodat Hesed* society in Kaplan, "The Portuguese Community and the Ashkenazi World," 32–33.

142. Bloom, *Economic Activities,* 25–26.

143. GAA, PA 334, No. 19, 242.

144. Ibid., 765.

145. Ibid., 194.

146. From the text of the merger agreement published in Pieterse, *Daniel Levi de Barrios,* 156.

147. See Kaplan, "The Portuguese Community and the Ashkenazi World," 35–36.

148. Ibid., 37–39, 42.

149. *TGP,* 114, 116.

150. Fuks and Fuks-Mansfeld, *Hebrew Typography,* 2: 236–37.

151. GAA, PA 334, No. 20, 293.

152. Fuks and Fuks-Mansfeld, *Hebrew Typography,* 2: 242.

153. English translation of ruling in Salomon, "Myth or Anti-Myth?" 297–98.

154. The best-known expression of this posture is the lengthy letter to Voltaire composed in 1762 by Isaac de Pinto (a great-grandson of a brother of the Isaac de Pinto who fled from Antwerp to Rotterdam), in which he protested Voltaire's failure in his article "Juifs" to distinguish between Ashkenazim and the culturally superior Sephardim ([Isaac de Pinto], *Apologie pour la nation juive, ou réflexions critiques sur le premier chapitre du VIIe tome des oeuvres de M. de Voltaire au sujet des*

juifs [Amsterdam 1762]). Similarly indignant is a letter of 1778 from a Portuguese Jew in Paris to the London *Mahamad*, in which, "zealous . . . for the welfare and honour of my nation," the author complained of the failure of the Paris authorities to honor the special privileges of the Sephardim over the Ashkenazim (*Transactions of the Jewish Historical Society of England* 20 [1959–61], 18).

155. Yosef Kaplan, "Jewish Proselytes from Portugal in 17th Century Amsterdam—The Case of Lorenzo Escudero" (Hebrew), *Proceedings of the Seventh World Congress of Jewish Studies* (Jerusalem 1981), 4: 99–101; idem, "Political Concepts in the World of the Portuguese Jews of Amsterdam during the Seventeenth Century," in Kaplan, Méchoulan, and Popkin, eds., *Menasseh ben Israel and His World* (Leiden 1989), 54–57.

156. A 1614 regulation set aside a separate burial plot for "slaves, servants, and Jewish girls who are not of our Nation" (Pieterse, *Livro de Bet Haim*, 4). Some modifications were made in 1647, but the principle of segregated burial was maintained (GAA, PA 334, No. 19, 224). In 1644 it was decided that a nonwhite male could not be called to the Torah or receive other synagogue honors (ibid., 173). The issue of attitudes to converted blacks or mulattos among the Portuguese Jews has yet to be explored thoroughly. Meanwhile, see the enlightening material in Robert Cohen, *Jews in Another Environment: Surinam in the Second Half of the Eighteenth Century* (Leiden, New York, Copenhagen, and Cologne 1991), 143–59.

157. Yosef Kaplan, "Relations between Spanish and Portuguese Jews and Ashkenazim in Seventeenth-Century Amsterdam," in *Transition and Change in Modern Jewish History: Essays in Honor of Shmuel Ettinger* (Hebrew) (Jerusalem 1987), 403.

158. GAA, PA 334, No. 19, 643.

159. GAA, PA 334, No. 20, 230. And indeed in the nineteenth century the community refused to bury in its cemetery a "Portuguese" Jew who had alienated himself by marrying an Ashkenazi woman. See J. Michman, "Between Sephardim and Ashkenazim in Amsterdam," in I. Ben-Ami, ed., *The Sephardi and Oriental Jewish Heritage* (Hebrew) (Jerusalem 1982), 136 n. 7.

160. GAA, PA 334, No. 20, 510.

6. Maintaining "the Nation" in Exile

1. See Yosef Kaplan, "Jewish Refugees from Germany and Poland," 587–622.

2. For a general description of the Jew's sense of separateness from Christian society in the early modern period, see Jacob Katz, *Out of the Ghetto: The Social Background of Jewish Emancipation, 1770–1870* (New York 1978), 25–27.

3. See Jacob Katz, "'Although He Has Sinned, He Remains a Jew,'" (Hebrew), *Tarbiz* 27 (1958), 203–17.

4. For a more detailed discussion of the *Dotar*, see Bodian, "'Portuguese' Dowry Societies," 30–61; idem, "The *Santa Companhia de dotar orfans e donzelas pobres* in Amsterdam, 1615–1639" (Hebrew) (Ph.D. diss., Hebrew University 1988). For the history of this institution after the seventeenth century (it is still in existence, though much altered), see W. Chr. Pieterse, *350 jaar Dotar. Gedenkschrift . . . ter gelegenheid van het 350-jarig bestaan, in opdracht van de vereniging Santa Companhia de Dotar Orphas e Donzellas te Amsterdam* (Amsterdam 1965).

5. Révah, "Premier règlement," 653. In the final version, the expression "a society of Portuguese" was changed to read "a sacred society" (ibid., 668).

6. Ibid., 659, 668.

7. Purely local activity was the accepted practice not only among the small parochial confraternities in Catholic Europe, but among the large ones as well

(including the Portuguese *Casa da Misericórdia*, each of whose branches, scattered throughout the Portuguese empire, operated solely within its own sphere). See A. J. R. Russell-Wood, *Fidalgos and Philanthropists: The Santa Casa da Misericórdia of Bahía, 1550–1755* (Berkeley 1968), 26–41 and passim.

8. Hebrew Union College Ms. 149, fol. 6v–7r, 12v.

9. Hebrew Union College Ms. 149, fol. 6v–7r.

10. For details on the founders, see Bodian, "The *Santa Companhia*," 26–29.

11. GAA, PA 334, No. 1142, 137. Halevi's granddaughter was a candidate each year from 1631 to 1641, when she won a dowry and, not surprisingly, married an Ashkenazi Jew (entry for 16 Adar, 1641).

12. For the decision concerning Mortera, see GAA, PA 334, No. 1143, fol. 8v. Published in H. P. Salomon, "La vraie excommunication de Spinoza," in *Forum Litterarum: Miscelânea de estudos literários, linguísticos e históricos oferecida a J. J. Van den Besselaar* (Amsterdam/Maarssen 1984), 189–90 n. 11.

13. See Bodian, "Amsterdam, Venice, and the Marrano Diaspora," 49–50.

14. Yosef Kaplan, "R. Shaul Levi Mortera and His Treatise *Te'anot ve-hassagot neged ha-dat ha-nozerit*" (Hebrew), *SDH* 1 (Jerusalem 1975), 10; H. P. Salomon, "Haham Saul Levi Morteira en de Portugese Nieuw-Christenen," *SR* 10 (1976), 127–41.

15. On Mortera, see Bodian, "Amsterdam, Venice, and the Marrano Diaspora," 49–50; H. P. Salomon, introduction to Saul Levi Mortera, *Tratado da verdade da lei de Moisés*, xxxvii-cxxii.

16. Révah, "Premier règlement," 674.

17. Ibid., 678.

18. GAA, PA 334, No. 1141, 37.

19. For a breakdown of the places of settlement of families seeking dowries from 1615–1639, see Bodian, "The *Santa Companhia*," Appendix 3, 305–307.

20. GAA, PA 334, No. 1141, entry of July 7, 1616; GAA, PA 334, No. 1143, entry of 1 Adar Sheni 1647.

21. Révah, "Premier règlement," 674.

22. In the period from 1615 to 1675, only twelve secret members joined the *Dotar.*

23. Révah, "Premier règlement," 671.

24. Ibid., 668, and see 671.

25. Samuel Aboab, *Devar Shemuel* (Venice 1720), No. 45.

26. Cecil Roth, "Quatre lettres," 137–65.

27. Ibid., 153.

28. Tirtsah Levie Bernfeld, "Caridade Escapa Da Morte: Legacies to the Poor in Sephardi Wills from Seventeenth-Century Amsterdam," *DJH* 3 (Jerusalem 1993), 181. Nahon mentions a case of a conditional legacy left to a relative in the Peninsula by a Portuguese Jew in France in the eighteenth century. Gérard Nahon, "From New Christians to the Portuguese Jewish Nation in France," in H. Beinart, ed., *The Sephardi Legacy*, 2 vols. (Jerusalem 1992), 2: 359.

29. GAA, PA 334, No. 19, 195.

30. GAA, PA 334, No. 19, 54.

31. This *Dotar* policy is revealed in a responsum by Jacob Sasportas; most likely it was established in the revised statutes of 1627, which have been lost. See Jacob Sasportas, *Sefer ohel ya'akov* (Amsterdam 1737), No. 59, fol. 64v. Cf. H. J. Zimmels, *Die Marranen in der rabbinischen Literatur* (Berlin 1932), 166–68.

32. Révah, "Premier règlement," 682.

33. In the first twenty-five years of its operation, 132 members were admitted; of these 104 were from Amsterdam, 17 from Hamburg, and only one from France. For details, see Bodian, "The *Santa Companhia*," 86.

34. As noted in connection with the decision to admit Mortera to the *Dotar*, relatives of members might apply for a dowry regardless of where they lived (thus the applications from Salonica, Corfu, Algiers, Jerusalem, etc.), while girls unrelated to members might apply only if they lived within the geographical orbit defined in the preamble, that is, "from St. Jean de Luz to Danzig, including France and the Netherlands, England, and Germany" (Révah, "Premier règlement," 681). Presumably, the *Dotar* founders took into account the fact that needy girls living in the Mediterranean orbit could easily apply to the Venetian dowry society.

35. GAA, PA 334, No. 1141, 64–65.

36. On the New Christian settlements in southwest France in the seventeenth century, see Nahon, "Les rapports," 37–78.

37. A. Detcheverry, *Histoire des Israelites de Bordeaux* (Bordeaux 1850), 59–62.

38. Nahon, "Rapports," 61.

39. *SR* 11, 84, No. 1106. This group of emigres may have been described in the testimony of Hector Mendes Bravo before the Lisbon Inquisition in December 1617. He testified that shortly before he left Amsterdam for Portugal, a ship arrived in Amsterdam carrying 73 Portuguese and Castilian passengers, who told him they had come from St. Jean de Luz to Amsterdam in order to live according to the Law of Moses (Roth, "Strange Case of Hector Mendes Bravo," 240).

40. For a similar instance of immigration by sea arranged between St. Jean de Luz and the Netherlands, see *SR* 17, 78 n. 72.

41. Jonathan Israel, "Spain and the Dutch Sephardim," 370–71.

42. GAA, PA 334, No. 1141, 75.

43. GAA, PA 334, No. 1141, 90. In 1627 the geographical quotas were dropped in favor of a system that controlled the number of dowries received by relatives of members, who had an advantage in the selection system. (The revised statutes of 1627 have been lost, but can be partially recontructed from other material in the *Dotar* records. See Bodian, "The *Santa Companhia*," 67–68 n. 98.)

44. GAA, PA 334, No. 13, 8–9, No. 29.

45. GAA, PA 334, No. 13, 7–8, No. 25.

46. Yosef Kaplan, "Jewish Refugees from Germany and Poland," 594–95; Yosef Kaplan and Israel Bartal, "The Emigration of Poor from Amsterdam to Eretz Israel" (Hebrew), *Shalem* 3 (1992), 175–92.

47. Kaplan, "Jewish Refugees from Germany and Poland," 594–96.

48. See GAA, PA 334, No. 1141, 37.

49. I. S. Révah, introduction to Delgado's *Poema de la Reyna Ester* (Lisbon 1954), xxviii.

50. Roth, "Marranes à Rouen," 113–55.

51. I. S. Révah, "Autobiographie d'un Marrane, edition partielle d'un manuscrit de João [Moseh] Pinto Delgado," *REJ* 119 (1961), 66.

52. The letter in the original Latin has been published by Roth, "Marranes à Rouen," 147–51. Cf. Révah, "Autobiographie d'un Marrane," 85–86 n. 1.

53. On royal policy concerning New Christian settlement in France, see Nahon, "From New Christians to the Portuguese Jewish Nation," 337–38.

54. Nahon, "Rapports," 43. But see the somewhat revised evaluation of Nahon in his "From New Christians to Portuguese Jewish Nation," where he points out the need to take emigration to other Jewish communities into consideration.

55. For a succinct discussion of the changing status of the "Portuguese" in France, see Hertzberg, *The French Enlightenment and the Jews*, 15–28.

56. Roth, "Quatre lettres," *REJ* 87 (1929), 137–65; idem, "Immanuel Aboab's Proselytization," 121–62.

57. Moses Rafael d'Aguilar, "Reposta e discurso sobre certas preguntas de

Bayona e foy em nome dos Hahamim Señores," Ms. EH 48A 11, 437. And see Kaplan, "Rabbi Moshe Rafael d'Aguilar," 95–106.

58. Sasportas, *Sefer ohel ya'akov*, No. 65, fol. 70r–71r. The responsum has been published in French translation by Gérard Nahon, *Les "Nations" Juives Portugaises de Sud-Ouest de la France (1684–1791)* (Paris 1981), 261–70.

59. Nahon, "Rapports," 55–57.

60. Révah, "Premier règlement," 681.

61. On Jewish visitors to post-Expulsion Spain, see Yosef Hayim Yerushalmi, "Professing Jews in Post-Expulsion Spain and Portugal," in Saul Lieberman, ed., *Salo Wittmayer Baron Jubilee Volume*, 3 vols. (Jerusalem 1974), 2: 1023–58; Beinart, "A Jew of Salonica," 189–97; Beinart, "Jews and Conversos of Italy and Spain," 275–88.

62. Salomon, *Portrait of a New Christian*, 285–86.

63. Teensma, "Fragmenten," 153–54.

64. Ibid., 154–55.

65. Azevedo, *História dos Christãos-Novos portugueses*, 374 n. 3.

66. Kaplan, "Travels of Portuguese Jews."

67. Caro Baroja, *Los judíos en la España*, 3: 361 (Appendix XXIX), and see Kaplan, *From Christianity*, 335–36.

68. Maximiano Lemos, *Zacuto Lusitano* (Porto 1909), p. 30, document no. 6. Menasseh ben Israel's lack of discretion in the presence of conversos who later returned to Spain reveals another aspect of Amsterdam Jews' activity in Spain. Menasseh revealed to someone who later testified before the Inquisition in Lisbon that "he had sent two crates of books that he himself had authored, one to Spain and one to Brazil, and that the name of the book was *Reconceliaçones de la sagrada escritura*"—clearly a reference to his *Conciliador* (Lemos, *Zacuto Lusitano*, 361 document no. 8).

69. Salomon, *Os primeiros portugueses*, 33 n. 30.

70. She is listed as such on the 1629 *pauta*, which noted that she was living in Salonica. GAA, PA 334, No. 1142, 110.

71. On Sasportas's unhappy rabbinic career, see Scholem, *Sabbatai Sevi*, 566–68.

72. The emergence of a differentiated Sephardi subgroup in the Jewish diaspora has yet to be analyzed thoroughly from a historical point of view. For an analysis from a rabbinic point of view, see H. J. Zimmels, *Ashkenazim and Sephardim: Their Relations, Differences, and Problems as Reflected in the Rabbinical Responsa* (London 1976).

73. See Aboab, *Nomologia*, 291–96.

74. Menasseh ben Israel, *Thesouro dos dinim*, dedication, n.p.

75. Abraham Farar, *Declaração das 613. Encomendancas de nossa Sancta Ley, conforme à Exposissão de nossos Sabios, muy neçessaria au Iudesmo* (Amsterdam 1627).

76. Benjamin Ravid, "The Establishment of the Ghetto Vecchio of Venice, 1541," *Proceedings of the Sixth World Congress of Jewish Studies* (Jerusalem 1975), 2: 153–67.

77. An English traveler in Venice noted that "western" (i.e., "Ponentine") Jews wore red hats, whereas Levantines wore yellow turbans. See David Malkiel, *A Separate Republic: The Mechanics and Dynamics of Venetian Jewish Self-Government, 1607–1624* (Jerusalem 1991), 106.

78. See Cecil Roth, "Les marranes à Venise," *REJ* 89 (1930), 205.

79. Benjamin Ravid, "The First Charter of the Jewish Merchants of Venice, 1589," *AJS Review* 1 (1976), 187–222.

80. On the complex relationship between the "Levantine" and "Ponentine" congregations, see Bodian, "Dowry Societies," 48 n. 48; Malkiel, *A Separate Republic*, 106–11; 313 n. 1.

Conclusion

1. Menasseh ben Israel, *Esperança de Israel* (Amsterdam 1650), 41.

2. Teensma, "Fragmenten," 149.

3. Cristobal Suarez de Figueroa, *El pasajero, Advertencias utilisimas a la vida humana* (Madrid 1617, ed. 1913), 78.

4. Quoted in José Antonio Maravall, *Estado moderno y mentalidad social* (Madrid 1971), 1: 158.

5. Hamburg Staatsarchiv, Gemeindearchiv AHW 993, I, 449 (photocopy at the Central Archives for the History of the Jewish People, Jerusalem).

6. Duarte Gomes Solís, *Alegación en favor de la Compañia de la India oriental* (1628), ed. M. Bensabat Amzalek (Lisbon 1955), 214. On Duarte Gomes Solís, see, inter alia, Carl Hanson, *Economy and Society in Baroque Portugal, 1668–1703* (Minneapolis 1981), 113–18.

7. See Révah, "Les Marranes," 53.

8. Among various discussions of this phenomenon, see Gerschom Scholem, *Major Trends in Jewish Mysticism* (New York 1954), 244–58; Shalom Rosenberg, "Exile and Redemption in Jewish Thought in the Sixteenth Century: Contending Conceptions," in Bernard Dov Cooperman, ed., *Jewish Thought in the Sixteenth Century* (Cambridge, Mass. 1983), 399–430.

9. This expectation is discussed in Kaplan, *From Christianity*, 339–43; Yerushalmi, *Spanish Court*, 302–306.

10. For a detailed discussion of this perception, see Kaplan, *From Christianity*, 363–77.

11. The impact of Iberian experience on ex-converso Judaism among two important "Portuguese" apologetes is analyzed in Yerushalmi, *Spanish Court*, 370–80, and Kaplan, *From Christianity*, 308–77.

12. Israel, "The Changing Role," 31–51.

13. See Isaac de Pinto, *Reflexoës politicas tocante a constitução da Nação Judaica* (Amsterdam 1748).

14. J. G. van Dillen, "De economische positie en betekenis der Joden in de Republiek en in de Nederlandse koloniale wereld," in *GJN*, 592–95.

15. One of the later emigres, Aron Vaz Dias, left Portugal for Amsterdam in about 1759; in Amsterdam, he married the daughter of a rabbi, but did not thrive. (J. J. Vaz Dias and B. N. Teensma, "Van onderdrukking naar vrijheid de Portugese achtergronden van een joodse Amsterdammer uit de achttiende eeuw," *SR* 21 (1987), 35–72. Among other documents, circumcision records reveal the arrival of new emigres from the Peninsula. In 1765, circumcisions were performed in Amsterdam on twenty-four persons who came from Lisbon (J. d'Ancona, "De Portugese Gemeente 'Talmoed Tora' te Amsterdam tot 1795," in *GJN*, 298).

16. There were some who continued to "judaize" in the Peninsula, like the converso in Lisbon who in 1765 asked his business partners in Amsterdam to send him prayer books, a Hebrew Bible, a prayer shawl, and phylacteries (M. M. Hirsch, ed., *Frucht vom Baum des Lebens (Peri Ets Haim)*, [Berlin/Antwerp 1936], No. 449, 145–46).

17. GAA, PA 334, No. 1143, 134v–136r.

18. Pieterse, *350 Jaar Dotar*, 30.

19. Ibid., 14.

20. Bloom, *Economic Activities*, 31.

21. On the eve of World War II there were about 3,000 Portuguese Jews in Amsterdam, and 67,000 Ashkenazim.

22. From *De Koopman, of Bijdragen ten Opbouw van Neêrlands Koophandel en Zeevaard* (Amsterdam), vol. 2 (1770), 430.

23. See Jozeph Michman, *The History of Dutch Jewry during the Emancipation Period, 1787–1815: Gothic Turrets on a Corinthian Building* (Amsterdam 1995), 6, 14.

24. Ibid., 90–157, 203–27.

25. David Franco Mendes, "Memorias do estabelecimento e progresso dos Judeos Portuguezes e Espanhoes nesta famosa cidade de Amsterdam," published in *SR* 9 (1975).

26. J. Vaz Dias, "The Ez-Hayyim Beit Midrash in Amsterdam" (Hebrew), *SDH* 5 (Jerusalem 1988), 283–84.

27. An outstanding case in point is that of Isaac da Costa (1798–1860). This scion of a distinguished "Portuguese" family in Amsterdam, like many of his generation, converted to Christianity, in his case while a student at the University of Leiden in 1822. In time he became a leader of the Dutch Reformed Church Party. Yet Da Costa continued to be fascinated both with his Jewish and his "Portuguese" ancestry, and worked out a set of beliefs that allowed him to value his ancestry from a decidedly Christian perspective. The most astonishing example of his idiosyncratic amalgam of values is his series of articles affirming the aristocratic status of certain Portuguese-Jewish families (including the Da Costa family), published in Dutch in the 1850s and in English translation in *Noble Families among the Sephardic Jews* (London 1936), 104–62.

BIBLIOGRAPHY

I. Archival Documents

Germany
Hamburg Staatsarchiv, Gemeindearchiv AHW 993, I, 449 (photocopy at the Central Archives for the History of the Jewish People, Jerusalem).

Italy
Venice. Archivio della Communità Israelitica, file 7. "Copie di lettere, Resc. de Schiavi de T.T."

The Netherlands
Gemeentelijke Archief, Amsterdam, PA 334, Nos. 13, 19, 20, 1051, 1141, 1142, 1143.

The United States
Cincinnati. Hebrew Union College Ms. 149.

II. Manuscripts

Amsterdam. Ets Haim collection.
Ms. EH 47B 4. *Copia do Livro das gerasoins prinsipiado p[or] o señor Jahacob Belmonte desde o anno 1599.*
Ms. EH 48B 12 Isaac Orobio de Castro. *Epístola invectiva contra Prado, un Philósopho Médico que dudava o no creía la verdad de la divina escriptura y pretendió encubrir su malicia con la afectada confessión de Dios y Ley de Naturaleza.*
Ms. EH 48D 6. Isaac Orobio de Castro. *Prevencionas divinas contra la vana Idolatría de las Gentes.*
Ms. EH 48D 6. Isaac Orobio de Castro. *Respuesta a un escrito que presentó un Predicante Francés a el Author contra la observancia de la Divina Ley de Mosseh.*

III. Primary Printed Sources

Aboab, Immanuel. *Nomologia.* Amsterdam 1629.
Aboab, Samuel. *Devar Shemuel.* Venice 1720.
———. *Sefer ha-zikhronot.* n.p., n.d.
Alting, Jacob. Hebrew letters printed at end of his *Fundamenta punctationis Linguae Sanctae.* Groningen 1673.
Barrios, Daniel Levi de. *Contra la verdad no ay fuerça, Panegirico a los tres bien-aventurados martires Abraham Athias, Yahacob Rodriguez Càceres, y Raquel Nuñes Fernandez, que fueron quemados vivos en Córdova, por santificar la unidad divina. En 16 de Tamuz, Año de 5425.* Amsterdam n.d.
———. *Triumpho del Govierno Popular y de la Antigüedad Holandesa.* Amsterdam 1683–84.
Broughton, Hugh. *Our Lordes Familie and many other poinctes depending upon it: opened against a Iew, Rabbi David Farar who disputed many houres, with hope to overthrow the Gospel.* Amsterdam 1608.

Cardoso, Isaac. *Las Excelencias de los Hebreos*. Amsterdam 1679.

Costa, Uriel da. *Examination of Pharisaic Traditions*. With facsimile of the original, translation, notes, and introduction by H. P. Salomon and I. S. D. Sassoon. Leiden/New York/Cologne 1993.

Coster, Abraham. *Historie der Joden . . . uyt verscheyde autheuren vergadert*. Rotterdam 1608.

De la Court, Pieter. *Interest van Holland ofte Gronden van Hollands-Welvaren*. Amsterdam 1662.

Elogios que zelosos dedicaron a la felice memoria de Abraham Nuñez Bernal, que fue quemado vivo santificando el Nombre de su criador en Cordova a 3 de Mayo 5415. [Amsterdam 1655].

Farar, Abraham. *Declaração das 613. Encomendanças de nossa Sancta Ley, conforme à Exposissão de nossos Sabios, muy neçessaria ao Iudesmo*. Amsterdam 1627.

Franco Mendes, David. *Memorias do estabelecimento e progresso dos judeos portuguezes e espanhoes nesta famosa cidade de Amsterdam . . .* Amsterdam 1769. L. Fuks and R. G. Fuks-Mansfeld, ed. Assen 1975. Also published appended to *SR* 9 (1975).

Gallego, Joseph ben Shalom. *Sefer imrei no'am*. Amsterdam 1628–30.

Hagiz, Moshe. *Sefer sefat emet*. Amsterdam 1707.

Halevi, Uri ben Aron. *Narração da Vinda dos Judeos espanhões a Amsterdam*. Amsterdam 1711. Reprinted in facsimile edition by J. S. da Silva Rosa, Amsterdam 1933.

Meldola, Rafael. *Mayim rabbim*. Amsterdam 1737.

Melo, David Abenatar. *Los CL Psalmos de David en lengua española, en varias rimas*. Frankfurt 1626.

Menasseh ben Israel. *Esperança de Israel*. Amsterdam 1650.

———. *Thesouro dos dinim que o povo de Israel e obrigado saber, e observar*. Amsterdam 1645–47.

Modena, Yehuda Aryeh. *Magen ve-Zinnah*. A. Geiger, ed. Breslau 1856.

———. *Responsa of R. Yehuda Aryeh of Modena*. Shlomo Simonsohn, ed. Jerusalem 1956.

Mortera, Saul Levi. *Tratado da verdade da lei de Moisés*. Facsimile edition with introduction and commentary by H. P. Salomon. Braga 1988.

Nieto, David. *Matteh Dan, y segunda parte de Cuzari*. London 1714.

Noordkerk, Hermanus. *Handvesten ofte Privilegien ende Octroyen . . . der Stad Amstelredam*. Amsterdam 1748.

Pieterse, W. Chr., ed. *Livro de Bet Haim do Kahal Kados de Bet Yahacob*. Assen 1970.

Pinto, Isaac de. *Reflexoës politicas tocante a constituição da Nação Judaica*. Amsterdam 1748.

Resolutiën van de Heeren Staten van Hollandt ende West-Vrieslandt . . . January . . . 1619 (n.d., n.p. Gemeentelijke Archief, Amsterdam, Arch. 5038, No. 52).

Sasportas, Jacob. *Sefer ohel ya'akov*. Amsterdam 1737.

Seder Brachot, Orden de Bendiciones y las ocaziones en que se deven dezir, con muchas adiciones a las precedentes impreciones, y por mejor methodo dispuestas. Amsterdam 1687.

Sermões que pregaraõ os doctos ingenios do K. K. de Talmud Torah, desta cidade de Amsterdam no alegre estreamento publica celebridade da Esnoga. Amsterdam 1675.

IV. Secondary Works

Altmann, Alexander. "Eternality of Punishment: A Theological Controversy within the Amsterdam Rabbinate in the Thirties of the Seventeenth Century," *Proceedings of the American Academy for Jewish Research* 40 (1972), 1–88.

Ancona, J. d'. "Komst der Marranen in Noord-Nederland: De Portugese gemeenten te Amsterdam tot de vereniging (1639)," in H. Brugmans and A. Frank, eds., *Geschiedenis der Joden in Nederland* (Amsterdam 1940), 201–69.

Azevedo, João Lúcio d'. *História dos Christãos-Novos portugueses*. Lisbon 1921.

Baer, Yitzhak. *A History of the Jews in Christian Spain*. 2 vols. Philadelphia 1978.

———. "The Messianic Movement in Spain at the Time of the Expulsion" (Hebrew), *Me'asef Zion* 5 (1933), 61–74.

Baião, Antonio. *A Inquisição em Portugal e no Brasil*. Lisbon 1921.

Baron, Salo. *A Social and Religious History of the Jews*. 18 vols. Vol. 15. Philadelphia 1973.

Beinart, Haim. *Conversos on Trial: The Inquisition in Ciudad Real*. Jerusalem 1981.

———. "The Exodus of Conversos from the Iberian Peninsula in the Fifteenth to Seventeenth Centuries" (Hebrew), *Scritti in Memoria di Umberto Nahon* (Jerusalem 1978), 63–106.

Benito Ruano, Eloy. *Toledo en el siglo XV*. Madrid 1961.

Ben-Sasson, H. H. "The Generation of Spanish Exiles on Itself" (Hebrew), *Zion* 26 (1961), 23–64.

Berg, J. van den. "Church and State Relations in the Netherlands," in J. A. Hebly, ed., *Lowland Highlights: Church and Oecumene in the Netherlands* (Kampen 1972), 32–39.

———. *Joden en christenen in Nederland gedurende de zeventiende eeuw*. Kampen 1969.

Berger, Shlomo. "Codices Gentium: Rabbi Isaac Aboab's Collection of Classical Literature," *SR* 29 (1995), 5–13.

Bloom, Herbert. *The Economic Activities of the Jews of Amsterdam in the Seventeenth and Eighteenth Centuries*. Williamsport 1937.

Bodian, Miriam. "Amsterdam, Venice, and the Marrano Diaspora," *DJH* 2 (Jerusalem 1989), 47–65.

———. "The 'Portuguese' Dowry Societies in Venice and Amsterdam: A Case Study in Communal Differentiation within the Marrano Diaspora," *Italia* 6 (1987), 30–61.

———. "The *Santa Companhia de dotar orfans e donzelas pobres* in Amsterdam, 1615–1639." Ph.D. diss., Hebrew University, 1988.

Boyajian, James. *Portuguese Bankers at the Court of Spain, 1626–1650*. New Brunswick 1983.

Brugmans, H. "De houding van Staat en Kerk ten opzichte van de Joden; hun betrekkingen tot de overige bevolking," *GJN* 617–42.

Caro Baroja, Julio. *Los judíos en la España moderna y contemporánea*. 3 vols. Madrid 1978.

———. *La sociedad criptojudía en la corte de Felipe IV*. Madrid 1963.

Carrete Parrondo, Carlos. "Nostalgia for the Past (and for the Future?) among Castilian Judeoconversos," *Mediterranean Historical Review* 6 (1991), 25–43.

Castro, Américo. *La realidad histórica de España*. Mexico 1954.

Coelho, António Borges. *Inquisição de Évora*. 2 vols. Lisbon 1987.

Cunha de Azevedo Mea, Elvira. "Orações judaicas na Inquisição Portuguesa—século XVI," in Y. Kaplan, ed., *Jews and Conversos, Studies in Society and the Inquisition* (Jerusalem 1985), 149–78.

———. *Sentenças da Inquisicão de Coimbra em metropolitanos de D. Frei Bartolomeu dos Mártires*. Porto 1982.

Denucé, J. "Een geheime Synagoge te Antwerpen in de XVI^{de} eeuw," *Antwerpsch Archievenblad*, 3rd ser. 4 (1929), 151–54.

Deursen, A. Th. van. *Plain Lives in a Golden Age: Popular Culture, Religion and Society in Seventeenth-Century Holland*. Cambridge 1991.

Dillen, J. G. van. "De economische positie en betekenis der Joden in de Republiek en in de Nederlandse koloniale wereld," in *GJN* 561–616.

Domínguez Ortiz, Antonio. *La clase social de los conversos en Castilla en la edad moderna*. Madrid 1955.

Edwards, John. "Race and Religion in Fifteenth- and Sixteenth-Century Spain: The 'Purity of Blood' Laws Revisited," *Proceedings of the Tenth World Congress of Jewish Studies*, B, 2 (Jerusalem 1990), 159–66.

———. "Religious Faith and Doubt in Late Medieval Spain: Soria circa 1450–1500," *Past and Present*, No. 120 (1988), 3–25.

Elliott, J. H. *Imperial Spain, 1469–1716*. London 1990.

Fuks, L., and R. G. Fuks-Mansfeld. *Hebrew Typography in the Northern Netherlands, 1585–1815*. 2 vols. Leiden 1984–87.

Fuks-Mansfeld, R. G. *De Sefardim in Amsterdam tot 1795*. Hilversum 1989.

Gans, M. H. *Memorbook: History of Dutch Jewry from the Renaissance to 1940*. Baarn 1977.

Gebhardt, Carl. *Die Schriften des Uriel da Costa*. Amsterdam 1922.

Gelderen, Martin van. *The Political Thought of the Dutch Revolt, 1555–1590*. Cambridge 1992.

Gracia Guillén, D. "Judaísmo, medicina y mentalidad inquisitorial en la España del siglo XVI," in A. Alcalá et al., *Inquisición española y mentalidad inquisitorial* (Barcelona 1984), 330–39.

Henriques de Castro, David. *Keur van Grafstenen op de Nederl.-Portug.-Israël. Begraafplaats te Ouderkerk aan den Amstel*. Leiden 1883.

Israel, Jonathan. "An Amsterdam Jewish Merchant of the Golden Age: Jeronimo Nunes da Costa (1620–1697), Agent of Portugal in the Dutch Republic," *SR* 18 (1984), 21–40.

———. "The Diplomatic Career of Jeronimo Nunes da Costa," *Bijdragen en Mededelingen betreffende de Geschiedenis der Nederlanden* 98 (1983), 167–90.

———. *The Dutch Republic: Its Rise, Greatness, and Fall, 1477–1806*. Oxford 1995.

———. *Empires and Entrepôts: The Dutch, the Spanish Monarchy and the Jews, 1585–1713*. London 1990.

———. *European Jewry in the Age of Mercantilism, 1550–1750*. Oxford 1991.

———. "The Jews of Venice and Their Links with Holland and with Dutch Jewry (1600–1710)," in *Gli Ebrei e Venezia, secoli XIV-XVIII* (Venice 1987), 95–116.

———. "Sephardic Immigration into the Dutch Republic, 1595–1672," *SR*, special issue published with vol. 23 (1989), 45–53.

Kamen, Henry. *Inquisition and Society in the Sixteenth and Seventeenth Centuries*. Bloomington 1985.

Kaplan, Yosef. "From Apostasy to Return to Judaism: The Portuguese Jews in Amsterdam," in Joseph Dan, ed., *Binah* 1 (New York 1989), 99–117.

———. *From Christianity to Judaism: The Story of Isaac Orobio de Castro.* New York 1989.

———. "Jewish Proselytes from Portugal in 17th Century Amsterdam—The Case of Lorenzo Escudero" (Hebrew), *Proceedings of the Seventh World Congress of Jewish Studies* (Jerusalem 1981), 87–101.

———. "Jewish Refugees from Germany and Poland in Amsterdam during the Thirty Years War and at the Time of the Chmielnitsky Massacres" (Hebrew), in *Culture and Society in Medieval Jewish History: A Collection in Memory of Haim Hillel Ben Sasson* (Hebrew) (Jerusalem 1989), 587–622.

———. "Rabbi Moshe Rafael d'Aguilar's Role with Spanish and Portuguese Emigres in the Seventeenth Century"(Hebrew), *Proceedings of the Sixth World Congress of Jewish Studies* (1976), Part B, 95–106.

———. "Relations between Spanish and Portuguese Jews and Ashkenazim in Seventeenth-Century Amsterdam," in *Transition and Change in Modern Jewish History: Essays in Honor of Shmuel Ettinger* (Hebrew) (Jerusalem 1987), 389–412.

———. "The Social Functions of the Herem in the Portuguese Jewish Community of Amsterdam in the Seventeenth Century," in *DJH* 1 (1984), 111–55.

———. "The Travels of Portuguese Jews from Amsterdam to the 'Lands of Idolatry' (1644–1724)," in Kaplan, ed., *Jews and Conversos: Studies in Society and the Inquisition* (Jerusalem 1985), 197–224.

———. "Wayward New Christians and Stubborn New Jews: The Shaping of a Jewish Identity," in Gartner and Stow, eds., *The Robert Cohen Memorial Volume* (Haifa 1994), 27–41.

Kaplan, Yosef, and Israel Bartal. "The Emigration of Poor from Amsterdam to Eretz Israel" (Hebrew), *Shalem* 3 (1992), 175–92.

Katchen, Aaron. *Christian Hebraists and Dutch Rabbis.* Cambridge, Mass. 1984.

Katz, Jacob. "'Although He Has Sinned, He Remains a Jew,'" (Hebrew), *Tarbiz* 27 (1958), 203–17.

———. *Out of the Ghetto: The Social Background of Jewish Emancipation, 1770–1870.* New York 1978.

———. *Tradition and Crisis.* New York 1993.

Kayserling, Meyer. *Biblioteca Española-Portugueza-Judaica.* Ed. Y. H. Yerushalmi. New York 1971.

Kellenbenz, Hermann. *Sephardim an der unteren Elbe.* Wiesbaden 1958.

———. "Tradiciones nobiliarias de los grupos sefardíes," *Actas del Primer Simposio de Estudios Sefardíes* (Madrid 1970), 49–54.

Kistemaker, Reneé, and Tirtsah Levie, eds. *Êxodo: Portugezen in Amsterdam, 1600–1680.* Amsterdam 1987.

Koen, E. M. "The Earliest Sources Relating to the Portuguese Jews in the Municipal Archives of Amsterdam up to 1620," *SR* 4 (1970), 25–42.

———. "Notarial Records in Amsterdam Relating to the Portuguese Jews up to 1639," *seriatum* in *SR* from *SR* 1 (1967).

Kohut, George Alexander. "Jewish Martyrs of the Inquisition in South America," *Publications of the American Jewish Historical Society* 4 (1896), 166–71.

Kuhn, A. K. "Hugo Grotius and the Emancipation of the Jews in Holland," *Publications of the American Jewish Historical Society* 31 (1928), 173–80.

Lecler, Joseph. *Toleration and the Reformation.* 2 vols. London 1960.

Lipiner, Elias. *Izaque de Castro: o mancebo que veio preso do Brasil*. Recife 1992.

Malkiel, David. *A Separate Republic: The Mechanics and Dynamics of Venetian Jewish Self-Government, 1607–1624*. Jerusalem 1991.

Maravall, José Antonio. *Estado moderno y mentalidad social*. Madrid 1971.

———. *Poder, honor y élites en el siglo XVII*. Madrid 1979.

Marín Padilla, Encarnación. "Relación judeoconversa durante la segunda mitad del siglo XV en Aragón," *Sefarad* 41 (1981), 273–300; 42 (1982), 59–77, 243–98; 43 (1983), 251–344.

Márquez Villanueva, Francisco. "Conversos y cargos consejiles en el siglo XV," *Revista de Archivos, Bibliotecas y Museos* 63 (1957), 503–40.

———. "El problema de los conversos: cuatro puntos cardinales," *Hispania Judaica* 1 (Barcelona 1980), 51–75.

Martz, Linda. "Pure Blood Statutes in Sixteenth-Century Toledo," *Sefarad* 54 (1994), 83–108.

Méchoulan, Henri. "Abraham Pereyra, juge des Marranes et censeur de ses coreligionnaires à Amsterdam au temps de Spinoza," *REJ* 138 (1979), 391–400.

———. "Le herem à Amsterdam et 'l'excommunication' de Spinoza," *Cahiers Spinoza* 3 (1979/80), 117–34.

Meijer, Jacob. "Hugo Grotius' *Remonstrantie*," *JSS* 17 (1955), 91–104.

Menasseh ben Israel. *The Hope of Israel*. Oxford 1987. Introduction by Henri Méchoulan and Gérard Nahon, 1–95.

Meyuhas Ginio, Alisa. "Las aspiraciones mesianicas de los conversos en la Castilla de mediados del siglo XV," *El Olivo* 13 (1989), 217–33.

———. "Self-Perception and Images of the Judeoconversos in Fifteenth-Century Spain and Portugal," *Tel Aviver Jahrbuch für deutsche Geschichte* 22 (1993), 127–52.

Michman, Jozeph. "Between Sephardim and Ashkenazim in Amsterdam," in I. Ben-Ami, ed., *The Sephardi and Oriental Jewish Heritage* (Hebrew) (Jerusalem 1982), 135–49.

———. *The History of Dutch Jewry during the Emancipation Period, 1781–1815: Gothic Turrets on a Corinthian Building*. Amsterdam 1995.

Monsalvo Antón, José María. "Herejía conversa y contestación religiosa a fines de la Edad Media: las denuncias a la Inquisición en el obispado de Osana," *Studia Historica* 2 (1984), 109–38.

Nahon, Gérard. "From New Christians to the Portuguese Jewish Nation in France," in H. Beinart, ed., *The Sephardi Legacy*, 2 vols. (Jerusalem 1992), 2: 336–64.

———. *Les "Nations" Juives Portugaises de Sud-Ouest de la France (1684–1791)*. Paris 1981.

———. "Les rapports des communautés judéo-portugaises de France avec celle d'Amsterdam au XVIIe siècle," *SR* 10 (1976), 37–78.

Netanyahu, Benzion. *The Marranos of Spain from the Late XIVth to the Early XVth Century*. New York 1966.

Nierop, H. F. K. *The Nobility of Holland: From Knights to Regents, 1500–1650*. Cambridge 1993.

Oelman, Timothy, trans. and ed. *Marrano Poets of the Seventeenth Century: An Anthology of the Poetry of João Pinto Delgado, Antonio Enríquez Gómez, and Miguel de Barrios*. Associated University Presses 1982.

Parker, Geoffrey. *The Dutch Revolt*. Ithaca 1977.

Pieterse, W. Chr. *Daniel Levi de Barrios als geschiedschrijver van de Portugees-Israel-itische Gemeente te Amsterdam in zijn "Triumpho del Govierno popular."* Amsterdam 1968.

Pohl, Hans. *Die Portugiesen in Antwerpen (1567–1648): zur Geschichte einer Minder-heit.* Wiesbaden 1977.

Popkin, Richard. "Scepticism, Theology and the Scientific Revolution in the Seventeenth Century," in I. Lakatos and A. Musgrave, eds., *Problems in the Philosophy of Science* (Amsterdam 1968).

Praag, J. A. van. *Gespleten Zielen.* Groningen 1948. Spanish trans. "Almas en litigio," *Clavileño* 1 (1950), 14–26.

Prins, J. H. "Prince William of Orange and the Jews" (Hebrew), *Zion* 15 (1950), 93–105.

Ravid, Benjamin. "The Establishment of the Ghetto Vecchio of Venice, 1541," *Proceedings of the Sixth World Congress of Jewish Studies,* 2 (Jerusalem 1975), 153–67.

———. "The First Charter of the Jewish Merchants of Venice, 1589," *AJS Review* 1 (1976), 187–222.

Révah, I. S. "Autobiographie d'un Marrane, edition partielle d'un manuscrit de João [Moseh] Pinto Delgado," *REJ* 119 (1961), 41–130.

———. "Aux origines de la rupture spinozienne: nouveaux documents sur l'incroyance dans la communauté judéo-portugaise d'Amsterdam à l'époque de l'excommunication de Spinoza," *REJ* 123 (1964), 359–83.

———."Les écrivains Manuel de Pina et Miguel de Barrios et la censure de la communauté judéo-portugaise d'Amsterdam," *Tesoro de los Judíos Españoles* 8 (1965), lxxxi-lxxxii.

———. "Une famille de 'nouveaux-chrétiens': les Bocarro Francês," *REJ* 116 (1957), 73–86.

———. "Les Marranes," *REJ* 118 (1959–60), 29–77.

———. "Pour l'histoire des Marranes à Anvers; recensements de la 'Nation Portugaise' de 1571 à 1666," *REJ* 122 (1963), 123–47.

———. "Le premier établissement des Marranes portugais à Rouen (1603–1607)," *Mélanges Isidore Lévy (Annuaire de l'Institut de Philologie et d'Histoires Orientales et Slaves* 13, 1953), Brussels 1955, 539–52.

———. "Le premier règlement imprimé de la 'Santa Companhia de dotar orfans e donzelas pobres,'" *Boletim internacional de bibliografia luso-brasileira* 4 (1963), 650–91.

———. "La religion d'Uriel da Costa, Marrane de Porto," *Revue de l'Histoire des Religions* 161 (1962), 45–76.

———. *Spinoza et le Dr. Juan de Prado.* Paris 1959.

Rooden, P. T. van, and J. W. Wesselius. "The Early Enlightenment and Judaism: The 'Civil Dispute' between Philippus van Limborch and Isaac Orobio de Castro (1687)," *SR* 21 (1987), 140–53.

Roth, Cecil. "An Elegy of João Pinto Delgado on Isaac de Castro Tartas," *REJ* 121 (1962), 355–66.

———. *A History of the Marranos.* Philadelphia 1932.

———. "Immanuel Aboab's Proselytization of the Marranos," *JQR* 23 (1932), 121–62.

———. *A Life of Menasseh ben Israel: Rabbi, Printer and Diplomat.* Philadelphia 1934.

———. "Les Marranes à Rouen: Un chapitre ignoré de l'histoire des Juifs de France," *REJ* 88 (1929), 113–55.

———. "Quatre lettres d'Elie de Montalte," *REJ* 87 (1929), 137–65.

———. "The Religion of the Marranos," *JQR* 22 (1931–32), 1–33.

———. "The Role of Spanish in the Marrano Diaspora," in Frank Pierce, ed., *Hispanic Studies in Honour of I. González Llubera* (Oxford 1959), 299–308.

———. "The Strange Case of Hector Mendes Bravo," *HUCA* 18 (1944), 221–45.

Ruderman, David. "Hope against Hope: Jewish and Christian Messianic Expectations in the Late Middle Ages," *Exile and Diaspora* (Jerusalem 1991), 185–202.

Salomon, H. P. "The 'De Pinto' Manuscript: A Seventeenth-Century Marrano Family History," *SR* 9 (1975), 1–62.

———. *Os primeiros portugueses de Amesterdão.* Braga 1983.

———. *Portrait of a New Christian: Fernão Alvares Melo (1569–1632).* Paris 1982.

Samuel, Edgar. "The Curiel Family in 16th-Century Portugal," *Transactions of the Jewish Historical Society of England* 31 (1990), 111–36.

Saraiva, António José. *Inquisição e Cristãos-Novos.* Porto 1969.

Schama, Simon. *The Embarrassment of Riches: An Interpretation of Dutch Culture in the Golden Age.* New York 1987.

Scholem, Gershom. *Sabbatai Sevi: The Mystical Messiah.* Princeton 1989.

Seeligmann, S., *Bibliographie en Historie, Bijdrage tot de Geschiedenis der eerste Sephardim in Amsterdam.* Amsterdam 1927.

Sicroff, Albert. *Les controverses des statuts de pureté de sang en Espagne du XVe au XVIIe siècle.* Paris 1960.

Silva Rosa, Jacob. *Over de verhouding tusschen Joden en niet-joden in de Republiek der vereenigde Nederlanden gedurende de 17e en 18e eeuw.* Amsterdam 1922.

Swetschinski, Daniel. "An Amsterdam Jewish Merchant-Diplomat: Jeronimo Nunes da Costa (1620–1697), Agent of the King of Portugal," in Dasberg and Cohen, eds., *Neveh Ja'akov: Jubilee Volume Presented to Dr. Jaap Meijer on the Occasion of His Seventieth Birthday.* Assen 1982.

———. "Kinship and Commerce: The Foundations of Portuguese Jewish Life in Seventeenth-Century Holland," *SR* 15 (1981), 58–74.

———."The Portuguese Jewish Merchants of Seventeenth-Century Amsterdam: A Social Profile." 2 vols., Ph.D. diss., Brandeis University, 1980.

———. "The Portuguese Jews of Seventeenth-Century Amsterdam: Cultural Continuity and Adaptation," in Malino and Albert, eds., *Essays in Modern Jewish History, A Tribute to Ben Halpern* (Rutherford, N.J. 1982), 56–80.

Teensma, Benjamin. "Fragmenten uit het Amsterdamse convolut van Abraham Idaña, alias Gaspar Mendez del Arroyo (1623–1690)," *SR* 11 (1977), 127–56.

———. "The Suffocation of Spanish and Portuguese among Amsterdam Sephardi Jews," *DJH* 3 (Jerusalem 1993), 137–77.

———. "De taal der Amsterdamse Sefardim in de 17e en 18e eeuw," in R. Kistemaker and T. Levie, eds., *Êxodo: Portugezen in Amsterdam, 1600–1680* (Amsterdam 1987), 70–72.

———. "Van Marraan tot Jood: 17e en 18e-eeuwse Amsterdamse Sephardim en hun iberische achtergrond," *Jaarboek Amstelodamum* 50 (1988), 105–25.

Teicher, Jacob. "Why Was Spinoza Banned?" *The Menorah Journal* 45 (1957), 41–60.

Tishby, Isaiah. "New Information on the 'Converso' Community in London According to the Letters of Sasportas from 1664/1665" (Hebrew), in *Exile and Diaspora: Studies in the History of the Jewish People Presented to Professor Haim Beinart on the Occasion of His Seventieth Birthday* (Hebrew volume). Jerusalem 1988, 470–96.

———. *Messianism in the Time of the Expulsion from Spain and Portugal* (Hebrew). Jerusalem 1985.

Vaz Dias, A. M. "De Stichters van Beth Jaäcob," *VA*, Dec. 25, 1931, 195–97; Jan. 1, 1932, 222–24; Jan. 15, 1932, 247–49.

Wiznitzer, Arnold. "Isaac de Castro, Brazilian Jewish Martyr," in Martin Cohen, ed., *The Jewish Experience in Latin America* (New York 1971), 205–17.

Yerushalmi, Yosef Hayim. "Assimilation and Racial Anti-Semitism: The Iberian and the German Models," *The Leo Baeck Memorial Lecture* 26 (New York 1982).

———. "Conversos Returning to Judaism in the Seventeenth Century: Their Jewish Knowledge and Psychological Readiness" (Hebrew), *Proceedings of the Fifth World Congress of Jewish Studies* (1969), vol. 2 (Jerusalem 1972), Hebrew section, 201–209.

———. *From Spanish Court to Italian Ghetto.* New York and London 1971.

———. "Professing Jews in Post-Expulsion Spain and Portugal," in *Salo Wittmayer Baron Jubilee Volume* (Jerusalem 1974), 2: 1023–58.

———. "The Re-education of Marranos in the Seventeenth Century," *The Third Annual Rabbi Louis Feinberg Memorial Lecture in Judaic Studies* (March 26, 1980).

Zernatto, Guido. "Nation: The History of a Word," *Review of Politics* 6 (1944), 352–55.

Zimmels, H. J. *Ashkenazim and Sephardim: Their Relations, Differences, and Problems as Reflected in the Rabbinical Responsa.* London 1976.

———. *Die Marranen in der rabbinischen Literatur.* Berlin 1932.

Zwarts, Jacob. "De eerste rabbijnen en synagogen van Amsterdam naar archivalische bronnen," *Bijdragen en Mededelingen van het Genootschap voor de Joodsche Wetenschap in Nederland* 4 (1928), 147–241.

INDEX

MIRIAM BODIAN, presently a visiting fellow at the Oxford Centre for Hebrew and Jewish Studies, Oxford, England, is a specialist in the history of post-Expulsion Spanish Jewry and has published a number of scholarly articles in this field.